26ᵗʰ Sept. AD MMXXII

For Ben ———

The book is at best a beta

The Sound of Silence

minus-plus-minus —— but

Fr Mankowski was alpha-

plus-plus — and it was a

PRIVILEGE to

meet him in 2019 . . .

Gasp †

Karen Hall

The Sound of Silence
The Life and Canceling
of a Heroic Jesuit Priest

CRISIS PUBLICATIONS

Manchester, New Hampshire

Copyright © 2024 by Karen Hall

Printed in the United States of America. All rights reserved.

Cover design by Updatefordesign Studio.

Cover photo (81959648) by kcherezoff/ Freepik.

Unless otherwise noted, biblical references in this book are taken from the Catholic Edition of the Revised Standard Version of the Bible, copyright 1965, 1966 by the Division of Christian Education of the National Council of the Churches of Christ in the United States of America. Used by permission. All rights reserved.

Excerpts from the English translation of the *Catechism of the Catholic Church* for use in the United States of America copyright © 1994, United States Catholic Conference, Inc.—Libreria Editrice Vaticana. English translation of the *Catechism of the Catholic Church: Modifications from the Editio Typica* copyright © 1997, United States Conference of Catholic Bishops—Libreria Editrice Vaticana.

No part of this book may be reproduced, stored in a retrieval system, or transmitted in any form, or by any means, electronic, mechanical, photocopying, or otherwise, without the prior written permission of the publisher, except by a reviewer, who may quote brief passages in a review.

Crisis Publications
Box 5284, Manchester, NH 03108
1-800-888-9344

www.CrisisMagazine.com

Sophia Institute Press˚ is a registered trademark of Sophia Institute.

paperback ISBN 979-8-88911-240-2

ebook ISBN 979-8-88911-241-9

Library of Congress Control Number: 2024934422

First printing

For Paul
AMDG

We've had enough exhortations to be silent.
Cry out with a thousand tongues.
I see the world is rotten because of silence.

— St. Catherine of Siena

Contents

Preface ix

1. Of Clerical Garb and Institutional Apostasy 1
2. Backstory 9
3. A Tree Grows in South Bend 17
   Interlude: Vocation Story 27
4. Epiphany 33
5. Rude Awakening 43
   Interlude: Canonical Warning Letter 49
6. The Noisy Years 61
7. Ghost Partner 83
   Interlude: Scenes from the *Vows* Pilot 97
8. Enemy at the Gates 101
   Interlude: "You Have to Tell Our Stories" 109
9. *Dark Debts* 117

Interlude: The Planes 129

10. The Wilderness Years (2008–2013). 133

11. The Pachamama Years 145

12. Blindsided 155

13. Goodbye, Farewell, and Amen 169

Appendix: More Mankowski

Paul on 179

Papers and Talks

    Truth Himself Speaks Truly 189

    Recent Work on the Patterning of Open-Syllable
    Vowel-Shifts in Pre-Masoretic Hebrew. 203

    The Priest as Evangelical Witness 211

    One Flesh: Reflections on the Biblical Meaning
    of Marriage 235

    Betrayal: Fr. Jason's Double Life 251

    The Truth about the Crisis in the Catholic Church 267

    Parody: All Things Bright and Fungible 283

    Baffled in Basingstoke 289

    My Favorite Things 291

Final Words: Why Stay Catholic? 293

Acknowledgments 297

About the Author 299

Preface

*A faithful friend is a sturdy shelter: he that
has found one has found a treasure.*

— Sirach 6:14

This book is a memoir of a friendship. Specifically, it is the story of my friendship with Fr. Paul Mankowski, S.J., a Jesuit from the Chicago Province, who died on September 3, 2020. It is the story of how that friendship came to be and how it changed my life. The story did not end when Paul died. In many ways, that was a new beginning. The Jesuits silenced him in 2007 (a story that I will tell you), and it took his death for much of the world to hear about him. This is the third major book written about Fr. Paul since his death. The first is George Weigel's *Jesuit at Large*,[1] a collection of articles and book reviews that Paul wrote before the Jesuits silenced him. The second book is *Diogenes Unveiled* by Phil Lawler,[2] a compilation of mostly satirical articles that Paul wrote under

---

[1] George Weigel, *Jesuit at Large: Essays and Reviews by Paul Mankowski, S.J.* (San Francisco: Ignatius Press, 2021).
[2] Philip Lawler, *Diogenes Unveiled: A Paul Mankowski, S.J. Collection* (San Francisco: Ignatius Press, 2022).

The Sound of Silence

the pseudonym Diogenes — a Jesuitical move he made after being told that he could no longer publish under his byline. Diogenes's column was published by Phil Lawler at *Catholic World News* (now Catholic Culture),[3] and Lawler compiled the best of Diogenes. Both books are highly recommended, and both go a long way in explaining who Paul was. Eventually the Jesuits also shut down Diogenes, but a lot of truth was unleashed before they did.

Paul chose the name Diogenes after the fourth-century Greek Cynic philosopher who was best known for holding a lantern to the faces of Athens' citizens, claiming he was searching for an honest man.

The Jesuits canceled Fr. Paul Mankowski long before there was such a thing as cancel culture. At least, they tried. Polymaths cannot easily be "canceled," so they really just kept him from publishing. Paul was many things to the people who knew him: a biblical scholar; a professor; a writer; a philologist; a satirist; a former boxer; a better-than-average cook; and the most loyal of friends. People who knew him describe him with a blizzard of words: brilliant; erudite; hilarious; scathing; convivial; droll; waggish; and any word that means hail-fellow-well-met. I know, from the forty-three years I've spent as a professional writer, those words won't make you *feel* anything. That's why "show, don't tell" is the most important rule in show business. So I'm going to try to show you who he was. My main purpose in writing this book is to try to share the joy that was knowing him.

My secondary reason for writing this book was that I, too, had a nice collection of Paul's writings — the result of a decade and a half of frequent e-mails on a wide variety of subjects. As you will see, Paul was my North Star as I struggled to become a loyal daughter of Holy

---

[3] Catholic Culture is a website that offers Catholic news, commentary, information, resources, and ways to observe the liturgical year: https://catholicculture.org.

Preface

Mother Church, even as she endured one shipwreck after another. As a morbid Scottish Southerner, I frequently reminded Paul that he had to outlive me; otherwise, I would be left rudderless. He made me no such promise, so no promise was broken.

Thirdly and finally, I wrote this book to shed some light, where little has been shed except by cryptic reference, on the problems that Paul had with his Jesuit superiors that led to his silencing. I wanted to share how it felt from *his* side. He was a white martyr if not a red one, and he was not allowed to tell his side of the story. Therefore, I am telling it for him.

What's in a Name?

In the course of this book, I refer to Fr. Paul Mankowski in several ways. When I met him, he told me to call him Paul. He was decidedly not a "call me Paul"–type priest, and I understood it to mean that we were going to be friends and foxhole buddies. I always called him "Paul," as I had been instructed to. I feel strongly about the importance of the priesthood, so it is never meant as disrespect. But as I explain later, he was my friend and not my spiritual director. As much as I am capable of being the peer of someone with an IQ that practically doubles mine, we were peers. When I refer to him by his full title or as Fr. Paul, I honestly just typed what I heard in my head. The fact is that Fr. Paul Mankowski, S.J., was a priest in every nuance of the word. I have never known anyone to embody the word the way he did.

Jesuit Disclaimer

I cannot send this book out into the world without a message to the good Jesuits who are true and faithful sons of St. Ignatius and therefore of Jesus Christ: I am not talking about you. I think most of you know that, because most of you are aware of Fr. Mankowski's story and have been praying for him for years. But for young Jesuits and Jesuits who have never heard of Fr. Mankowski: when I speak harshly about Jesuits, I am referring to the current power brokers. I asked every Jesuit I know to give me the percentage of modernist — as opposed to old-school — Jesuits who currently are in power; every one gave me an answer between 90 and 100 percent.

I have high hopes that most of the Jesuits who are not movers and shakers are men who are faithful to God when He is directly opposed to modernists (which is often these days). I love St. Ignatius, my patron saint, with all my heart, and I love Ignatian spirituality, and many of my heroes are Jesuit martyrs. Many of my present-day heroes are Jesuits. But right now the face of Jesuitdom is Fr. James Martin, S.J., who is enabled by a Jesuit pope who loves and supports his work, which is inarguably directly opposed to the catechism of the two-thousand-plus-year-old Magisterium of the Holy Roman Catholic Church.

Aristotle on Friendship

Aristotle, in *Nicomachean Ethics*, book 8, declares that there are three kinds of friendship.[4] The first is a friendship that is based on pleasure. Two people are friends because they enjoy the same things and have fun on outings. There isn't a lot of depth involved, but for this kind of friendship, none is needed. The second kind, Aristotle says, is a friendship of utility: a friendship based on what the two friends can do for each other. These might be friends from work or from a book club or a study group. These friendships can end rapidly, as soon as any use for the other person is gone. The third and best kind of friendship, according to Aristotle, is a friendship based on virtue. In this kind of friendship, the friends care about each other for each other's sake

---

[4] Aristotle, *On Friendship: Being an Expanded Translation of the Nicomachean Ethics, Books VIII & IX* (Cambridge, UK: Cambridge University Press, 2000).

Preface

rather than because of any exchange of benefits. This is the rarest kind of friendship, Aristotle says, and people are lucky to find one such friendship in a lifetime. These are the friends who will tell each other the brutal truth in order to help each other grow. These friendships, being unconditional, are permanent. These are sometimes known as "holy friendships," and though it took me years to make that claim about my friendship with Paul, the fact is that I knew it from day one.

Truth and Consequences

When I first sat down to write this book, I spent three days sifting through words, trying to come up with one that best explained why Paul and I had a friendship of virtue. Having thrown out scores of alternatives, the word that I settled on was "truth." Or, more to point, Truth, which is not something but someone, Jesus Christ. We shared a near obsession with wanting to know and live in Truth. I never asked Paul when that quest started for him, but for me, it has been the thing that has hounded me the most since my earliest memory. At the time I met Paul, I had been sold a big lie (more about that as we go) and I was particularly in need of a friend who knew the Truth and would teach it to me. Paul's adherence to the Magisterium and to the deposit of faith let me know that I was on solid ground. I had always *wanted* to believe that all the most archaic biblical teachings were true, and meeting a great biblical scholar who believed that they were was like a new sunrise, after so many years of confusion. What I did not foresee, however, was the vicious backlash that would come from embracing the truth.

Creed or Chaos?

In addition to truth, Paul and I also bonded over the importance of dogma, though to us they were the same thing. Having been all the way down the road of "I don't need no stinkin' dogma," I had returned to dogma with a vengeance. I saw where its absence had left me, and

The Sound of Silence

I did not want to go back there. Tossing it out had led me to a life of chaos, and I now agree with everything Dorothy Sayers says in this quote from *Creed or Chaos?*:

> It is worse than useless for Christians to talk about the importance of Christian morality, unless they are prepared to take their stand upon the fundamentals of Christian theology. It is a lie to say that dogma does not matter; it matters enormously. It is fatal to let people suppose that Christianity is only a mode of feeling; it is vitally necessary to insist that it is first and foremost a rational explanation of the universe. It is hopeless to offer Christianity as a vaguely idealistic aspiration of a simple and consoling kind; it is, on the contrary, a hard, tough, exacting, and complex doctrine, steeped in a drastic and uncompromising realism. And it is fatal to imagine that everybody knows quite well what Christianity is and needs only a little encouragement to practice it. The brutal fact is that in this Christian country not one person in a hundred has the faintest notion what the Church teaches about God or man or society or the person of Jesus Christ.... Theologically this country is at present in a state of utter chaos established in the name of religious toleration and rapidly degenerating into flight from reason and the death of hope.[5]

We have only to turn on the news to see how right she was. My mother's constant admonition was, "If you don't stand for something, you'll fall for anything." I have seen this proven vividly in the last few years. You will fall for there being more than two genders. You will fall for the idea that children benefit from being taken to sexually explicit drag shows.

---

[5] Dorothy Leigh Sayers, *Creed or Chaos?: Why Christians Must Choose Either Dogma or Disaster; Or, Why It Really Does Matter What You Believe* (Manchester, NH: Sophia Institute Press, 1995), 44–45.

Preface

You will fall for the "truth" that a man can put on a skirt and call himself a woman, and that makes him a woman. Sadly, I could go on and on.

Without dogma, chaos is now reigning in the Church too. We have "devout Catholic" politicians supporting abortion on demand, even infanticide. We have find-a-priest-who-agrees-with-you Confession. We have a pope who puts on a full display of idol worship in St. Peter's Basilica. And that same pope has all the tolerance in the world for atheists, heretics, and religions that are diametrically opposed to Christianity but no tolerance for faithful Catholics who want to preserve their ancient form of liturgy. In short, chaos.

Obedience

God wants obedience, which leads to order. He has made that clear throughout salvation history. He explained it to Adam and Eve, He repeated it with Moses, and He spelled it out in exquisite detail to Job. And His consistent message is this: "I'm God, and you're not." We have been told, in no uncertain terms, that His ways are not our ways. He has given us the following:

- Moses, Abraham, the prophets (major and minor)
- His Son (!)
- The apostles
- St. Paul
- The Holy Spirit
- The Church
- The Fathers and Doctors of the Church
- The Council of Nicaea
- The Council of Trent
- Many apparitions that the Church has investigated and declared worthy of belief
- More than two thousand years of popes, biblical scholars, and consistent Church teaching

The Sound of Silence

- ❖ The Magisterium and the deposit of faith
- ❖ The Bible

The modern world has declared all of that to be of minimum or no value and has adopted in its stead what I call "I just think theology." False modern theology replaces all that God has given us with the idea that a mere mortal's best reasoning is enough. "I'm God, and you're not" has been replaced by "I just think." As in: "I just think a benevolent God wouldn't throw anyone into Hell." (So Jesus lied about that?) "I just think God would never see any kind of love as a bad thing." (St. Paul spells it out for you. Do you know better than a man that Jesus handpicked and knocked off a horse?) "I just think all religions are equally good." So "no one comes to the Father, but by me" (John 14:6) was another lie? (Evidently modernists "just think" that Jesus was a pathological liar.)

The hubris and the insanity of thinking that a mortal can understand the mind of the God of the universe is breathtaking to me. And Fr. Paul Mankowski, the most brilliant person I have ever met, agreed. This brings me to another thing that he and I had in common: an extreme fear of Hell. I have full faith that God will not fault me for following the Bible and the Magisterium, and so did Fr. Paul. But when it comes to the question of eternal destiny, the thought of Hell terrified us, though very little scared either of us. We were not so bold as those who say, "I just think a loving God could never send anyone to Hell."

Silence

In his book *The Day Is Now Far Spent*, Cardinal Sarah says, "We bishops ought to tremble at the thought of our guilty silences, our complicit silences, our over-indulgent silences in dealing with the world."[6]

---

[6] Robert Cardinal Sarah and Nicolas Diat, *The Day Is Now Far Spent* (San Francisco: Ignatius Press, 2019).

Preface

Interesting words from a cardinal who also wrote a book called *The Power of Silence*, but he is correct. I have often thought how different the entire world would be right now if the clergy had spoken out (loudly and boldly) in support of the Church's two-thousand-year-old "hard teachings" instead of watering them down so as not to make waves or forfeit tax exemptions. If they had, I dare say we would not be in the mess that we are in.

I now donate money to an organization called Coalition for Canceled Priests. These are priests who have, for all intents and purposes, been kicked out of the priesthood, stopping just short of excommunication. In every case, these priests have suffered this sad fate for standing up for the Magisterium of the Church in instances where doing so is unpopular with the world. Such a thing would have been unthinkable to me had I not been privy to Fr. Paul's story, since I watched him be tortured by his Jesuit brethren for exactly the same reason.

The Paul Who Never Was

Paul was frequently a victim of the straw-man fallacy. People who barely knew him nonetheless felt qualified to describe him, in great detail, to anyone who would listen. The words used to describe Paul when the speakers are modernist Jesuits are very different from the ones used to describe him in tributes and memorials. I have heard him called all of the following: hater, bigot, homophobe, totalitarian, obscurantist, dogmatist, and misogynist. I have heard the following adjectives used to describe him: intransigent, narrow-minded, rigid, cold, dictatorial, fanatical, and, my personal favorite, contumacious. (One thing about Jesuits: they insult people with great eloquence.) I have heard many more words that are not suitable for polite company. Most of the time, the Jesuits who were describing Paul to me (under the heading of "keep away from that guy") had never met him. They were merely spouting the Jesuit party line. I have said to more than one such Jesuit, "I don't know the man you are describing, and I certainly wouldn't be friends with him."

Paul's friend and colleague Thomas Levergood, the recently deceased director of the Lumen Christi Institute,[7] where Paul worked, tells the following story in his tribute to Paul:

> The difference between Fr. Paul and me was clear when we organized a symposium on "Dominus Iesus," a declaration issued by the Congregation for the Doctrine of the Faith under Cardinal Joseph Ratzinger. The document clarifies concepts concerning the relation of the Catholic Church to other Christian communities. To join Fr. Paul on a panel on the text, I had invited Fr. Franz Jozef van Beeck, SJ, a Dutch Jesuit, who was a member of our Board of Advisers. Besides organizing a lively, thoughtful event, I intended also to allow Fr. Paul to get to know van Beeck, then holding a top chair at Loyola University. The event and subsequent conversation over dinner succeeded according to my designs. Fr. "Joep" van Beeck said afterwards: "My, that was a wonderful event. Fr. Mankowski is learned and thoughtful. He was nothing like the monster I'd been told I'd encounter." Fr. Paul had a different view. He said something like, "It went well, but I was rather disappointed that there was not more disagreement, conflict, and pugilism."[8]

The people who knew Paul adored him. That is clear if you read the tributes and memorials written by his friends. Paul's friend Onsi Kamel wrote, "The loss of a friend like Fr. Paul loosens one's grip on this

---

[7] See the website of the Lumen Christi Institute: https://www.lumen christi.org.

[8] "Remembering Fr. Paul Mankowski, S.J.," Lumen Christi Institute, https://www.lumenchristi.org/news/2020/09/update-prayer-request-for-fr-paul-mankowski-s-j.

Preface

life. There is much yet to love in this world, but much less than there was."[9] Those were my exact feelings in the days right after Paul's death.

Yet this was a man whom the Jesuits had admonished to the point of silencing. This book will shed some light on how Paul came to be repugnant to some and a hero to others. As you will read later in an e-mail, Paul's goal in writing (before he was silenced) was that "sixty years from now the half a dozen eccentrics interested in Jesuit history will study the records and say, 'Well, it seems that not EVERYONE went along with the flakiness' "[10]

The world has never heard a detailed version of what the Jesuits put him through because they silenced him, and Paul had taken a vow of obedience. I have no such vow.

---

[9] Onsi A. Kamel, "The World Was Not Worthy: In Memoriam Fr Paul Mankowski," *Mere Orthodoxy*, September 15, 2020, https://mereorthodoxy.com/fr-paul-mankowski/.

[10] "More Questions," April 2007. Most citations for e-mails between Fr. Mankowski and the author are listed by subject line and date; some are listed by one or the other.

1

Of Clerical Garb and Institutional Apostasy

*The temple of truth has never suffered so much
from woodpeckers on the outside
as from termites within.*

— Vance Havner

Fr. Paul Mankowski, S.J., is not a common Catholic household name like Archbishop Fulton Sheen, Fr. Mike Schmitz, or Fr. James Martin, S.J. He would have been had he not been silenced by the superiors of his religious order, the Society of Jesus, the Jesuits. In 2003, the Jesuits banned him from writing and from speaking on anything other than his area of expertise — ancient Semitic languages. He lived forty-four years as a Jesuit and was forced to remain silent for many of those years. He was carefully kept away from impressionable young minds, as well as other old-school Jesuits, lest they pool forces and become, as liberal Jesuits refer to them, *Shadow Formatores* — men who are a bad influence on novitiates because they are "rigid traditionalists." What was Fr. Mankowski's crime? Faithful obedience to the Magisterium of Holy Mother Church. That, and a severe love of the Truth, and an inability to keep his mouth shut about it.

The Sound of Silence

The obituaries that came out after his death were written by scholars, fellow priests, close friends, a famous cardinal, and even a prime minister. All of them do as good a job as possible in describing Fr. Paul, yet none of them do him justice in describing the whole man. A thorough reading of all the tributes might begin to give you an idea. What makes Fr. Paul Mankowski, S.J., so elusive and yet so striking is that he was a mixture of many things that do not go together. He was a mental giant but also a self-proclaimed jock. He was a serious scholar, but he was scathingly funny and extremely playful. He could and did eviscerate people with the written word as his weapon, but he was one of the kindest, gentlest, most compassionate people I've ever known. He was a Jesuit's Jesuit, but only if you go by the standards of *dead* Jesuits. He was, for my money, a miracle of a person.

There is a glaring absence in the obituaries and tributes, though, and that is the story of what he suffered at the hands of his Jesuit brothers. There are cryptic references, and one writer went so far as to say this: "He was silenced by the Society, the ultimate tribute which those who cannot bear the truth bestow upon those who forcefully proclaim it."[11] Highly accurate, but there is no room in a short tribute article to go into detail. The persecution that Paul Mankowski suffered lasted many years and took on many forms. Someone would have to write a book to describe it fully. I decided that maybe it wasn't a coincidence that Paul had befriended a writer, so I volunteered for the job.

I wanted to come up with a story that would serve well as an introduction, for those who needed one, to Paul Mankowski the man and would also give insight into the problems he had with his fellow

---

[11] Raymond de Souza, "Fr Mankowski Was Silenced by the Jesuits. It Was a Kind of Tribute," *Catholic Herald*, December 2, 2020, https://catholicherald.co.uk/fr-mankowski-was-silenced-by-the-jesuits-it-was-a-kind-of-tribute/.

Of Clerical Garb and Institutional Apostasy

Jesuits. There is a story that serves both purposes, and I will let Paul tell it himself. Way back in 2007, I had asked him (in an e-mail) why he always wore clerics. The following was his response:

> As a scholastic, I didn't wear clerics. Partly this was because clerics confuse people who took them as a sign of priesthood. ("Well, like, what priest-things can you do and not do?") But mostly it was because life is just a lot easier when you're not wearing them. My mind on the subject was changed by one offhand comment and one not-so-offhand event, both of which occurred in my first year of priesthood (when I was studying at Weston, in Cambridge, MA). The offhand comment was by a layman and a Harvard grad student who knew the Jesuit community very well and remarked to me, "You know, if you guys did nothing different from what you do now, but started wearing clerics, it would stun Harvard. You'd have ninety men walking around Harvard Yard every day whose dress announced that they take Christ seriously." I thought: damn. He's right.
>
> The event was a mandatory all-community morning on Jesuits with AIDS (there were a number of AIDS deaths in those years), in which the Vice Rector told a story about his lying on a beach in Provincetown two years previously with two men talking about AIDS, one of whom had since died and the other of whom was HIV-positive, etc. He, and the other community leadership, went on to declare (in effect, not in so many words) that the Society of Jesus rejected Church teaching on homosexuality. It was a kind of institutional apostasy happening before my eyes. I went for a long, long walk afterwards, during which I promised myself that I would never appear at another Jesuit function (be it even breakfast in my own house) not wearing clerics. It was a sign of protest, a kind of full-body

black armband. Unless I'm deluding myself, it's a promise I've never broken, either.

Returning to the more general level, and repeating myself, things are more comfortable for a priest who's not wearing clerics, but there's nothing especially noble about the comforts enjoyed. E.g., black is hot and hard to keep clean and the collar is tight. Civvies are not only more comfortable, but they give you anonymity. Civvies let a priest go to the kind of bars and restaurants that a man in clerics would be shy of entering.... They let the priest buy the kind of reading material that would raise eyebrows otherwise. They free the priest from the obligation to edify — or at least not be disedifying. In civvies the priest can flip off people who cut him off in traffic and yell nasty things at panhandlers and argue with salespeople and waiters and airline personnel without regard to an institutional reputation to uphold. And, of course, civvies give the priest the prerogative to reveal his priesthood to those he wants and withhold from those he wants. Though it's a temptation I resist, the biggest temptation for me to crawl into civvies comes just before a long flight, so I don't have to get into discussions about my fellow passengers' problems with divorce, their anger at (or loud, loud, LOUD enthusiasm for) the Church, their fight with Father Murphy, their mystical experiences on the beach, their certainty that the true church is the church of Mormon of the disciples of Christ, etc., etc. Sometimes you just want to be Mister Average Passenger.

However, turning yourself into Mister Average Passenger — for a priest — is like Frodo Baggins putting on the Ring in order to disappear. It's a sneaky way out that makes you a tiny bit more cowardly every time you take it.

Regarding the freedom to misbehave in civvies, one of the priests I admire was known to say: if you feel the need to remove your clerics to go someplace, you shouldn't be going there. Regarding the witness value generally, the bottom line is that priesthood is not a job that you take up at 8:30 and put down at 4, but a lifetime vocation. As I say, except for showering, bass fishing (and yes, sleeping), there's almost nothing I do that I can't do in clerics if I really want to.

One Jesuit I know — not a flake, but 65 years old and a man of his time — doesn't wear clerics, he says, because people associate them with diocesan priests rather than Jesuits, and he says he doesn't want to be seen as a diocesan priest. I think he's sincere, but the reality is that he's seen as nothing-in-particular by all except those very few people who happen to know what a Jesuit is and happen to know him well enough to realize he belongs to the order. I think most liberal Jesuits don't wear clerics (1) for convenience and (2) because they're embarrassed by the Catholic Church and want to be able to choose the when, the where, and the how of their public association with her. When you wear clerics, you're stuck with the whole schmeer.

One final point. St. Ignatius says we should pray for humiliations because humiliations make us humble. I've never been very good at this. However, it did occur to me that wearing clerics is a kind of freebie in this respect, because all kinds of humiliations come your way, gratuitously, so to speak, when you're in clerics. This was always true since I was ordained, and especially so after the clerical sex abuse crisis blew up. It really hurt to see, e.g., a woman on the L in Chicago look at me in fear and sort of shepherd her children away from me to the other side of the train car. Another time I was heading into the men's room at the airport at the same time as a six- or seven-year-old boy when his mother came up behind him and pulled him back. I understand their concern, and even agree with the steps they took, but it's no less painful for that. So when someone yells, "How many kids did you molest today, Father?" ... I figure: heck, I'm not in Iraq getting shot at. This is the least I can take as part of the job.

"Do you tell people some version of that story (clerics as a protest)," I asked him, "or do you let them assume whatever they want to assume about your reasoning?" He replied:

Every now and then someone's curiosity will get the better of him and he'll ask what the story is. If he's capable of understanding the story I'll tell him; if not, not. There were a couple of 95-year-old pious Italian Jesuits here who would bring it up with me — pleased at my non-conformity — but the notion of actively gay Jesuit superiors was simply beyond their ability to grasp and it was pointless to try to explain.

The conversation about clerics is almost always edgy. Think of a group of married co-workers who head off in a group to a bar on Friday evening, and before entering all yank off their wedding rings except one. The ring-hiders are generally going to be disinclined to ask the ring-displayer the reason for holding out (suspecting the answer they get will not reflect well on themselves), and if they do so at all they'll be edgy and aggressive.

Sometimes, to take a little off the punch when explaining things to a curious and good-willed Jesuit, I downplay the real reason and stress the poverty angle. If you wear civvies you need a whole set of clothes for every occasion (plus neckties, shoes, socks, etc.). If you wear clerics, well, that's that. I've got a total of about six shirts, four of which are wearable in public and the others of which are greyed and frayed enough for use while I'm laundering the others or just hanging around the house. I average a new shirt about every year and a half, cycling the new one into the closet and the old one into the community rag bag, and roughly the same with trousers. Mean annual clothing expenditure: say, $90; if shoes were included, $140. Of course, many Jesuits, even those who wear clerics often, like to present a nattier image to the public, but personally I've never trusted a priest who wasn't at least a little bit seedy, and so rarely feel inclined toward spit-and-polish. At any rate, there are some guys who aren't ready to deal with the sacerdotal/theological reasons for clerics who can at least understand and appreciate the fact that it's the more economical option.[12]

The term "institutional apostasy" is not as hard-hitting today as it was when I first read it in 2007 because in 2023 it seems to be the norm rather than the exception. It was something that Paul and I discussed at great length over the years, and the arc of that conversation went from "it *has* to get better" to "I'm waiting for the asteroid." The incident that Paul describes above was one of many times in which he drew a line in the sand. His decision to wear his clerics faithfully only further increased his brother Jesuits' opposition toward him. The Jesuits interpreted the move (as I have heard them describe it) as Paul having declared himself holier than the rest of them. If Paul ever had any such thought, it was along the lines of his being more faithful to the Magisterium of Holy Mother Church than his detractors. His critics hardly had an argument there.

The bad treatment that Paul received at the hands of liberal Jesuits was extremely distressing to those close to him, but it never kept *him* up nights. And when he would speak of it, it was only in unemotional, factual terms. I have many e-mails in which he presented distressing

---

[12] "Clerics," April 2007.

news under the heading of "this is where things currently stand." I think it would have been easier on the rest of us had he thrown the occasional tantrum, but that was not who he was. There was the occasional e-mail in which he would voice his frustration, but out of fourteen years of e-mails, I could count those on one hand. He expressed his frustrations in jokes, sarcastic one-liners, satire, and parody. That is where you will see his pain. It was not insignificant.

When God formed Paul Mankowski in his mother's womb, He knew exactly what He was doing. He knew that the times were going to call for a man who could stand up to them, and He knew how badly the rest of us would need the leadership of this man. He did a perfect job. He just couldn't do anything about the free will of men with disordered affections. Or maybe He's doing something now, as Paul's words are being spread far and wide by people who have no vow of obedience to the Jesuit order. This is the third book to put Paul's words into print. I hope it is the third of many.

2

Backstory

Every story has a beginning, a middle, and an end. Not necessarily in that order.

— Tim Burton

While there is a chance that you have heard of Paul Mankowski, there is little chance that you have heard of me, unless you are in the small population of extreme nerds who read the credits on television shows. If you are, then you have seen my name on many popular television series, including *M*A*S*H*, *Hill Street Blues*, *Moonlighting*, *Northern Exposure*, *Judging Amy*, and *The Good Wife*. If you are an extreme nerd and you watch everything, then you will have seen my name on lesser-known shows such as *Brotherhood*, *The Glades*, *Jericho*, *Cupid*, and an excellent show from the early nineties called *I'll Fly Away*. I have also written TV movies and miniseries, including *Toughlove*, *The Betty Ford Story*, and *The Women of Brewster Place*. Forty-three years in television has earned for me seven Emmy nominations, six Writers Guild of America (WGA) Award nominations, one WGA Award, the Women in Film Luminas Award, the Women in Film Muse Award, and many other accolades.[13]

---

[13] The rest of my credits are available at the following URL: https://www.imdb.com/name/nm1027107/?ref_=nv_sr_srsg_3.

The Sound of Silence

TV or Not TV

In the face of what really matters, my résumé plus $4.25 will get me a tall salted-caramel mocha at my local Starbucks, a fact that God pointed out by having me befriend a man who, in sixty-six years of life, never owned a television. My accomplishments were meaningless to him. He wasn't opposed to the idea of television. He encouraged my endeavors, and he even helped me with them. But pop culture was not one of his many interests, except when it coughed up a perfect illustration for one of his essays. (I often wondered, for example, how on earth Diogenes knew who Beyoncé was.) None of that mattered, though, because by the time we met, the question of whether one valued pop culture was the least of either of our problems.

The Long and Winding Road

I wish to tell you a short version of my own story because it will eventually be pertinent. To understand my friendship with Fr. Paul, you need to understand what led up to our meeting. Here is a little about my "faith journey." I hate the term "faith journey," which sounds as if it comes with felt banners, enthusiastic clapping, and a warm, fuzzy homily. But I don't know what else to call it. I started out in one place, covered a lot of miles, and ended up somewhere entirely different. And that journey has everything to do with how I became friends with Paul Mankowski.

I grew up Methodist with a wandering eye. By the time I graduated from high school, I had visited every mainline Protestant church in town, dropped in on my best friend's Pentecostal church, and even dipped my toe into Mormonism. All of this started at age eight, when I began to recognize that there were a lot of churches, and I shouldn't belong to just one because the stork had dropped me down a Methodist chimney. I also could not believe that for the rest of my life, my only experience of God (according to my child's mind) would be sitting on a hard pew and listening to some man lecturing at me for forty-five minutes. After I had tried the other churches, I resigned myself to my liturgical fate because whatever was leaving me restless at the Methodist church was the same, no matter where I went. But God works in mysterious ways, and in my senior year of high school, what should show up but a Catholic boyfriend? That is a long story that is fodder for a separate book, but for now I'll just say that the first time I walked into a Catholic church, I wanted to yell, "*That's* what I'm talking about!"

The Wayward Years

The Catholic boyfriend and I went our separate ways — for twenty-five years before he came back and married me. Those were, shall we say, twenty-five highly educational years. (I frequently tell my husband that he is responsible for every sin I committed between 1974 and 1997.)

Like many other people of my generation, I lost my faith in college. Ironically, it started with a former Jesuit professor who informed my history of Western religion class that everything we'd learned from our parents was a lie, to be believed only by bumpkins. (He didn't say "bumpkins," but that was the gist.) I had grown up in a town of twelve hundred people in the rural South, and one of my biggest fears, as I went out into the world, was being a bumpkin, so he did not have to tell me twice.

When I went to college, I had continued going to Mass. It was folk Mass — with a groovy priest who played the guitar — rather than the beautiful Mass I had fallen in love with, but there was an advantage to that. It made going to church completely painless. I could wear jeans, the homily was only fifteen minutes, and I really liked singing folk songs. My parents would ask if I had gone to church, and I would happily chirp, "Of course!" I wanted to join the Church, but since I knew it would not thrill my parents, I was in no rush. Finally, in my senior year, my best (Catholic) friend told the priest that I wanted to join the Church, and he made an appointment for me with the pastor. I knew and liked the young priest who said our Mass, but I had never met the pastor. He turned out to be around 137 years old, and let's just say that his enthusiasm for new Catholics was not what it had once been. He gave me some literature and told me to come back in a week. I gave him two single-spaced pages of questions. He looked them over and then said, "Just read the literature and come back." Since I was an angry young idiot at the time, I marched off in a collegiate huff and stayed away for fifteen years.

I declared myself an agnostic and announced to God that He could explain it all to me when I got there. Shortly thereafter, I moved to Los Angeles to become a screenwriter. I quickly discovered that in L.A., agnosticism was both supported and encouraged (if you were too much of a wimp to go for full-blown atheism). I married an atheist television writer and producer. As you might suspect, that trajectory led me to something short of Nirvana.

Rethinking Agnosticism

There is a joke about an agnostic mountain climber who loses his footing and begins to fall down the mountain. He manages to grab a scrubby tree and stop the fall. He looks down and sees that the tree is the only thing preventing him from certain death. At this point, he begins to rethink his agnosticism. He turns his gaze skyward and, in a timid voice, asks, "Is there anybody up there?" Immediately he hears a booming voice that says, "Let go of the branch." Since that makes no sense, he seeks clarification. "Excuse me?" The voice booms even louder: "Let go of the branch. I'll catch you." The mountain climber takes that in, then looks skyward again and calls out, "Is there anybody *else* up there?"

That joke sums up my theological position in 1990, when I decided to take some time off from television to write a novel. I knew I needed help, but I was too proud to accept it from God, who wanted blind trust. I buried myself in the novel as a way of avoiding my quandary.

No Evil without Good

The novel was born from listening to the dysfunctional family-of-origin stories of a close friend. He had three brothers with impressive criminal records, one of whom had eventually been executed for a murderous rampage. His mother, he told me, had been convinced that there was a demonic curse on the family. While I wasn't ordinarily one to believe in such things (a demonic curse really messes with agnosticism), I knew all the details, and I thought his mother had a case that would hold up in court. So I set out to write a book that would make as intelligent a case as could be made of the idea of a generational demonic curse. As the book began to take shape, I went to Hollywood cocktail parties and informed all listeners that I was writing a book about the nature of evil. I felt oh so wise and sophisticated.

Somewhere around page 250, it began to dawn on me that it is not possible to examine the nature of evil without looking at the nature of good, and that was something I had abandoned completely. I also realized that I was writing myself into the buzz saw of an exorcism, which meant that I was going to need a priest character. Because I wanted the priest to spout a lot of my own questions, I needed him to be a malcontent with a thin grasp on his faith. I also wanted him to be intelligent and skeptical, so I asked my Catholic friends, "What kind of priest would be the least likely to believe in the devil?" They all gave me the same answer, and quite enthusiastically: a Jesuit. So I made him a Jesuit. That necessitated finding out what a Jesuit was, so I found a couple of Jesuits from the California Province who were willing to help me with that.

At the same time, I also knew that I had to go back to church for research purposes. I knew that I would not be able to create a convincing priest protagonist unless I could understand why, in 1990, an intelligent man would give up everything in his life for something so archaic as Christianity. I bought two dresses because I thought I'd go to church twice. That shows you how long it had been since I'd been inside a church — I thought women still wore dresses! I remember being nervous about entering the church, thinking that if there was a God, He would surely smite me for the fifteen years I had been away. (Later, when all the dust had settled, my sister said something that I realized was true: "God doesn't hit back.") I also thought that the parishioners could look at me and know that I wasn't a believer. But they paid no attention to me, and I settled in for an hour of what I thought would be research with a side of nostalgia.

Conversion in Four Steps

The friend who had taken me to Mass invited me to return the following week. I accepted her offer, mostly because I realized how much I had missed having ritual in my life. And I had to admit that I envied the people who believed it could make a difference.

On the second Sunday, I felt the tug of nostalgia for the beliefs of my childhood, which had made life make much more sense than agnosticism did. On the third Sunday, I told myself, "If there is any way on earth that an intelligent case can be made for this, I will believe it." I didn't really think that was possible, but I set out to give it a chance. I made two large piles of books by my bed. In one pile were the books that had made me stop believing in Christianity, some of them just by their titles. (Having never read anything about them, I had concluded that the Dead Sea scrolls were proof enough that the Jesus fairy tale was the invention of people who wanted the illusion of an afterlife.) In the other pile, I placed newly purchased books written by Catholic apologists and biblical scholars. I started to read. I was three books into the stack of naysayers when something became abundantly clear to me: the people who wrote those books did not believe in the supernatural. Having grown up in a haunted house, I had always known that there was something going on behind the scenes. This realization made me abandon the anti-Christian books and turn to the biblical scholars. These, I soon realized, were very intelligent men and women who could come darned close to proving what they believed, based on sciences: archaeology, psychology, and geography. They also had historical accounts from contemporaries of Jesus who had no dog in the Christian fight. All of this did not drive me home, but it dropped me off at the closest exit. It was my choice whether to make the final hike. That took place on the fourth Sunday, when I found myself singing loudly and grinning, and the thought came to me, "Oh, hell. I believe this."

I had let go of the branch. The rest was up to God.

3

A Tree Grows in South Bend

You know, I'm from the Midwest. That shapes my personality much more than having gone to Harvard.

— Dean Norris

Fr. Paul grew up in a blue-collar home in the Midwest; his father worked at a factory; his mother was a teacher; he worked in the steel mills to help pay for his college tuition. All of that is true, but the lack of nuance causes people to fill in the blanks with stereotypes. Commonsense imagination would conjure up pictures of the family sitting around the television at night to watch *Let's Go to the Races* while yelling for the victory of the horse that would earn them $100 for groceries that week. I knew from Paul that his family had only briefly owned a television set (during Watergate), but we never really talked about his family in anything other than present tense, so I had made the same assumption as everyone else. I wondered at the miracle of Paul's having grown up in a blue-collar-factory-worker house and having become who he became. I never dug deeply into it until I decided to write this book. There was so little time and so many important things to discuss.

The Sound of Silence

The Mankowski Family

One day, many years ago, I was online searching for a particular article that Paul had written when I came across his name on a blog called *The Musical Almanac*. It turned out that the blog was written by one of Paul's best high school friends, who had spent a lot of time at the Mankowski house and was quite taken by Paul's family. He wrote about them in detail, which was how I began to understand what Paul's family was like. I sent an e-mail to the blog writer, Kurt Nemes, and we spent time — in e-mails and in person — talking about Paul behind his back.

Here is an excerpt from one of Kurt's blog posts:

> The year I joined the team, there were a number of fast swimmers who were to be admired, but the real leaders were two brothers, who had high I.Q.s and SAT scores *and* swam well — the Mankowski brothers. Paul and Mark (respectively one and two years older than I) came from a family everyone regarded as smart. Their mother taught high school English and the father, though a quality control engineer in a factory, had gone to the University of Chicago for two years on the G.I. Bill after World War II. They had three bright sisters as well: a set of twins my age and a little sister two years younger. Some of us used to rendez-vous at their house on weekends before going out to parties.
>
> Their household was completely different from mine. They all listened to classical music, read the *New Yorker*, discussed classic works of literature, and studied languages. This opened up a whole other world for me. I felt so uncultured in their presence that I devoted myself to turning myself into an "intellectual." (Partly because I had a crush on one of the sisters.) I read voraciously, studied the works of great artists, and began

buying or checking out from the library classical albums that the family recommended.

My three years in high school, therefore, turned out to be some of the most fertile in my intellectual life. The family introduced me to quite a few pieces....

One of the first pieces I remember the Mankowski's telling me about was Brahm's *Fourth Symphony*. The recording they had was by Carlo Maria Giulini, who had taken over the baton of the Chicago Symphony Orchestra after Fritz Reiner died. The daughters pointed out to me that the rock group "Yes" had done a synthesized version on one of their albums, and the parents didn't seem to particularly mind.

Mr. Mankowski would sit in his comfy chair in the living room, chomping a cigar, listening to a symphony. Every once in a while he would look up from his book to read aloud a humorous passage from Ring Lardner or S. J. Perlman or to quote a James Thurber cartoon. One time I arrived to find the whole household in an uproar. *The Mary Tyler Moore* show, a '70s American sitcom, had depicted a dinner party in which one of the characters raised a glass of wine and said, "It's a naive domestic Burgundy, without any breeding, but I'm sure you'll be amused by its presumption." The Mankowskis weren't enraged by the use of the quote, but rather that the writers hadn't attributed it to James Thurber, who had created it as the caption of one of his cartoons in the *New Yorker*.[14]

---

[14] Kurt Nemes, "Johannes Brahms: Symphony Number 4, in E minor," *Kurt Nemes' Classical Music Almanac*, May 14, 2012, https://musical almanac.wordpress.com/2013/05/30/johannes-brahms-symphony -number-4-in-e-minor-2/.

The Sound of Silence

A Dog Ran Out in Front of It

Also from Nemes, here is one of my favorite stories from Paul's high school years, and one that Paul and I did discuss.

One rainy summer weekend evening, Paul Mankowski called me up to go out drinking. He had a friend named Dave Baker whose parents had a big, hulking Chevrolet station wagon. "Road party!" Paul said, and I was in. We loved to go get a case of beer, climb into a big boat of a car, and then drive around the countryside until about two in the morning.

When we started toward home, I said we should take the alternate route. "It has a great hill!" "Yeah!" said Paul, who knew the road as well. Unfortunately, Dave didn't. At the top of the hill, we yelled "Gun it!" and Dave took off. At the first curve, Dave lost control on the wet road, and the car went sailing into the woods and hit a tree head-on. I was sitting in the back seat and was hurled forward, hit the seat with my left hip and flew over and landed in Paul's lap. The pain at first was sharp and blinding. We all checked each other. Dave's head had hit the windshield, and he had a gash on his forehead, and his nose was swollen. Paul had managed to block his impact and somehow was unscathed. He left us and ran to get help.

An ambulance soon arrived and packed Dave and me off to the hospital. My parents were greatly relieved when the X-rays showed no broken bones. When quizzed about how it had happened, we only told them that Dave didn't know the road and had lost control on the wet pavement. We omitted the fact that we had told Dave to gun the car and had done it for the thrill of it.[15]

---

[15] Kurt Nemes, "Franz Schubert: (The Witch King)," *Kurt Nemes' Classical Music Almanac*, October 22, 2014, https://musicalalmanac.wordpress.com/2014/10/23/franz-schubert-the-witch-king-2/.

Paul told me that while Kurt and the others were at the hospital, he was at home explaining to his parents that a dog had run out in front of the car. He said that his parents seemed to believe him, but years later, he got a belated birthday card from one of his sisters with a scribbled note: "This would have been there on time, but a dog ran out in front of it."

Long before I had read anything by Kurt Nemes, on one of the first days that Paul and I spent time together, we were walking down a cobblestone road in Rome and discussing his background, and he said, "I was a jock in high school." I stopped walking and asked, "What did you just say?" He repeated it as I stood astounded. "*How* were you a jock in high school?" What I meant was, "How was someone with your brain a jock in high school?" but he answered by telling me about the various sports teams he'd been on. He added that he had boxed at Oxford. And then he told me the story of how he and a friend had resurrected the dead football team at the University of Chicago — let that sink in — where he played middle linebacker. (He was under six feet and skinny at the time.) When the team, which had been defunct for thirty years, was being resurrected, Paul had joined as the result of losing a bet — all it took to be on the team was a pulse. He didn't get to play often, because he hadn't played football since junior high and therefore wasn't very good, but during the last game of his senior year, the coach decided to let him play. This is a classic Paul story: he fractured his shinbone on the first play but didn't tell anyone about it until the game was over. He also went to the aftergame party before going to the emergency room.

He loved sports — one of the many things we had in common. (I was not a jock in high school, although I was captain of the cheerleading squad, and I have the ruined knees to show for it.) He had a strong competitive streak (I have heard many stories of things that he had to do as a result of a lost bet), and he was also a big fan of anything that involved detailed rules and a clear hierarchy. Hence, he was enamored of the military. It wasn't — as I'm sure a modernist Jesuit would tell you — that he was rigid and liked black-and-white rules. It was that he had a lot of respect for anything that was clearly ordered for a higher good, whether that good was serving God or taking one for the team.

Thanks to Nemes's blog and what he and Paul had told me, I thought I had a good understanding of Paul's family when I sat down to write this book, but I went on a research trip to South Bend just to get a feel for the place. When I wrote on Facebook about my plan to do that, I discovered that one of my Facebook friends, Kate Adams, not only lived in South Bend but had grown up with the Mankowski kids. She invited me to stay at her house, and she gave me the Mankowski tour of South Bend. That trip allowed me to see the rest of the story.

The Eagle Lake Yacht Club

Paul never told me that the blue-collar Mankowski family belonged to a yacht club. Kate's father had belonged to the club, and she spent time there on weekends with the Mankowskis. She took me to see it. It had never been modernized and probably looks the same way now as it did when the Mankowskis were members, so it was easy to imagine the time they spent there. Once I saw it, I could understand why Paul had never mentioned it. The *biggest* reason, I think, was that Paul was unable to make the words "yacht club" come out of his mouth; but I am also sure that he thought — justifiably — that I would have gotten a mistaken impression. The Eagle Lake Yacht Club, where he spent many impressionable young years, has since been given the more accurate name Eagle Lake Sailing Club. There are no yachts involved, merely different classifications of sailboats. An entire new dimension of Paul's father, Jim Mankowski, was made known to me by discovering that the "yacht club" was an important part of his life. First of all, he loved to race sailboats, and he taught his sons to race sailboats. That probably explains a lot about Paul's love of both competition and chain of command. Paul and his brother had crewed for their father until they became old enough to have penguins (the first sailboat for junior sailors) of their own. Paul had even crewed for Kate's father for a while.

There was a beach with a swing set for the kids who weren't old enough (or willing) to crew sailboats, and Kate had spent a lot of time playing in the sand with Paul's sisters. Basically, if your family owned a sailboat, your weekends were spent at the sailboat club. Paul's mother and sisters also provided the cheering section for Jim Mankowski's boat.

The Mankowski world was further opened up to me as I went into the clubhouse and Kate described the men who hung out there when they weren't racing sailboats. (These were the days when the women were either watching small kids or in the kitchen making something for the men to eat.) Most of the men who were Jim Mankowski's closest friends were college professors. Kate's father, Dr. Marshall Smelser, was the chair of the Notre Dame History Department. Jim Mankowski had dropped out of the University of Chicago to take the job at Bendix. Still, Kate said that he could hold his own with the professors on any topic, and, while mostly self-educated, he was by far the *most* educated. So instead of swilling beer at the local watering hole, Paul's father was at the yacht club, talking about history, philosophy, and literature with the college professors who were his closest friends.

Kate also insisted that I revisit the "factory worker" aspect of Jim Mankowski's life. Yes, he technically worked at a factory, but he worked for Bendix, which made things such as brakes for commercial aircraft. As a quality-control expert, Jim wasn't checking to see that a toy car had all four wheels. He was reading complicated schematics and comparing them with intricate airplane parts on which a great many lives depended. Kate always considered the Mankowskis to be upper-middle-class and had never thought of them as blue-collar.

The Sound of Silence

I have always thought that the traits that made Paul legendary had come from his father's influence. Kate confirmed this when she called Jim Mankowski "a pistol" and said that he used to greet her family with "Tyger, tyger, my mistake, I thought you were William Blake."

Eulogies

Paul's parents died in 2014, within a month of each other, and Paul offered the funeral Masses for both of them. In the eulogy for his father, Paul describes Jim Mankowski in terms that will sound very familiar to people who knew Paul:

> My father's preeminent strengths were, I think, the ability to distinguish the bogus from the genuine article — true of his reading of persons, and true of his response to ideas propounded by politicians, merchants, or churchmen — and the ability to recognize what is of primary versus what is of secondary importance. He was, as I said, no theologian, but anyone — *anyone* — who tried to get Jim Mankowski to move away from Catholic doctrine found a man
> Who.
> Would.
> Not.
> Be.
> Budged.[16]

Who is to say what was inherited and what was taken from a role model, but Paul was, in all ways, Jim Mankowski's son.

What I knew about Paul's mother, from him, was that she was highly intelligent and relatively quiet and had a great sense of humor but was never caustic (Paul must have gotten that from his dad). She was an

---

[16] Paul Mankowski, Homily for the Mass of Christian Burial for James Mankowski, November 19, 2014.

artist, but she was losing her eyesight to macular degeneration. My own mother was losing her eyesight to glaucoma, so most of the time when we discussed our mothers, we talked about their vision or lack thereof. As a result, I did not have a good take on who Paul's mother was. When he sent me the eulogy he had written for her funeral Mass, he filled in the blanks for me:

> In the instructions she left for her funeral my mother insisted there be no eulogy delivered at any part of the liturgy. But her son is a member of the Society of Jesus, and for that reason, alert to the dictum of Fr. Peter Hans Kolvenbach that the unique gift of the Jesuits to the Church is that of *creative fidelity*. Consequently, in the spirit of creative fidelity to my mother's wishes, I will make no mention of her manifold virtues as teacher, disciple, mother, wife. I will pass over in silence her concern for the weak, her lack of self-pity and self-display. Nor will I make reference to her neglect of her own pain and fatigue in tending to others, to her profound faithfulness to the Church, to her absolute incapacity to tell a lie. Obedient son that I am, I shall omit all of this and draw your attention instead to a remark made in the 1940s by the archbishop of Paris to his priests. Having reminded them of their duty to bear witness to the Catholic Faith, he went on to say, "To be a witness does not consist in engaging in propaganda, nor even in stirring people up, but in being a living mystery. It means to live in such a way that one's life would not make sense if God did not exist."[17]

From everything I have heard about Alice Mankowski, that is indeed how she lived her life. And so did her son.

---

[17] Paul Mankowski, Homily for the Mass of Christian Burial for Alice Mankowski, October 20, 2014.

The Sound of Silence

The Best-Laid Plans

As an exceptionally smart kid, it only made sense that Paul spent his college years at the University of Chicago, majoring in the classics. He also had an absolute gift for languages. By the time he died, Paul had mastered about a dozen languages, including the dead languages of ancient Hebrew, Akkadian, and Sumerian. He didn't do it to be pretentious. As he told me one day over lunch, "I just kept taking languages because they were always an easy A." The best summation of Paul's college years is to say that while he was studying the classics and learning languages, he was also on the football team *and* hosting a college radio show called *The Baroque Masters*. By his senior year, he had a Hawaiian fiancée named Eva, he had applied for graduate school at the University of Chicago for the following year, and he had his entire life planned all the way through retirement.

And then everything changed.

Interlude: Vocation Story

Early on, I asked Paul to tell me his vocation story. It follows, from e-mails we wrote near Easter of 2007.

My vocation story, at least until I actually entered the Jesuits, is simple. I was never one of those little boys who always dreamed of being a priest, but I never doubted the truth of the Catholic Faith. Even in college, while I got up to most of the usual iniquities, I never missed Sunday Mass. Late in my senior year at the U of Chicago, I had my future pretty neatly planned out. I was going on in ancient history at the U of Chicago and would become a tweed-and-briar-pipe classics prof, sire a large Catholic family, and spend a comfortable life fishing and hunting and reading Horace and bringing home good wines and Mass books to the wife and kiddies.

In early May of 1976, I was clobbered, out of nowhere, by the very strong certainty that God was calling me to give up that future and become a Jesuit. I knew no Jesuits personally, had never gone to a Jesuit school, had no particular knowledge of the Society beyond its history in religious controversy and missionary work. Yet it was clear that "Jesuit" was part of the message. I prayed in response: "Thanks, but no thanks. I'll be a good Catholic family man, kick in my share and more into the collection plate, fight my corner doctrinally, but please pick someone else for your priest." The answer kept coming back: "No. You." I told none of this to anyone else, including my girlfriend (who had plans of her own for us), my friends, or my family. I knew no priest to talk to, and I wasn't particularly pious. I steered clear of the campus chaplaincy and always attended the local parish instead. In fact (odd as it sounds), even though there was a Jesuit theologate at the University of Chicago at the time, including probably 120 Jesuits all told, I was totally unaware of this until I entered the novitiate.

After three or four weeks of the same give-and-take in prayer, I eventually gave in, telling God, "OK, you win." That was all there was to it. I'd read no vocational material or done any other "shopping" or discernment. On May 30 or 31, I picked up a phone book, found something called the Jesuit Seminary Association listed, rightly figured that it was a fund-raising office, and called to ask for the phone number of a vocation director. I still remember how flustered the secretary was in scrambling to get the number for me, as if she was afraid I'd hang up and become a Dominican if she didn't find it in time. At any rate, I got the number, made an appointment with the vocation guy, and started the candidacy program.

At this point, within a few days of my graduation, I went home to see my parents (who'd had absolutely zero inkling of this) and told them out of the blue that I was not going to grad school but would be becoming a Jesuit. Then, and in every subsequent vicissitude up to the present, they handled it about as well as it could possibly be handled: "It's your life, your decision; we wish you the best but will not interfere." They were

Interlude: Vocation Story

admirably neutral. I suspect my father was secretly pleased and that my mother was secretly displeased (at the time, I was the best prospect of providing grandchildren), but neither tipped their hand. For me, it couldn't have been better. Telling my girlfriend was harder. She was as unsuspecting and unprepared as my parents, and it was a real shock. Part of the difficulty is that a boyfriend and girlfriend carry on a life of intimacy that rarely includes an explicit statement of commitment. Yet the nature of the intimacy precludes a discussion of the boy's becoming a priest as a frank and objectively considered option; it's not the kind of thing the boy can hint at or bring in gradually into the usual conversations ("You know, I've been wondering lately whether Roman history might be more interesting than Greek, also whether I should become a priest or not"). So, understandably, the girl feels sucker punched at the news, since she was cut out of the deliberations and handed only the conclusion. Though Catholic, my girlfriend's churchmanship was based more on sharing my interest than in her own conviction, and she had little or no understanding of the morally imperative feel of a religious vocation that might help ease the hurt she felt. It took three or four years before she could talk about it with equanimity. Apart from my roommate (who was to marry my youngest sister six years later), whom I put under a promise of silence, I told none of my friends until the acceptance came through (in August). They were all stunned as well — again, I was not a campus ministry puppy and had everything geared up to return to classes in the Fall. With the exception of one very intelligent Jew, who since became a Catholic, none could see the change-of-career move as other than weird. I visited the novitiate (in Detroit) for a long weekend, probably in July. I was shocked by the fact that not even the priests wore clerics: that should tell you how clued in I was to the reality of the Society of Jesus — this was 1976. I remember having Mass standing around the usual round altar with the fabric covering and the colored candles, and I remember that they looked at me funny when I dropped to my knees during the Consecration. Believe it or not, I had never been to Mass before (with a bizarre exception in 1968) that wasn't in a standard chapel with kneelers, and I couldn't imagine the nonordained wouldn't kneel for the Eucharistic Prayer. The priest-formatores at the novitiate, who included some prominent liberal Jesuits, liked me and were encouraging. With the advantage of hindsight, I realize they were somewhat amused by my old-fashioned scruples but were confident that I'd lose them in time and get with the program. A misjudgment. I was, in turn, shocked by the opinions I heard — or thought I heard — from the mouths of the Jesuits, but I figured I must be misunderstanding their real meaning and at some deeper level they were doing what Jesuits always do and rooting for Holy Mother Church against her enemies. Why else would someone become a Jesuit, after all?

So, in barest outline, that's the story. When my brother dropped me off at the novitiate on September 5, I was the most clueless novice in the whole U.S. of A. One remark made to me that day by a fellow novice (during the post-liturgy get-to-know-you cocktails) still sticks with me: "You are exactly the kind of man I'd hoped I wouldn't find in the Jesuits."

My sibs (an older brother, three youngers sisters) were all surprised but supportive of my vocation. All remain practicing Catholics, though one of my sisters sort of flaked out for a fifteen-year period. The difficulty I had — and this was also true of my parents — was in making them understand what things were really like inside. They simply didn't believe it could have been as wacky as I said it was. There's a line in Michael Rose's *Goodbye, Good Men* where someone says, "When I tried to explain to my family what it was like in the seminary they couldn't believe me. So after a while I stopped trying." Exactly my own experience. In fact, one of the silver linings to the sex abuse crisis came home the day my dad said to me, "You know, I never knew what to make of the stuff you used to tell us about what went on. Now I see. In fact, in some respects, you may have been down-playing it." In some respects, I had to.[18]

---

[18] April 2007.

4

Epiphany

The truth will set you free. But not until it is finished with you.
— David Foster Wallace

In 1994, I was once again a person of faith, and I was decidedly "unequally yoked" with an atheist. I wasn't worried about it, initially, because my then-husband was an extreme liberal and therefore tolerant of all things. Surely my choice of religion would fall under that umbrella.

We were in a session with our couples' therapist (an L.A. must-have) when he informed the therapist that he had no problem with my going to RCIA classes, as long as I did not join the Catholic Church. That surprised me, and I said I wasn't going to make any promises, and he became more than a little angry.

We had driven separate cars to the therapist, and when I got home, he was sitting in a rocker, waiting. (The fact that it was a rocker has always been particularly cloying to me.) As I entered the room, he said, "If you're going to join the Catholic Church, I want a divorce because I never would have married a Catholic." I was so sure he was kidding, I said "fine" and asked him what I should wear to a dinner that night. As it turns out, he was not kidding. Not long after his initial proclamation, he made my decision easy by telling me that I had to choose between him and Jesus. "I never want to hear that man's name in my house again." Then, obviously, we could no longer live in the same house.

The rest of that story is better told elsewhere, but suffice it to say that I walked out on my life. I left an extremely expensive house in a prestigious neighborhood and moved into a Residence Inn. I left my life as part of a Hollywood power couple. Our friends chose one or the other of us to side with, so I lost good friends whose loss I still mourn. But in the long run, for having made that decision, I gained everything.

Kinder, Gentler Jesus

I was received into the Church on April 2, 1994. What I did not know at the time was that I was Cardinal Roger Mahony's version of a Catholic. The vast majority of the priests in L.A. were following his lead at that time, and that included the one who taught my RCIA class.

One of the first things I learned in RCIA class was the word "pastoral." I did not realize, for a long time, that "pastoral" is not so much a word as it is a wink. As hypothetical examples of "pastoral" were laid out for me, I learned that God had softened up a bit from the days of my youth. I naively asked one priest, "But we still believe in the Ten Commandments, don't we?" With a slight tilt of the head and squint of the eyes he answered, "Well... *ideally*." I also learned that the Church, the Bible, and the *Catechism* were living documents and that they had therefore evolved as the world had. It was the answer to one of my prayers: God grades on a curve!

This all sounded a little too good to be true, but it was coming from priests and catechists, and they certainly knew more than I did. So for my first few years of Catholicism, I enjoyed freedom from the burden of God's rules and regulations. I tried my best to be an overachiever and reach for the "ideals," but when I fell short, I went with the now-standard "I'm a good person; it'll be fine."

Epiphany

Wait, What?

It was when one of my liberal Jesuit friends told me that God was okay with abortion that I first saw a chink in the armor. I was still a babe in the woods in terms of fully understanding Catholicism, but that one was a no-brainer. And much like the first time I realized that my parents were wrong, it opened up all sorts of possibilities as to what else my Catholic-lite friends might be wrong about. By then I had observed Catholics' practice of parish-hopping until they found a priest who agreed with them, especially as to what was and wasn't sinful. In the early days of my desire to convert, I had assumed that the *Catechism* was the be-all and end-all and that all Catholics agreed on that. I also assumed that the pope (or at least a bishop) would leap on any deviation like a pig on a biscuit. But after a few years of being a Catholic, I realized that no such correction was taking place, and the *Catechism* was treated like a friend's advice, at which you nod politely with no intention of following.

"You Knew That"

My mother used to say, "God protects chaps and fools." ("Chaps" was a derogatory term my mother's side of the family always used for children. I assumed it was Scottish.) And because my mother was always right, God sent me help in the form of a woman named Barbara Nicolosi. She has since become Catholic-famous, but at the time, she was mostly unknown and working as the head of development for Paulist Productions in Los Angeles. She had heard about me, and she invited me to speak on a panel about Christians in show business. By that time, I had a foot out of the closet and figured I might as well go the rest of the way. Besides, Barbara seemed nice on the phone and would probably not find a plethora of people who would accept her invitation. The night of the panel, Barbara introduced herself to me and asked me if I'd like to have lunch, and we have been best friends ever since.

The Sound of Silence

Barbara had told me that she had been a nun for nine years, so I knew that she was well-versed in all things Catholic. Being a recent convert, I was happy to find a friend who did not tire of my proclaiming my love for the Church. One day I casually said to her, "I really like how the Church has changed since I last left it." She froze in place, then turned and stared at me in shock, and said, "*Nothing* has changed." I ran through some of the things I had learned in RCIA, and she was horrified. I also told her things that I had learned from the Jesuits who were helping me with my novel, and her horror doubled. She said, "First of all, don't listen to Jesuits." She spent the rest of the afternoon deprogramming me, and explaining to me both the basic tenets of Catholicism and the reasons for my being told the wrong thing by priests, of all people. It made sense to me, having watched society devolve over the course of my life. Why wouldn't priests lose their minds, as everyone else had?

I knew that I had some work to do. I had to find my way through the murkiness and "sophistication" of the modern Church to return to what was, as my mother had constantly reminded me, "good enough for Paul and Silas."

This was all made easier by a minor miracle that happened the moment after Barbara said, "*Nothing* has changed." Immediately, a loud voice in my head — that did not belong to me — said, "You *know* that." And I realized that the voice was right.

God Answers a Twenty-Five-Year-Old Prayer

At the same time, I was going through the annulment process, which was almost worse than the divorce. Ironically, it is much more difficult for an agnostic or atheist marriage to be annulled than a Catholic one if the marriage took place in a Christian church — even if the atheist had kicked the agnostic out for wanting to become Catholic. And it mattered now because a great miracle had taken place. My high school boyfriend — the Catholic — whose loss I had mourned for twenty-five years — appeared out of nowhere. Or rather, out of my Gmail inbox. (My mother always claimed that she "prayed him back," and I don't doubt it.) And then the woman who had made him break up with me in high school because I wasn't Catholic became my mother-in-law. Her name was Dorothy Walker, and she was more Catholic than the pope back when that really meant something. Remember her. She'll be back.

Chris and I were married in the Church in the year 2000. We went to the Jubilee in Rome that year, along with Barbara Nicolosi and a couple of habited nun friends. (If you want to know, *that's* how to get a good seat at a restaurant in Rome.) A few months after the trip to Rome, Chris and I discovered that we were about to be parents, at the ripe old age of forty-five. That gift from God is now a senior in college, and Chris and I recently celebrated our twenty-third wedding anniversary.

Gather Faithlessly Together

I had mostly recovered from my years as a Mahony-ite, but I still had no idea of the extent of the damage that the cardinal was doing. That changed in 1997, when he released a "pastoral letter" entitled *Gather Faithfully Together: A Guide to Sunday Mass, Pastoral Letter on the Liturgy*. *Gather Faithfully Together* was full of all of the modern language of unity and community and accompaniment. But Cardinal Mahony was trying to change the Mass in ways that affected my life, and I was not happy about it. Said pastoral letter detailed a set of instructions that were, for my money, aimed at devaluing both the priesthood and the Eucharist.

There were many things wrong with the letter; I don't have the room in a book of this scope to get into many details. If you'd like to seek them out, I would point you to the "Adoremus Statement on 'Gather

The Sound of Silence

Faithfully Together' — Cardinal Mahony's Letter on the Liturgy."[19] There Mahony's letter is taken point by point and addressed by Fr. Joseph Fessio, S.J.; Helen Hull Hitchcock; and Fr. Jerry Pokorsky. I read and agreed with that statement, but my nonscholarly mind was stuck on what I thought were the two gravest errors: (1) the faithful were told not to kneel for the Eucharistic Prayer and (2) we were instructed that when we received Communion, we were to look the eucharistic ministers in the eyes. Both, I thought, were blatant affronts to Jesus. By following those instructions, we would not be kneeling for His arrival, and when He was held up before us, we would be turning our gaze away from Him and toward Betty-from-row-three.

I knew that the letter was wrong. It was wrong to the point that it had to be resisted. I refused to stand for the Eucharistic Prayer, and so did many other Catholics in Los Angeles. So instead of creating the "unity" he was proposing, Mahony turned the Catholic Church in Los Angeles into a chaotic mess. During the Eucharistic Prayer, some people knelt, some people stood, and the rest paused mid-squat, looking around, trying to decide what to do. It would have been comical if it hadn't been so infuriating.

I consider it a badge of honor that I was once scolded — from the pulpit — for kneeling. I had gone to noon Mass at the Jesuit parish on Sunset Boulevard, and when I knelt, the presiding Jesuit priest looked at me (the only kneeler) and said, "It is our practice here in Los Angeles to remain standing as a show of community." I did not budge. He then said, in a firmer tone, "So if you are *able-bodied*, you should be standing." I kept kneeling. When I went up for Holy Communion, he hesitated

---

[19] Fr. Joseph Fessio, S.J., Helen Hull Hitchcock, and Fr. Jerry Pokorsky, "Adoremus Statement on 'Gather Faithfully Together' — Cardinal Mahony's Letter on the Liturgy," *Adoremus*, December 31, 2007, https://adoremus.org/2007/12/adoremus-statement-on-quotgather-faithfully-togetherquot-cardinal-mahonys-letter-on-the-liturgy/.

Epiphany

while he considered denying Communion to me. As this was during the papacy of John Paul II, I gave him a look that said, "Oh yes, please. I *want* to write that letter." He relented, and after Communion I knelt before the gorgeous statue of St. Ignatius and prayed, "Did you *see* that?"

Meanwhile, my mother-in-law, Dot, was thrilled to see that I was beginning to understand the full extent of the modernist rot. She belonged to the Third Order of St. Dominic, the Lay Dominicans. She was a daily communicant, and one of Cardinal Burke's Marian catechists. She established something called the Catholic Studies Center, where she catechized hundreds of people over the years. Her two spiritual directors were Cardinal Burke and Fr. John Hardon, S.J., so she was rock-solid in terms of orthodoxy. And while she was happy that I had converted, she had concerns — rightfully — about the state of my soul, after all of those years in L.A. under Mahony and after the years I had spent listening to liberal Jesuits. She could see that my eyes were being opened to the truth, but it wasn't happening fast enough to suit her.

One day she informed me that I was going to go to Kansas City, to a meeting of the Fellowship of Catholic Scholars (FCS), where a Fr. Paul Mankowski, S.J., would be one of the speakers. She knew him from her years at FCS, before she became too old to travel, and she had decided that what I needed was to spend some time with him. She gave me marching orders: "Do not get on the plane to come back home if you have not introduced yourself to Fr. Mankowski." Dorothy Walker was a woman who could silence a sports stadium with a look. She did not have to tell me twice.

Because I didn't yet understand the importance of meeting Paul, I had other things on my mind when I got to the conference. At that time, I was particularly upset about the fact that *Gather Faithfully Together* had begun to spread to other places in the country. So when there was a time to ask questions, I asked the panel of scholars what seemed to me an obvious question: "What are we going to do about this?" The panel of scholars all exchanged looks that reminded me of the old commercial, "*I'm* not going to try it. *You* try it." And then, in a "let's get Mikey to try it!" silent exchange, they all turned to look at Paul. I don't remember exactly what Paul said, but I do remember that he gave me very pragmatic suggestions along the lines of "write to this guy, not that guy" and "say this."

Throughout the rest of the conference, Paul and I continued our discussion across the crowded room, so he "knew" me before I came up to introduce myself. During a brief break, I introduced myself (and identified myself as Dot Walker's daughter-in-law), and I asked, "Could I have your e-mail address if I promise not to abuse it?" He cheerfully wrote it down, handed it to me, and said, "Abuse it all you want to." A few days after I returned home, I received the following e-mail from him:

> I was delighted to make your acquaintance at the FCS convention and wished I could have stayed around a little longer to talk to you and to old friends as well. I was very much struck by the point you made about the way in which sin and grace are mingled in our lives, and how God makes use of unlikely people and circumstances to call us back to Himself — and how, almost perversely, pious biographers (and autobiographers) choose to ignore this by downplaying the sinful choices made by saints — and by other Christians — as well as papering over the unseemly passages of our lives. I think your project of trying to restore the other side of the picture is a noble one and one that will help a lot of other folks who are hesitant to bring themselves into contact with the Church. A lot of folks who have lived fast and loose and begun to regret it feel they'd be hypocritical by coming to church, because they think they'd be claiming, deceitfully, to be godly and upright and pious by showing up on Sunday. It's hard to convince them that they've

Epiphany

got it backwards: you come to church because you know you're a sinner in need of God's forgiveness. For this reason it's good to remind them, or inform them, that some of the greatest saints were in the same position and that the strength of their holiness couldn't have taken the form it did without the corresponding boldness of their sins. So, power to your right hand!
— Paul[20]

I wasn't aware of it at the time, but my life had just changed.

---

[20] "Fellowship," October 2006. He was speaking about an idea I had told him: I wanted to write a movie about the unsaintly years of St. Ignatius. In 2022, I finally sold the idea to a Spanish production company as a miniseries, and it will be coming eventually to a streaming service near you.

5

Rude Awakening

*Shot through the heart
and you're to blame
Darling, you give love a bad name.*

— Bon Jovi

Paul knew little about the Jesuits before joining them, but he knew that his vocation involved not just being a priest but being a Jesuit. That might have been because his father had given Jesuitdom a go but had left early. He had declared that the "obedience" thing was a deal-breaker for him. Paul might have had an issue with that, too, had he not been so certain that "Jesuit" was part of his vocation. He had grown up in a place and in a family where "Catholic" meant "Catholic," and it would never have dawned on him that he might be placing a phone call to a religious order whose leaders held the Magisterium in contempt. It wouldn't have occurred to him that people who hated the Church's Magisterium would become priests. Ever the pragmatist, he would have asked, "*Why?*"

It is impossible to understand Paul Mankowski's life — especially his priesthood — without understanding the current state of the

The Sound of Silence

Society of Jesus and how the modernists came to control it. But first, here is another disclaimer: since St. Ignatius founded the Jesuits in 1540, there have always been amazing Jesuits: men who have given their very lives — sometimes literally — for Holy Mother Church. I know Jesuits who can be so described. Those men used to be the majority. It is possible that they still are, but they do not hold — aren't allowed to hold — positions of power, so it doesn't matter. The Jesuits in power positions are the ones who control the order and what the order presents to the outside world as "Jesuit." Otherwise, the current face of the Jesuits would be Fr. Mitch Pacwa of EWTN or Fr. Joseph Fessio of Ignatius Press instead of Fr. James Martin of the LGBTQ movement.

How did the Jesuits go from being men who would risk their lives climbing the Iguazu Falls to bring Christianity to the Guarani to being men who are proud that their colleges have hosted productions of *The Vagina Monologues*? (I checked. Every Jesuit college in America has hosted a production of *The Vagina Monologues*.) If I were to boil it down to the shortest possible answer, that answer would be "the sixties." The real answer is more complicated, but not by much. If you would like the answer in extreme detail, you should find a copy of *The Pope and the Jesuits*[21] by Church historian James Hitchcock. He details what happened to Jesuits all around the globe. The American Jesuits were hit by a perfect storm made up of the following: the sixties, the "spirit" of Vatican II, liberation theology, the Land O' Lakes Conference (whereby, for all intents and purposes, Catholic colleges declared themselves free from Catholicism), *Humanae Vitae*[22] (and their objection to it), and the abdication of logic (and the Magisterium) in

---

[21] James Hitchcock, *The Pope and the Jesuits: John Paul II and the New Order in the Catholic Church* (New York: National Committee of Catholic Laymen, 1984).

[22] With the papal encyclical *Humanae Vitae* (July 25, 1968), Pope Paul VI reaffirmed the Church's traditional teachings on birth control.

favor of feelings. Volumes have been written about modernist Jesuits and how they got that way. I invite you to do the research rather than take my word for it.

Novitiate Years

Paul's first clue that something was amiss involved a painful discovery: roughly half of his novitiate class was gay. Paul knew that the Church provided a good hiding place for men who were tired of answering "Why aren't you married yet?" but he was surprised at the number of them. He was also alarmed by the many modernists (who were known merely as liberals back then). Furthermore, he was bothered by the numerous pictures of Pedro Arrupe, the Jesuits' (liberal) father general, that adorned his community's walls rather than pictures of John Paul II, who was the pope at the time. As described previously, he became extremely concerned after he learned of the Jesuits' "institutional apostasy" on the Church's teaching regarding homosexuality, and he quickly learned that this was not the only way in which the Jesuits disagreed — openly — with the Church. He was especially dedicated to the "teaching Church," and any disagreement with her bothered him immensely.

He quickly learned that the majority of modern Jesuits bore little resemblance to those martyrs he admired. He found other men in his novitiate class who were equally bothered, and they formed a de facto support group. During their years in theology at Weston, Paul and company cobbled together their own theology program, meeting together to read and discuss St. Aquinas and St. Augustine rather than the modernist theologians they were being made to read in their classes.

The formatores who had been convinced that Paul would grow out of (or be brainwashed out of) his orthodoxy were becoming disturbed as that did not happen. Paul posed a threat to them, given his intelligence and his writing skill. The last thing they needed was for him to grow a fan club, so by the time he went to Harvard to work on his master's degree, his superiors were watching him closely.

The Drinan Affair

Paul's first official fall from Jesuit grace was brought on by something that can now be easily googled as "the Drinan Affair." George Weigel has written about it extensively in *Jesuit at Large*, but I will give you the "coverage," as we say in showbiz.

As you may or may not be aware, there has been a Jesuit congressman. His name was Robert Drinan, and he ran for and was elected to Congress in 1971. He was re-elected twice and served until 1981.

Because of Drinan, canon law now bars any priest from public office,[23] but it had not been spelled out before then. St. Ignatius admonished early Jesuits not to run for clerical office. He did not address their running for secular office, but I think we can extrapolate.

It would be an exaggeration to say that Drinan is almost single-handedly responsible for the number of abortion mills we see in the United States today, but I'm not sure how much of an exaggeration. He was a liberal who ran on an anti-war platform, and in almost everything, he sided with the Democratic Party. There was, of course, the not-so-small matter of abortion, but Drinan did the liberal Catholic sidestep and declared himself against abortion "personally" but not as a matter of public policy. He didn't leave it there, though. In 1964, he was one of three priests who went to Hyannis Port, Massachusetts, and convinced the rising-star Kennedy brothers that they could support abortion with clear consciences. Where might the country be had that not happened? How many abortions did Drinan open the door to on that day? The number, if we could know it, would be staggering.

---

[23] *Code of Canon Law* (Washington, D.C.: Canon Law Society of America, 1999), 208–329.

Rude Awakening

Can you imagine, instead, if the three Catholic Kennedy brothers had voiced their opposition to abortion?

As a congressman, Drinan continued to support and defend abortion rights. He voted, with the other Democrats, for abortion in all forms. Sadly, he was one of the strongest defenders of abortion in Congress.

Paul, who was a Harvard graduate student at the time, set out to write an article about Drinan. As he explained to me, the point of the article was to exonerate the Jesuit father general, Pedro Arrupe, from any responsibility for Drinan's career because Arrupe had told Drinan not to run for office. As Paul further explained, the more he worked on the research, the more he realized that Arrupe could not be fully exonerated. Arrupe had allowed Drinan's operatives to dupe him, and once he discovered that he had been duped, Arrupe caved and did not step up to declare opposition to Drinan. Paul abandoned the article but gave his research to Church historian James Hitchcock, for whatever good it might do for posterity.

Hitchcock did nothing with the research from 1992 until 1996. However, when Drinan wrote an op-ed in the *New York Times* in 1996 defending President Bill Clinton's veto of a bill banning partial-birth abortion, both Paul and Hitchcock decided it was time to do something with the information that Paul had unearthed. Hitchcock wrote the article,[24] and he offered to keep Paul's name out of it entirely. Paul wouldn't have that. He wanted to take full credit for the research, so the expected ire would fall on him and not on Hitchcock. And fall it did.

The Jesuits, who were infuriated by the besmirching not only of *their* congressman but also of their father general, commenced to spread

---

[24] James Hitchcock, "The Strange Political Career of Robert Drinan," Catholic Culture, June 27, 1996, https://www.catholicculture.org/news/features/index.cfm?recnum=775.

the absolute lie that Paul had sneaked into the archives and taken the research material without permission. That lie is still alive today in Jesuitdom, I would assume. It was still alive when I researched a project in 2007:

> Fr. XXXX, (SJ) and I did discuss Paul again, and they (the Chicago Jesuits) have the belief that he entered the space of the Provincial and literally took files out and gave them to the press ... whatever that is worth.[25]

I advised my research assistant that it was worth nothing because it was a lie. Paul asked for and received full permission from the archivist before copying any of the Drinan material. When he had been trying to make Arrupe look better, there was no problem with him taking the material. When the truth turned out to make Arrupe look, at best, like a wimp, then history was revised and Paul was a thief.

The lie, however, was not enough. Paul had to be punished for airing their dirty laundry. (I remember asking him, when I first heard the story, "Don't they see that the problem is that they *have* dirty laundry?" That, to this day, never has been considered a problem.)

The hell that rained down on Paul as a result of the publishing of his Drinan research was, as George Weigel puts it, draconian.[26] Luckily, it is also well-documented. Paul sent me a copy of the letter he received from his superior. The next "interlude" includes the "canonical warning" letter in its entirety, with the exception of the opening amenities. This was the letter that robbed the world of ten years of the brilliant mind of Paul Mankowski.

---

[25] Anonymous, "Photos," e-mail to the author, September 2007.
[26] George Weigel, *Jesuit at Large: Essays and Reviews by Paul Mankowski, S.J.* (San Francisco: Ignatius Press, 2021), 13.

Interlude: Canonical Warning Letter

In 2003, long before we met, Paul had received the following canonical warning letter from his provincial. The debate at hand had to do with Paul's request for final vows. (What that means will be dealt with in detail later; for now, it is enough to know that Jesuits take two different sets of vows. The first set is taken when they are novices and the "final" vows are taken later in the process, after which the men are fully incorporated into the Jesuits.)

From Paul's direct superior:

[Amenities excluded]

Of even greater concern to me are some remarks you made in our conversation that indicate almost no trust in the leadership of the Society of Jesus. To say that many or most of the superiors in the Society are in material heresy is a rather sweeping condemnation. To dismiss the decrees of our 34th General Congregation and to question their approval by the Holy See because of a lack of vigilance in the Secretary of State's office at the Vatican reflects a remarkable arrogance on your part.

As I indicated to you in my previous letter on this matter, my primary concern in all this has been your apparent lack of trust in superiors and in the ordinary governance of the Society, manifested in your actions. After talking with you, this concern is only heightened.

You tell me you want to remain in the Society, that this is where God has called you. While I want to believe that, with all my heart, your present behavior and underlying attitude continue to trouble me. I really do wonder, Paul, whether you can or should remain in the Society. It truly saddens me to say that. You're a good man, passionate in your love of the Lord, the Church, and the Gospel. I find myself agreeing with some things you say and sharing many of your concerns. And yet your almost total mistrust of the legitimately established authority of the Society and of the Society's articulated presence in the Church as Servants of Christ's mission is deeply disturbing.

Because of this substantive, underlying mistrust of the Society's superiors and our most recent congregation, questions of obedience and your ability to live at peace and be governed by superiors remain. I have had to give very serious consideration to whether or not I ought to begin at this time the process that would lead to your dismissal from the Society. As serious as these issues are and clearly worthy, in my judgment, of such action, I have decided against it at this time. This remains, however, a real option.

Let me indicate why I have decided against beginning such an action at this time. Perhaps the most encouraging thing to me in all this is the honesty with which you have always presented yourself and, in particular, during our recent conversation. Such candor may allow a provincial to govern as directed by the Society. It is the sign to me that, despite your judgments of those in authority, you are desirous of not being deceptive. And you have told me that you will be obedient. I presume you

Interlude: Canonical Warning Letter

mean this to be the case in more than just the letter of the law but in its spirit as well. In these next months and years, however, it will be important for you to demonstrate that willingness to live according to our way of proceeding by your actual conduct.

In order for the Society to judge whether or not you are apt for tertianship and final incorporation, you must take this matter to prayer, rebuild the trust with your superiors and brothers which has been significantly damaged, demonstrate the quality of obedience expected of Jesuits, and attend fully to the mission assigned you by the Society. Specifically, this is what I want you to do:

1. Find a spiritual director with whom you will work closely in considering these matters in prayer;
2. Destroy immediately any materials from the New England archives which are in your possession;
3. Direct anyone to whom such materials have been transmitted that these are not to be used in any way;
4. Complete and defend your dissertation in the timely fashion you outlined;
5. Dedicate yourself fully to the mission assigned you at the Biblicum and to your "professional development" as a Scripture scholar through research, writing, and participation in professional organizations and conferences;
6. Get the specific approval of your local superior for any ministry beyond your work at the Biblicum;
7. Get the permission of your rector to publish anything, make any public statement, or take any public action. If he judges any of these to be "controversial," then the Delegate and the Chicago Provincial are to be consulted for their respective permissions in such matters. You are to abide by their judgment.

The Sound of Silence

As I have said, I am hopeful that someday you can be fully incorporated into the Society of Jesus. I have listed above my clear expectations that would serve as very positive indicators that final vows could be a real option for you. These are not my personal expectations; through my office, I am presenting them to you as the expectations of the Society of Jesus. Things cannot stay as they are, Paul. If you fail to fulfill these expectations to the satisfaction of your major superior, then it is not likely you can be fully incorporated into the Society of Jesus. You need to move genuinely and obviously into the Society of Jesus, while remaining who you in conscience are and must be; otherwise, there is little likelihood you will ever be fully incorporated into the Society. While currently no canonical process is underway concerning you, please know that all this material would be quite pertinent should such a process be deemed necessary in the future.

I am deeply saddened in writing this letter. Out of care for you and for the whole Society, however, I feel compelled to do so. I would have preferred to communicate this to you in person, but the time needed to reflect on our conversation and the current distances between us require this format. This is a crucial moment, Paul, for all of us. Are you willing to put your marvelous gifts at the genuine service of the Society? I surely hope so. The decisions you make will tell the story.[27]

Follow-Up Letter

Soon afterward, Paul received the following e-mail from the same superior:

---

[27] "Canonical Warning Letter," May 2007.

Interlude: Canonical Warning Letter

I thought it'd be best to write out for you the questions I mentioned. I'm glad for your willingness to respond to these matters. I'd also like to add a further area (#3) which I voiced in a summary way at the conclusion of our conversation. I'd appreciate your reflection, as well, to #3 below:

1. What was the grace of your Tertianship experience?
2. Why do you wish to become a Jesuit, fully incorporated?
3. Related to the first two questions, my underlying concern is about whether you feel a pervading sense of trust in the Society and its governance as it is today.
4. Finally, do you have any additional comment about or reflections to the three specific areas I raised as my chief concerns with respect to your advancement to final vows?[28]

Paul's Response

Paul responded to the canonical warning as follows:

Paul Mankowski, SJ — Statement of Intent

January 10, 2003

I wish to make my final profession in the Society of Jesus. The ground of this desire is my conviction — which since I first acknowledged it has never wavered — that it is God's will that I serve him as a Jesuit. For my part, this is both a necessary and a sufficient condition of my request. All other considerations are ultimately of negligible importance.

My vocation came to me when I was finishing college, and my response was motivated by three factors: my deep love of the Church, especially the teaching Church; my distress at

---

[28] May 2007.

the assault on Catholic doctrine by anti-Christian forces both inside and outside the Church; my respect for and delight in the Jesuit knack for turning up in the front lines wherever the battle was fiercest. Other orders were directed ad intra, aimed at consolidating the gains already made by the Church. But the uniquely Ignatian spirit was, I believed, expressed by the cheerful and lucid intellectual fearlessness of an Edmund Campion:

> When you shall have heard these questions of religion opened faithfully, which many times by our adversaries are huddled up and confounded, [you] will see upon what substantial grounds our Catholic Faith is builded, how feeble that side is that by sway of the time prevaileth against us, and so at last for your own souls that depend on your government, will discountenance error when it is betrayed, and hearken to those who would spend the best blood in their bodies for our salvation.

Campion happened also to possess outstanding physical courage, but it was the moral and intellectual gutsiness of the Jesuits — believing, and acting on the belief, that truth will prevail — that attracted me in 1976 and attracts me still.

If my picture of the Society of Jesus was naively rosy when I entered the novitiate, the intervening twenty-six years have provided many corrective shocks. That said, when I made my request to do tertianship, my deepest desires were different in no important way from those that first led me to pick up the phone and dial Pat Darcy. I had, and have, no doubts that the promise made in the same vow formula "to live and die in this same Society" persists in full force, and that by seeking to leave the Society I would jeopardize the salvation of my soul. The vows were made not to men but to God.

Interlude: Canonical Warning Letter

❖ ❖ ❖

My tertian year brought with it many profoundly satisfying moments. Yet the prime grace of tertianship — which in default of every other blessing would still have made the experience worthwhile — was stumbling upon these passages in the autobiographical works of St. Ignatius:

> When [Ignatius] wondered in Barcelona whether he should study and how much, it was a question of whether after his studies he should enter a religious order or go through the world as he was. And when he thought of entering a religious order, then he thought and desired to enter one that was corrupt and unreformed — to be able to suffer more, and also perhaps thinking that God would help them. [Autobiography 71]

He finally decided on this, that if he had to become a religious, he would enter some order that was further from its fervent beginnings and had forgotten the observance of its rules. For on the one hand it seemed to him that perhaps our Lord would be served if that order reformed itself by his work and example, and on the other hand he would have more opportunity to suffer and put up with the many contradictions and persecutions that would come from those who, content merely with the name and habit of religious, would be unwilling to have their discipline and religious life reformed. [Fontes Narrativi IV 199]

Clearly Ignatius was able to recognize and call it by its proper name, without recourse to euphemistic evasions. Clearly he was "judgmental," though in a sane and honest way; he could frankly acknowledge his own defects, but had the guts not to become complicit in falsehood. Clearly too his astuteness did not lessen his charity. Ignatius didn't flinch at naming the contradictions in the religious life of his day, yet his impulse was not to begin a campaign to suppress the wayward congregations but to throw in his lot with theirs and take the inevitable hits. He was a man's man.

That Ignatius did not in fact enter a corrupt order but, against his own inclinations, became the founder of a new one is irrelevant. The point is that he taught me that charity, if it tells the truth about itself, gives positive value to suffering.

In tertianship I came to see that the question, "Are you happy in your vocation?" is a boy's question. Except for the desperately wretched, every man experiences a mixture of happiness and frustration in his life. The key question is: are your frustrations — the frustrations consequent on the choices you've made — meaningful frustrations or meaningless frustrations? Ignatius' own autobiography makes it clear that "contradictions" in religious life, provided one is not responsible for them, can be meaningful, can contribute to one's own salvation and to the salvation of others. Coming face-to-face with this truth was the prime grace of my tertianship. In asking for final vows I am asking for a life in which failure (i.e., failure to accomplish what I desire to accomplish as a religious) is probable and in which frustrations are certain.

❖ ❖ ❖

The principle concern I was asked to address in this statement regards doubts — doubts voiced by my superiors — as to whether I "feel a pervading sense of trust in the Society and its governance as it is today." Having reflected on this question at length, my answer is this: I trust the Church. I trust

Interlude: Canonical Warning Letter

that God works through his Church; that it is his Church he has protected from error; and that, to the extent that my life as a vowed religious is conformable to Church teaching and discipline, it will be pleasing to God. Hence I trust the Society of Jesus when and where it thinks with the Church, and not elsewhere.

In October of 19[XX] I had a meeting with [name withheld] (then my provincial) in which the issue of trusting the Society of Jesus came up. Here is the central part of that conversation, verbatim or very nearly so:

Paul, do you trust your superiors in the Society of Jesus?

I trust my superiors in all the unimportant things but not in the important things.

Explain.

Taking the hot-button issues — remarriage, the ordination of women, gay sex, contraception — my surmise is that you and your colleagues all dissent from defined doctrine on at least one of these issues, and that the majority of you dissent on the majority. Am I wrong in my surmise?

No.

In fact, your general attitude regarding your doctrinal dissent is: What the bishops and Vatican don't know won't hurt them — right?

Right.

So then, what you're asking from me is precisely the kind of trust that you superiors are unwilling to extend to the Holy See and the bishops — am I right or wrong?

But Paul, how can we govern you if you don't trust us?

Absolutely no problem. You give me a command and I'll obey it. But you're asking for a purely subjective declaration of confidence. You've just told me yourself the reasons I can't honestly offer this.

But why would you want to be a part of a group of men whose superiors hold theological opinions so different from your own?

The opinions of superiors are irrelevant. Opinions are historical contingents. They are different now from what they were in 1960, and they will change again. But I'm a vowed man, and vows concern responsibilities which are not contingent, responsibilities based on things that never change.

Except for [name withheld]'s unusual frankness, this account differs in no essential way from dozens of my discussions with other superiors on the same subject. For me, the bottom line is this: Where the superiors of the Society of Jesus are at variance with the pope, I'm on the side of the pope. Would a better Jesuit act otherwise?

❖ ❖ ❖

Had Ignatius pursued his aspiration to enter an unreformed congregation, how candid and explicit could he have been to the examiners regarding his own motivations and regarding corrupt aspects of religious life in need of remedy? The question is not idle. I find myself in a similarly paradoxical position: obliged by circumstances to manifest my desire for incorporation into a religious institute to the very men who have power of refusal, yet obliged in conscience to manifest

Interlude: Canonical Warning Letter

my conviction that the same men — corporately, at least — dissent from orthodox Catholic faith and have failed seriously in their own responsibilities to that faith. I am asking of my superiors, not that they come to believe that I'm right, but that they decide that, even if I be mistaken I may be allowed to go forward in the Society. I am asking that they view my judgments not as the arrogance of an outside critic but as the candor of a brother Jesuit. I am asking that they forbear to make use of their canonical prerogatives to eliminate a gadfly. In fact, I am asking quite a lot.

It may be that I am asking too much. But I hope not. I still hold to the words of the vow formula: As You have given me the grace to desire this, so will You also bestow abundant grace to fulfill it.

Paul Mankowski, SJ

Paul had to wait six months for the answer, and it came in the following letter from the same superior:

[Amenities missing]

Let me quote directly from Fr. General's letter to me. It goes to the heart of the matter:

> ... taking into account his declarations about superiors and about the Society, we cannot at this time admit him to final vows. On the other hand, we cannot let the present situation continue year after year without any attention given to it on the part of the superiors. You and his future provincials should take up this issue each year with him, making him aware that his stand is not "normal" and cannot last forever.

> Paul, I know how difficult this is for you. Yet I know Fr. General's decision was made in light of as caring and thorough a process as I could facilitate. Fr. General had at his hand a very wide range of information and recommendations, including your own perspectives.
>
> God's peace and light be with you in your current work and service of the Society and the Church.[29]

Besides the above responses, Paul's email to me included a personal note:

> My takeaway, among all the obvious things, is this: no one — not the provincial and not the Father General — said, "Wait, WHO told you that we don't agree with the Church on all the categories you mentioned????" In this case, the silence roars.[30]
>
> In our Lord,

---

[29] Anonymous superior to Paul Mankowski, "More Knowledge I'm Trying to Fake," e-mail to the author, May 2008.

[30] "More Knowledge I'm Trying to Fake."

6

The Noisy Years

*Truth tellers are not often palatable.
There is a preference for candy bars.*

— Gwendolyn Brooks, *Gottschalk and the Grande Tarantelle*

One of the many things on which Paul and I agreed was the importance of work. We were both raised with a strong work ethic and were both aware of the gifts God had given us and the importance of using them. I have a vivid memory of the first time I heard a pastor read, "Unto whomsoever much is given, of him much shall be required." I was only six years old at the time, but I got it. I remember thinking, "Uh-oh. That means me." I wish I had discussed Luke 12:48 with Paul, but I didn't because I felt certain that I already knew what he would say. Ironically, the evidence of how strongly we both felt about work is there because we never mentioned it. We were too busy doing it.

When Paul was silenced in 2003, it wasn't simply the Drinan affair (1996) that had made him the enemy. Although his superiors had pinned it on that, Paul had, shall we say, been begging for it for a decade. In that decade, he'd written and published many articles on hot-button topics and had received, much to the Jesuits' dismay, a wide readership and a lot of respect. Many people, my mother-in-law among them, saw the young Jesuit Mankowski as a ray of hope in a darkening Catholic world. My mother-in-law first heard Paul speak at a Fellowship of Catholic Scholars conference, and she told me that when he finished his talk, everyone in the room gave him a standing ovation, while exchanging "Do you believe this?" looks with each other. Could this be true? Could a young priest have given such a remarkable talk? And a *Jesuit*? Dot told me that everyone in the room had new hope, not only for the Church but also, of all things, for the Jesuits!

A brief look at his body of work during that decade will explain a lot. (Note: These articles can be read in their entirety in George Weigel's *Jesuit at Large*, and I highly recommend reading them all.)

Here is the list, with snippets from each article.

1989: Why the Immaculate Conception?

Among all the articles that Paul wrote, "Why the Immaculate Conception?" is one of my favorites. He wrote it long before we met, but I reread it every year on the feast of the Immaculate Conception. The world that he describes sounds innocent compared with what we see today, but the article (originally a homily) was daring at the time.

> I live in an age, and a country, wherein the largest single cause of death of infants under one year of age is homicide. I live at a time when, according to those who claim to know these things, Ronald McDonald has surpassed Jesus Christ in popularity among children. I live at a time when the best-known moral theologians have despaired of leading people to a more virtuous life but are principally concerned to insulate the sinner from the consequences of his sin; logic has given way to latex as the preferred medium of instruction. I live in a country where, this very day, in the time between my rising and my standing here

before you, four thousand of our fellow citizens, four thousand human beings with an eternal destiny, were summarily killed by abortion. I live at a time when most promises will be broken, most vows will be repudiated, most marriages will fail. I live at a time when it is virtually impossible to go through a day without using some commodity that, however innocent in itself, is not hawked in terms of some base or venal allure. I am promised prosperous and intriguing companions by the folks who brew my beer; and those who sell my shaving cream are at pains to assure me that it will provoke the women I encounter into sexual frenzy. (The last claim, I might add, is an exaggeration.)

It may seem pointless at such a time, in such a place, to hold up the Virgin Mary, and especially her Immaculate Conception, as a source of nourishment for our lives as Christians. For her perfection can appear so remote from the moral sweatiness and squalor in which our personal struggles occur that it recedes entirely into the background; it is swallowed up by our furious temptations and enthusiasms and so is lost to us. This remoteness is widened, and not helped, by a way of speaking that would present the Virgin Mary to us as "the representation of an Ideal," that is, as an abstraction, or at best a personified Virtue, like the Roman goddesses of Wisdom or Moderation. Thus, she, who begins as a real flesh-and-blood woman, "a virgin, betrothed to a man named Joseph," as today's Gospel has it, becomes in the end an abstract noun, a figure of speech.

And of course it's not hard to see why, in and of itself, a personified Ideal is of little consequence to the moral or spiritual life. To use an analogy from a more trivial world, we might imagine a mythological golfer who scored 18 in every round he ever played, yet few instructors would "hold up" such a figure as an example to his pupils, and even fewer players would tell themselves in preparing to make a treacherous shot, "Steady now. Remember that the Great McTavish always did the 530-yard fifth hole in one stroke." Ideals can be beacons to guide us, but they are seldom fires at which we can warm our hands; they may be necessary to our thinking, but they don't strengthen the will. In terms of discipleship, humanity needs prodding in order to be spurred on to a companionship in godliness. If you think about the two or three saints to whom you yourself have the deepest devotion, is it not the case that part of what attracts and fascinates you about these saints is that you can recognize a certain kinship in the kind of fragility they possess, a fragility against which their heroism blazes with particular glory in your eyes, in your heart? Isn't it the case that, since you can see God's work in their weakness, you can come to accept the possibility of God's working in your weakness too?[31]

The following year he took on the feminists.

1990: Feminist Pilgrims

In this article, Paul writes about Western feminist fans of Marxism who descended upon Managua to cheer on the Sandinistas, "clutching their Nikons and their dissertations, anxious for a cure or an imprimatur."

It is hardly surprising, for example, that Western feminists should have mounted their own fact-finding tours to assess the progress of the Daughters of the Revolution. In May 1988 Maxine Molyneux published an article in the *Feminist Review*, "The Politics of Abortion in Nicaragua: Revolutionary Pragmatism — or Feminism in the Realm of Necessity?" Molyneux

---

[31] Paul Mankowski, "Why the Immaculate Conception?," posted at Women for Faith and Family, http://archive.wf-f.org/mankowski.html.

was grieved to learn that "Nicaragua is an anomaly among socialist states. Its comparatively advanced record on general political issues — pluralism, democracy, abolition of the death penalty — contrasts with a surprisingly conservative position on reproductive rights."

The chief villain was, of course, the Catholic Church, and particularly its hierarchy, which exercised a kind of mind control even over emancipated Sandinistas, which Molyneux was at a loss to account for. But a second factor was the rather embarrassing one that the National Directorate of Nicaragua — though a splendid thing in itself — was overwhelmingly composed of *Latino* males, with predictable consequences: "The cults of *machismo* and *hombria* [manliness] place considerable store on being able to father large numbers of children, biologically if not socially."

It is interesting that leftists constitutionally averse to negative stereotypes of "ethnic minorities" find their scruples only too vincible when the ethnics in question fail to measure up. Nor is it only Nicaraguan men who are at fault. As Molyneux laments, "in Catholic countries where women's identification with motherhood is positive and particularly strong," even the sisters themselves can fall short of full enlightenment. One Nicaraguan feminist told the author:

> The losses of war have strengthened rather than diminished the emotional significance of motherhood. There are 11,000 women in Managua alone who are mothers of soldiers who have died in the fighting. Abortion in such a context is associated with more death; for some women it's unthinkable.

Our researcher does not explicitly draw the conclusion, but we are meant to feel that not the least of the tragedies of war is that it robs a young woman of her normal, wholesome urge for the surgical termination of pregnancy.[32]

1991: Of Rome and Runnymede

This article is about Pope St. John Paul II's *Ex Corde Ecclesiae*, a papal declaration on the mission of Catholic universities. He begins like this:

> Curious. Why should the *New York Times,* the *Washington Post,* and the *Boston Globe* all see fit to carry the story of the promulgation of *Ex Corde Ecclesiae,* the papal declaration on the mission of Catholic universities? On the face of it, Vatican norms for higher education hardly seem to have national "news value," especially from the perspective of those papers that have frequently strained the bounds of responsible journalism to the breaking point in order to reinforce the notion that the Vatican view of *anything* is hopelessly inapplicable to our contemporary situation. Could it be that they protest just a little too much, that this is yet another instance in which the power brokers of a militant secularism see more clearly than Christians themselves how the teaching Church cuts too close to the bone for anyone's comfort?

And later:

> Perhaps the Pope is onto something overlooked by others, that the secular academy in our century has abetted partisan attempts to discredit methods proper to science and scholarship, and this with a vigor unparalleled in the history of the West. We have seen Marxists condemn Mendelian genetics as

---

[32] Paul Mankowski, "Feminist Pilgrims," *Commentary*, September 3, 2015, https://www.commentary.org/articles/paul-mankowski/feminist-pilgrims/.

a counterrevolutionary intrigue, Nazis reject the theory of relativity as a Jewish fabrication, feminists dismiss propositional logic as a white male conspiracy — all with the (rather uneasy) connivance of the university authorities. Would an impartial observer find more political contamination in Renaissance scholarship than in our own, or less intellectual independence among the orthodox churchmen than among the dissenters of our time? Is Scaliger more a child of his age than Stanley Fish? Charles Curran less a product of politics than Henri de Lubac? Is there doubt any longer that the proper distinction is not between dogmatists and free inquirers, but between those who are aware of their dogmas (and to this extent free) and those who are unaware that they hold any dogmas at all (and thus their unwitting slaves)?

The terms of the *magna carta* are these: (1) that genuine scholarship and scientific independence are in grave danger of forfeiting their rightful prerogatives to an increasingly tyrannous politicization of knowledge, a tyranny that has made itself felt by placing ideological constraints on nearly every field of enquiry; and (2) that Catholic scholars have in this document a charter of their duty "to speak uncomfortable truths which do not please public opinion, but which are necessary to safeguard the authentic good of society," and their freedom "to preserve the sense of the human person over the world and of God over the human person."

He concludes:

The professoriate is extremely uneasy with the notion of evangelization as a task of the Catholic university, precisely because a true Gospel freedom runs counter to that politicization of knowledge, and especially of theology, which the professoriate has been at such pains to advance. The authority by which evangelical liberty is safeguarded is the enemy of every Goliath, and most commentators have chosen to ignore the central place this document gives to evangelization in the university's mission, for reasons that are not hard to find. For if the message of *Ex Corde Ecclesiae* is taken seriously by Catholic scholars, it is all too likely that the tyranny of ideology over the search for truth — a tyranny so long complacent, so long indulged — will have met, if not its Waterloo, then at least its Runnymede.[33]

1991: In Praise of Conformity: Why Priests Should Stop Fooling Around with the Liturgy

I doubt this article needs any explanation. At least, it doesn't to anyone who has regularly attended a Novus Ordo Mass in the last few decades.

A side-effect of this emphasis is that Catholic culture has become much more haute-bourgeois, more suburban, than ever before. In effect the new liturgists disenfranchised working-class Catholics, and in particular working men, from reasonably wholehearted participation in the Mass. Say what you will, you cannot get a congregation of plumbers and foundry-workers to join in Ray Repp's hit "Al-lelu! Allelu! Ev'body sing Allelu!" and *mean* it. It might come off in Lake Forest but not in Gary. One of the main reasons the Church got fewer vocations from blue-collar families after the Council is the precious tone set by the parish liturgy. Few fathers who earn their living with their hands and shoulders are going to smile on the prospect of their sons' leading a congregation in "Eagle's Wings."

---

[33] Paul V. Mankowski, "Of Rome and Runnymede," *First Things*, March 1, 1991, https://www.firstthings.com/article/1991/03/of-rome-and-runnymede.

The Noisy Years

What I say about liturgical music applies *a fortiori* to dance and "movement." Unless the Church consciously decides that it is in her best interests to further distance herself from humble working people, I cannot imagine why she continues to flirt with these diversions. I do not think it impossible that liturgical dance may have a limited place in certain peripheral, para-liturgical situations, but I would doubt the canniness or the sincerity of anyone who claimed that it should be part of the liturgical life of the conventional parish.

Once again this is more than simply a question of taste; a vision of the Church is at stake. One of the moments of most acute embarrassment for me as a religious occurred during a weekend gathering, as part of which we were formed in a circle and led in a Shaker "movement exercise." We bobbed and bowed and raised our hands like toy puppets as we sang:

> *When true simplicity is gained*
> *To bend and to bow we won't be ashamed.*
> *So we'll turn to the left and turn to the right*
> *And turn and turn till we come 'round right.*

I wince as I remember the sight of the faces of grown men — whom I had come to admire in office and classroom and chapel — freeze in obedience as they shuffled back and forth in their Docksiders. And for what? For "true simplicity"? Hardly. No authentic simplicity requires a man to lay aside the benign dignity of adulthood. No, it was for the image of a New Church.[34]

---

[34] Paul Mankowski, "In Praise of Conformity: Why Priests Should Stop Fooling Around with the Liturgy," *Crisis Magazine*, February 1, 1991, https://www.crisismagazine.com/vault/in-praise-of-conformity-why-priests-should-stop-fooling-around-with-the-liturgy.

The Sound of Silence

1992: What I Saw at the American Academy of Religion

This article was published in *First Things* in March of 1992 and is a fan favorite. In it Paul writes about attending a conference of, well, I'm not sure what, even having read the article. I'll let him explain how he got there:

> The American Academy of Religion, in its statement of purpose, calls itself "an inclusive learned society and professional association in the field of the study of religion. The Academy [we are told] fosters teaching, research, scholarship, and critical awareness about the study of religion as a humanistic field of learning." The AAR was formed in 1964, grafted onto the stock of an organization called the National Association of Biblical Instructors, which had its own beginnings in 1909. Curious about the treatment of religion in the university and about the functioning of this learned society, I decided to attend its Annual Meeting, to be held in November of 1991 in Kansas City. Never having been a member of the organization, I came not as a participant but simply to observe and (as will be seen) to take notes.

The event consisted of sessions on various topics, and participants chose the talks they wanted to hear. Paul writes about all of the sessions he attended. Here is another excerpt:

> In the third (and, for me, final) afternoon of the Annual Meeting a session was listed of the Theology and Science Group on the theme: The Natural and Moral Origins of Sin and Evil. I was looking forward to this forum with particular interest, inasmuch as the topic promised a change of intellectual diet and because Langdon Gilkey of the University of Chicago — a scholar of considerable influence — was scheduled to speak. To my disappointment, Prof. Gilkey was unable to attend. I did hear Mary Hunt, of the Women's Alliance for Theology, Ethics, and Ritual (WATER).

The Noisy Years

In a paper titled "If Biology Isn't Destiny, What Is?" Hunt deplored the "dangerous hegemony of the U.S. in the construction of a New World Order," and spoke hopefully of the contributions to be made by "feminist/womanist/mujerista advances in theology" in refocusing our energies for social change, as such theology provides "a critique of power through a hermeneutics of suspicion." Hunt expressed satisfaction that "the myth of objectivity has been put to rest in science as well as theology," and applauded the paradigm shifts in virtue of which both have moved "from value-free to advocacy-based priorities." Orthodox Christian theology has worked to encourage violence; for example, the story of "God sacrificing 'his' Son legitimizes child abuse." Chaos theory in contemporary physics can help lead us to a reassessment of the category of sin. Through the prompting of feminism, Hunt suggested, we are invited "to move from Chaos (capital 'C') to chaos (small 'c'), from ethics to ecology." If we are respectful of the insights from chaos, it was argued, the concept of sin may fall away.

While it was not made explicit, Hunt's reasoning seemed to follow this course: sin belongs to a structure of natural morality, which in turn requires that nature be fundamentally rational. But if nature is ultimately chaotic, it is irrational. Therefore natural morality, and sin, are illusory. Certainly Hunt viewed natural morality as a malignant doctrine. "Women taught not to sin are taught not to change," she insisted, and affirmed the insight of Boston College's Mary Daly: "Elemental Being *is* sinning; it requires the courage to sin." The final note I made, the last bit of wisdom I carried away from the American Academy of Religion, was the dictum that served as the keystone of Mary Hunt's address. Our present task, she concluded, is to explore fully the implications of the first and the greatest commandment of the new dispensation: "Go, and sin some more!"[35]

1993: The Prayer of Lady Macbeth: How the Contraceptive Mentality Has Neutered Religious Life[36]

This article was originally published in *Faith & Reason* 19, no. 1 (Spring 1993) and was adapted from an address to the national meeting of the Institute of Religious Life held in Chicago, April 16–18, 1993. The question Paul had been asked to address was "Has the contraceptive mentality affected religious life?" His answer was an unqualified yes.

> Consider once again all that is consequent upon the change from serving the good to effecting the good. Call to mind the direction of change in religious communities in their apostolic involvement over the past 25 years, the de-emphasis on adoration, catechesis, spiritual works of mercy (even the term has become comically antiquated); the new stress on consciousness raising, political action, community organizing, world peace, environmental awareness. I want to stress that none of these latter activities need be pursued in a manner incompatible with traditional moral reasoning, but the fact that this reasoning plays a small part in the motivations of religious men and women who champion these causes is evidenced by the rationale commonly given for the moral compromises these tasks ask of them. Call to mind the excuses and justifications

---

[35] Paul V. Mankowski, "What I Saw at the American Academy of Religion," *First Things*, March 1, 1992, https://www.firstthings.com/article/1992/03/what-i-saw-at-the-american-academy-of-religion.

[36] Paul V. Mankowski, S.J., "The Prayer of Lady Macbeth: How the Contraceptive Mentality Has Neutered Religious Life," EWTN, https://www.ewtn.com/catholicism/library/prayer-of-lady-macbeth-how-the-contraceptive-mentality-has-neutered-religious-life-11926.

frequently offered by priests and nuns acting as university officials or appointed agents of state for their complicity in scandals of political and public life, for their actions that are contrary to Church teaching. Is it not the case, almost without exception, that their plea is to a higher responsibility to effect the good, rather than to serve it? Is it not the case that those whose aim is to cause a certain effect regard their more scrupulous brothers and sisters with Lady Macbeth's exasperation?

> Yet I do fear thy nature. / It is too full o' the milk of human kindness / To catch the nearest way. Thou wouldst be great, Art not without ambition, but without / The illness should attend it. What thou wouldst highly, / That wouldst thou holily; wouldst not play false, And yet wouldst wrongly win. Thou'dst have, great Glamis, / That which cries, 'Thus thou must do, if thou have it'; / And that which rather thou dost fear to do / Than wishest should be undone.

Translated into contemporary terms, the message runs thus: "Only weaklings let moral principles stand in the way of social change. You can accomplish nothing great if you let yourself be trapped by the snare of holiness. If you're going to succeed, you have to regard success itself as the only gauge of morality. True charity, after all, is not serving the Good, but delivering the goods."

And so it goes, step-by-step, on a gentle downslope, in the lives of religious: Faith in a provident God gives way to the Faith That Does Justice, which in turn gives way to the Justice That Brings Itself into Being, which turns out, in practical terms, to mean an ideologized justice that must dispense with faith when faith would hinder its full realization. Thus in the space of 25 years the voices that urged us to follow the patriarch Moses in his exodus of liberation now urge us to believe that patriarchy — indeed the very Law by which Moses vindicated himself — constitutes the final and most formidable obstacle to true human freedom. The God of the Patriarchs is worse than the bondage of Pharaoh.

1996: Tames in Clerical Life

Written in 1996, this article was published anonymously. I don't know where it was first published, but it was widely read and well-remembered. "Tames" has become a part of the lingo of conservative Catholics.

What is here proposed is that the contemporary priesthood exhibits a disturbingly high number of one sociopsychological type, to be designated by the neologism "tame," and what follows is a first attempt to sketch a profile of the tame priest.

He then goes into details about "tame" priests, and if your experience of the last two decades is the same as mine has been, you will instantly recognize the priests he is talking about. I can best explain it this way: in our Anglican Ordinariate parish,[37] our priest is a former Marine and a former cop and former member of the Orlando SWAT team. He is not a "tame." At our previous Novus Ordo parish, there was a priest who, before Mass started, made us turn to the person next to us and say, "Good evening, sweet pumpkin." (In his defense, it *was*

---

[37] The Ordinariate of the Chair of Saint Peter is a structure, similar to a diocese, that was created by Pope Benedict XVI in 2012 for former Anglican communities and clergy seeking to become Catholic. The Mass is in English, but is very similar to the Traditional Latin Mass. At present the Ordinariate has become home to many non-Anglican Catholics who seek refuge from the liturgical abuses frequently found in the Novus Ordo Mass.

fall.) The woman next to me did as directed and didn't know what to make of me when I said, "I *cannot* do that." That priest was a tame.

Paul has much to say about "tame" priests, and it makes me think about how he once described them to me: "They want to save you from despondency, not damnation." From the article:

> In one-on-one situations, tames in positions of authority will rarely flatly deny the validity of a complaint of corruption lodged by a subordinate. More often they will admit the reality and seriousness of the problem raised, and then pretend to take the appellant into their confidence, assuring him that those in charge are fully aware of the crisis and that steps are being taken, quietly, behind the scenes, to remedy it. Thus the burden of discretion is shifted onto the subordinate in the name of concern for the good of the institution and personal loyalty to the administrator: he must not go public with his evidence of malfeasance lest he disrupt the process — invariably hidden from view — by which it is being put right. This ruse has been called the Secret Santa maneuver: "There are no presents underneath the tree for you, but that's because Daddy is down in the basement making you something special. It's supposed to be a surprise, so don't breathe a word or you'll spoil everything." And, of course, Christmas never comes. Perhaps most of the well-intentioned efforts for reform in the past quarter century have been tabled indefinitely by high-ranking tames using this ploy to buy their way out of tough situations for which they are temperamentally unsuited.

1995: Pastoral Proposals for the Problem of Clerical Sexual Abuse

This is another article that Paul wrote for *Catholic World Report*. It was published in October 1995. Please note the date. This article came out seven years before the *Boston Globe* made the subject public knowledge.

Most of the public discussion by church officials regarding the pastoral response to sexual abuse by priests has centered on the therapy to be provided. Now it is a good thing and a necessary part of the Church's response that psychological and physical therapy be offered to the victims, the victims' families, and to the offender. But if the Church puts the emphasis on therapy she sends the wrong message to the public. It suggests that the principal harm inflicted by a priest engaged in sexual abuse is psychological or social, and that a primarily psychological approach to healing, combined with a prudential caution about restoring the offender to ministry, discharges the Church's responsibilities in the matter. Yet the chief damage wrought by sexual abuse is moral and spiritual, and even complete success in restoring the psychological equilibrium of victim and offender will not right these wrongs.

The priest sexual abuser objectively commits a mortal sin. In no official commentary on this issue have I heard any recognition of or concern for the fact that these men must be living as priests and performing the sacraments in a state of mortal sin for a large part of their ministerial lives. The validity of the sacraments themselves is unaffected by the unworthiness of the minister, of course, but what about the counseling, homilizing, confessional judgments, instruction in prayer, retreats, marriage preparations, and the whole business of daily human interactions conducted outside the state of grace? It is reckless and contrary to all human wisdom to assume that a man who can live in outrageous violation of common decency in one area of his life, and in defiance of his solemn commitment to chastity as well, can be expected to discharge his other responsibilities with integrity. Even if we entertain the possibility that abusers themselves resort to confession now and again our concerns are not allayed, because the pastoral efficacy of that sacrament is thereby called into question: either abusers would be resorting to priests of their own kind for a purely formal fix, or to priests unwilling or unable to convince their penitents to leave the ministry while seeking the help they need.

Superficially, of course, abusers can lead commonplace lives, and the fact that priest abusers often go a long time without arousing suspicion is an indication that the nature of their perversion is not obvious in all instances. But this underscores the moral crisis at the center of these men's existence, the grotesque contrast between the foulness of their sexual behavior and the role of priestly sanctity which serves as a mask. These priests are either tortured by their hypocrisy or *not* tortured by it — and in either case there must be incalculable pastoral harm done to those lay people whom they have to help in overcoming temptations and in accepting the Church's harsher demands. A priest capable of justifying his own sexual predation to himself is not going to be able to give spiritual aid to those who need it most and will almost certainly compound the problems of those who seek his counsel. Once it can be determined that a priest has lived as an abuser, it should be assumed that *all* his pastoral work was defective, and the diocese should take it for granted than any parish (or other apostolate) at which he worked for more than a short time requires re-catechesis. A pharmaceutical company that wrongly batches a drug does not simply issue a press release saying, "we've become more forthcoming about our quality-control failures," and let the matter drop. Rather, it makes some effort to track down those who may have used the defective product and educates them in order to minimize harm. By the same token, it is not enough for a diocese to offer counseling to an abuser's parish in order to bring about "healing"; it should actively investigate the condition of the parish in terms of its understanding of and adherence to Church doctrine, and take whatever steps are necessary to put things right. The souls put at risk by the sexually predatory priest are not just those of his victims, but of everyone whom he has given ill counsel, bad example, empty promises, misplaced hope, and above all false doctrine. They deserve to know the truth.[38]

2001: Jesus, Son of Humankind?

Since Paul was a linguist, it only made sense that he would weigh in on the subject of "inclusive language." Here again, he made no friends among liberals.

In linguistic terms, there is no such thing as inclusive or exclusive language. Language is a vehicle of thought, capable of being steered in any direction by any speaker. Of course a man may use language as a vehicle for urging the exclusion of women, just as he may use his car as a vehicle for traveling westward, but the language by means of which he communicates can no more be called "exclusive" than his Ford can be called "occidental."

The project that is termed "inclusive language" is in fact an etiquette. As an etiquette it is a complex system of rules, mainly

---

[38] Paul Mankowski, "Pastoral Proposals for the Problem of Clerical Sexual Abuse," July 1995, posted at Bishop Accountability, https://www.bishop-accountability.org/news/1995_07_Mankowski_Pastoral Proposals.htm.

prohibitions, used to encourage certain attitudes and types of behavior and discourage others, and to allow those who accept a particular code of conduct to recognize both conformists and non-conformists. This etiquette operates in the service of feminism in the broadest sense; to adopt inclusive language is to signal, if not personal agreement with specific feminist claims, at least a personal unwillingness to risk social unpleasantness resulting from rejection of such claims.

If I translate Mark 10:9 (with the Revised New American Bible) "what God has joined together, no human being must separate," I make no advance in accuracy or intelligibility over the customary translation — no one says, "Ah, now I get it!" — but I do indicate that, at minimum, I am not willing to do battle with those for whom generic "man" is a fighting word: a line has been drawn that I have declined to step over. On the other hand, when the English *Catechism of the Catholic Church* headlines its opening paragraph "The Life of Man — To Know and Love God," there is no question of a defect of intelligibility. This is tacitly admitted even by inclusive-language advocates. An editor of *America* magazine, in reviewing the translation, objected to what he termed "the 'in your face' response to feminist concerns" conveyed by the language. His complaint was not of a breakdown in communication but of an insult; the etiquette had been ignored.[39]

2003: What Went Wrong?

I believe this article was the final nail in Paul's coffin. And when liberal Jesuits try to convince me that Paul was Satan, they most often cite

---

[39] Paul Mankowski, "Jesus, Son of Humankind?," *Touchstone*, October 2001, http://touchstonemag.com/archives/article.php?id=14-08-033-f.

this article. Following is an excerpt, but you should read the article in its entirety.

A third answer to "What went wrong?" concerns a factor that is at once a result of earlier failures and a cause of many subsequent ones: I mean sexual blackmail. Most of the men who are bishops and superiors today were in the seminary or graduate school in the 1960s and 1970s. In most countries of the Western world these places were in a kind of disciplinary free-fall for ten or fifteen years. A very high percentage of churchmen who are now in positions of authority were sexually compromised during that period. Perhaps they had a homosexual encounter with a fellow seminarian; perhaps they had a brief heterosexual affair with a fellow theology student. Provided they did not cause grave scandal, such men were frequently promoted, according to their talents and ambition. Many are competent administrators, but they have a time-bomb in their past, and they have very little appetite for reform measures of any sort — even doctrinal reforms — and they have zero appetite for reform proposals that entail cleaning up sexual mischief. In some cases perhaps, there is out-and-out blackmail, where a bishop moves to discipline a priest and the priest threatens to report the bishop's homosexual affair in the seminary to the Nuncio or to the press, and so the bishop backs off. More often I suspect the blackmail is indirect. No overt threat is made by anyone, but the responsible ecclesiastic is troubled by the ghost of his past and has no stomach for taking a hard line. Even if personally uneasy with homosexuality, he will not impede the admission and promotion of gays. He will almost always treat sexuality in psychological terms, as a matter of human maturation, and is chary of the language of morality and asceticism. He will act only when it is impossible not to act, as when a case of a priest's or seminarian's sexual misconduct is known to the police or the media. He will characteristically require of the offender no discipline but will send him to counseling, usually for as brief a period as possible, and will restore him to the best position that diocesan procedures and public opinion will allow him to.

Note: sexual blackmail operates far beyond the arena of sexual misconduct. When your Aunt Margaret complains about the pro-abortion teachers at the Catholic high school, or the Sisters of St. Jude worshiping the Eight Winds, or Father's home-made eucharistic prayer, and nothing is done, it is eminently likely that the bishop's reluctance to intervene stems from the consciousness that he is living on borrowed time. In short, many bishops and superiors, lacking integrity, lack moral courage. Lacking moral courage, they can never be reformers, can never uproot a problem, but can only plead for tolerance and healing and reconciliation. I am here sketching only the best-case scenario, where the bishop's adventures were brief, without issue, and twenty years in his past. In cases where the man continues his sexual exploits as a bishop, he is of course wholly compromised and the blackmail proportionately disastrous.[40]

Put simply, sexual blackmail was a bridge too far, even though the sexual abuse scandal of 2001 had made most of us suspect that it was going on. The Jesuits had, as of 2003, let the Drinan affair be merely a

---

[40] Paul Mankowski, "What Went Wrong?," July 15, 2003, posted at Catholic Culture, https://www.catholicculture.org/culture/library/view.cfm?recnum=5915.

source of anger, irritation, and gossip. After the "What Went Wrong?" article was published, his superiors dragged the Drinan affair out of the dusty file drawers and used it as the excuse for silencing the mighty pen of Paul Mankowski before it could do them any more harm.

7

Ghost Partner

*It's amazing what you can accomplish when
you do not care who gets the credit.*

— Harry S. Truman

After I had converted myself (through the process of writing a novel — more about that later), and my mother-in-law had sent me to Kansas with the instruction of introducing myself to Fr. Paul Mankowski, S.J., and my eyes had become open to real Catholicism, I continued to be fascinated by the Jesuits. In fact, they were even more interesting to me now that I knew about the warring factions.

Around this time, I had lunch with my agent, and he wanted to hear my ideas for TV pilots. This is a question to which one does not answer, "I don't have any." If you don't have any, you make one up on the spot. At least, you do if you're everyone else in show business, and this is why a large part of what you see on the small screen is horrible. It's extremely difficult to come up with a pilot idea that you know will last for at least a season, as I have been explaining to agents since my earliest days in showbiz. Not satisfied with my response, I explained again to my agent that I didn't have a pilot idea. Finally, he said, "If someone told you that they'd buy your pilot no matter what it was, what would you do?" Solely to get him off my back, I said, "I'd do a show set at a Jesuit seminary." (Jesuits do not have seminaries, but he was Jewish, and I wasn't going to explain the process of Jesuit formation to him, especially since this was a moot exercise anyway.)

The next day, my agent called me and said, "AMC is interested in your pilot." Confused, I asked, "*What* pilot?" He replied, "Your thing with the priests." I had four days to come up with a show before meeting with AMC; this is why Paul became my protagonist. I had no time to research, and I knew him. To my absolute shock, I sold the pilot when I pitched it. As fate would have it, a couple of days before my pitch, the guy who ran the network had said to his young executives, "We should do a show with a priest protagonist." Go figure.

The Invisible Staff Writer

I had suggested doing a show set in a Jesuit house of formation because I knew the network would want it to appeal to the coveted eighteen-to-twenty-five demographic. I also knew that I was going to make Paul the protagonist because he was, at that point, the only Jesuit I knew well and talked to frequently. The only way to make those worlds meet — since the Jesuits always made sure that Paul never got close to impressionable young minds — was to have him sent to the community as a punishment for something, so that's what I did. I made the protagonist Paul in all ways other than circumstances (where he lived, what his job was, and so forth)

Here's the thing about writing a television pilot: it is *the* most difficult job in show business because it is a job with a lot of huge working parts and the writer, unlike every other person in show business, has no one with whom to collaborate. A pilot is created in a way that has nothing to do with the way show business actually works. Television writers rarely stare at the wall and try to come up with ideas. They have

Ghost Partner

a staff with whom they can spitball, fly trial balloons, and mold stories into what they need to be. Not so with a pilot. It's the writer in a room alone, trying to put together something that is necessarily very complicated, with no help. No writer I know actually does it that way. We all have "staffs" made up of our friends, and we run things by each other, and there is always someone who is willing to help. I had my friend and frequent writing partner Joe Garcia, who had the added benefit of knowing all about the Jesuit wars and would therefore understand anything I was pitching. I also had Barbara Nicolosi, who knew all of the same. And I had Paul, who *was* my protagonist and could therefore work with me on all of his storylines. And since I had a model for a protagonist who was also a fine writer, we would work out stories by working through dialogue. As we would pitch things back and forth, it quickly began to dawn on me that were I to get this show on the air, Paul would effectively be unsilenced. My character could not only be his voice but could spout dialogue actually written by him. And while the Jesuits had told him that he couldn't write under his own name or under a pseudonym, they had said nothing about ghostwriting. We were off to the races!

My biggest challenge in writing the pilot was to explain to the audience why Crae (the protagonist based on Paul) wouldn't simply leave the club that didn't want him for a member. I had to explain, to a modern audience, that Crae absolutely believed in Hell and absolutely believed that he'd end up in Hell if he broke the vows he had made. And I needed for Crae to sound intelligent while explaining this. I always tell my graduate students, "Don't declare a character to be brilliant unless you yourself are brilliant." I had broken one of my own rules, but I had done it because I knew that I could get Paul to write Paul.

In addition to getting help from a brilliant writer, I also began really to understand Paul as we worked on this "fictitious" protagonist. Things that he would not have said to me — or anyone — in first person were much easier for him to convey in terms of a "fictitious" character. We discussed many things in terms of what the "character" would do or say, and these discussions went much deeper than a regular conversation between us ever would have. For example, in the *Vows* pilot, there is a scene in which Crae explains to his lapsed-Catholic sister why he can't simply walk away from the Jesuits. Paul wrote the following speech:

> Look, Kath, I knew what I was saying yes to. I didn't think it would turn out as bad as it did, but I knew I was committing myself — my soul, the salvation or damnation of my soul — to a future that included that contingency. It's like being married to a woman who turns schizophrenic: you pray it never happens, but when it does, it doesn't change your obligations, even if she no longer recognizes her own. The clueless superiors I have can no more free my soul from its bond than a crazy wife can free her husband from his — if he believes his word is his word. The meaning of a man's life is, when all is said and done, how he keeps his most solemn commitments in circumstances when it's difficult to do so and to his advantage to oil out of them. Sure, my life would be more comfortable, gratifying, and suited to my abilities if I were to bail out — but the "Father Black Sheep" who left to live that life is someone I would despise, to the extent I couldn't fall asleep in the same bed with him. I'd become one of the walking damned.[41]

For anyone who ever wondered why he never left the Jesuits, the above speech should thoroughly answer the question. We did a lot of "talking" about the state of things by my asking him questions for research and his answering them. He was especially edifying when it came to the lay of the land in Jesuitdom. Like this:

---

[41] Paul Mankowski, e-mail to author, July 2007.

KAREN. I have to write the "okay, this time you really did it" scene with the superior, and I want the superior to be a "nice" guy because I don't want to establish all superiors as bad guys within the first five minutes. So the scene is basically "this time you did something that I can't get you out of." My questions are things like how are people (black-sheep Jesuits) silenced? Is it believable that there is a "last straw" action? Is it believable that he had no warning, other than common sense?

PAUL. Realistically, the confrontation wouldn't be like a choleric major chewing out a second lieutenant. It would take the line of hurt feelings. "You disappointed me. I had hoped for better things from you. You violated the trust I thought we had built up." A man of the superior's generation and accomplishment will not know how to discuss human ends or issues that are connected to them. He will be adept at the language of human belonging, etc. The "this time you did something I can't get you out of" scene is entirely plausible in itself (I've had a number of them in real time), but the line the black sheep would have crossed is not a clearly stated norm or regulation but a human bond. "You wounded men who deserved better from you. I can no longer protect you from the consequences of your own actions." Thus the tension will be in the communication breakdown: the black sheep speaking the language of "these are the goods that explain why I'm a Catholic and a priest in the first place," while his superior speaks the fuzzier language of healing and expectations and openness — not that the superior is necessarily a fool or insincere, but he can fix only problems he's been trained to fix, and he can't make anything else real to himself. In fact, the higher the regard the two men have for each other's basic goodness, the more frustrating their inability to find a common language.

Also important: the concept of punishment has totally dropped out of the vocabulary. In its place is "growth" or "a growth experience." So even when a course of action is clearly disciplinary in intention and effect, it's never called by that name. Instead, e.g., "we're sending you to the Fordham community (or to St. Luke's) to provide an opportunity for growth, because there are some growth issues that you haven't dealt with and which need to be addressed." Or maybe, "It hurts me to say this, but I think I'd be irresponsible if I didn't provide the space for you to become the Jesuit God wants you to be." The prospect of returning to the state of grace, by the same token, is framed in relational terms: "when you can integrate yourself better in our life ... when you show you can be more accepting of your brothers," etc.

What may be puzzling to your viewers (if you keep it real) is the near-total absence of God or the Church as a decisive factor in the superior's worldview. When mentioned at all, it's something flimsy, like "I want you to realize God's dreams for you."

One of the things that I needed him to explain, in order for me to write a character that was based on him, was why that character would want to continue to belong to a club that didn't want him as a member. This is one of the (e-mail) conversations we had about it:

KAREN. Why does Crae feel so strongly about remaining in this club where he is so obviously not wanted?

Paul: He knows he has a vocation. The call isn't necessarily voices in his head — though Crae (not I) may have heard a voice he couldn't account for naturally — but we've all had crossroad decisions to make in which, when we stopped kidding ourselves, we knew that one option involved facing the music and the other option involved running away from something. This is a gut-level feeling, but it is or can be just as unambiguous as a voice rumbling from the parted clouds.

Crae doesn't care that he's not wanted because — granted the authenticity of his vocation — whether he's wanted or not doesn't matter. On one level Crae wants to be wanted for the same reason a husband wants his wife to love him fifteen years into their marriage, but if she ceases to do so, that fact doesn't end the marriage, doesn't alter his commitment.

KAREN. What does he think will happen to him if he leaves?

PAUL. If he leaves, he goes to Hell. It's that simple. He knows that canon lawyers can get him a dispensation, but he knows in his heart of hearts that the vow he made was to God — who, unlike us, doesn't change His mind — and that he was plunking down the whole wad on black. Almost no one understands this because they think taking a vow is something like taking a dare: "I dare you to join the Marines!" your roommates taunt you; so you take them up on it, enlist, wash out after eight months during jungle-warfare school, and turn up back on the streets a little sheepish, but with no damage except to your pride. To make this concrete, you might contrive a conversation with Crae's sister or another Jesuit in which Crae explains that, even in secular terms, a man is no more real or solid than his trustworthiness, and when he doesn't keep his word, "he" ceases to exist: there's no there, there. So in sending away the damned, God says, "I never knew you" (see Matt. 7:23).

In medieval chivalry, a captured knight gave his word of honor (parole) that he would not try to escape if he were unchained and unshackled and would not take up arms against his captors if, say, his own army were later to make a raid into his captors' camp. That's where the notion of parole comes from in our criminal justice system. Thus, the captive knight, having given his word, would be treated with respect, fed well, allowed to move about, etc. until such time as a prisoner exchange took place or a ransom was paid. If a knight broke his word (by taking advantage of his captors in a weak moment) and escaped, he forfeited his honor — even among his own family and allies — and was even obliged to display a disfigurement on his coat of arms (what they call a "blot on the escutcheon"). He was thereafter incapable of making marriages, contracts, etc. and was, in fact, a nonbeing. De-romanticize this and recast it in terms of religious profession, and you see that, for a guy who understands what giving his word means, any incidental frustration, indignity, humiliation, defeat, or disappointment is preferable to forfeiting his vow. As long as his promise is intact, his sense of purpose is intact. He'd rather wash dishes at an Indian reservation in South Dakota [my note: the Jesuits have a ministry at an Indian reservation in South Dakota — he wasn't picking on Indian reservations] than mortgage the word he gave to God. The audience should be able to grasp this even without images of hellfire in the background. And images of hellfire are, and belong, in the background of Crae's consciousness.

KAREN. I think this is a large part of what I need to make the audience understand. They need to understand that even if *they* have decided that Hell doesn't exist, that is still what is at stake for Crae. (And if I end up making one or two of them believe in Hell, so much the better.) Is there anyone else in Crae's life who believes this? I know his sister doesn't. She doesn't believe in Hell. His parents think that might be true for another order but that the Jesuits *are* Hell and God would only be thrilled to have Crae leave them. I can't imagine he's met another Jesuit recently who believes that. I think it makes for an interesting situation to have a protagonist who thinks there is the most enormous possible thing at stake, and he's surrounded by people who equate it to thinking you're going to be mauled by Bigfoot.[42]

---

[42] "Provincial Language," October 2007.

Ghost Partner

❖ ❖ ❖

After I had written the pilot for *Vows,* the executives asked me to start thinking about future episodes. Because the show took place in a college setting, and because the protagonist was a scholar, I decided to do a story whose idea prompt was the public squabble between Paul and (alleged) scholar Elaine Pagels, author, Princeton professor, and "religious historian." In April 2006, Paul had written for *Catholic World News* an article titled "The Pagels Imposture," in which he took to task Pagels, who was the go-to source on the Gnostic gospels whenever the news media needed one. Paul, as an actual scholar, was annoyed by Ms. Pagels's claim to be one. Here is a brief excerpt from his article:

> Put simply, Irenaeus did not write what Prof. Pagels wished he would have written, so she made good the defect by silently changing the text. Creativity, when applied to one's sources, is not a compliment. She is a very naughty historian.
>
> Or she would be, were she judged by the conventional canons of scholarship. At the post-graduate institute where I teach, and at any university with which I am familiar, for a professor or a grad student intentionally to falsify a source is a career-ending offense. Among professional scholars, witness tampering is no joke: once the charge is proven, the miscreant is dismissed from the guild and not re-admitted.[43]

I wrote to ask Paul for help in fictionalizing a story about a hypothetical encounter between them. I proposed some possibilities, and he replied.

---

[43] Paul Mankowski, S.J., "The Pagels Imposture," Catholic Culture, April 26, 2006, https://www.catholicculture.org/news/features/index.cfm?recnum=43736.

The Sound of Silence

KAREN. I want to have as little backstory as possible, so here is what I am thinking of doing:
1. In episode 1, the provincial tells Crae that the president is trying to figure out how to best make use of Crae's scholarly gifts, since there is no Semitics Department here at Fictitious Jesuit University. So in the first beat of the Crae story, the president tells Crae that he's going to be teaching English as a second language to the children of the groundskeepers, or whatever ... something lowly and awful. Crae says some version of "But I could teach [fill in the blank]" ... and the president says something wherein the subtext is, "And if you behave, we might talk about that later."
2. Crae discovers that Elaine Pagels (character's name is Dana Hollister) has been awarded (is about to be awarded?) the Extremely Prestigious and Well-Funded So-and-So Chair. Crae's provincial says, "And at the [whatever event] on Friday, you will be sitting front row center, with a smile on your face, clapping with enthusiasm."
3. Crae grumbles and explains to someone (and therefore the audience) why he's so angry about it.
4. At the event, Crae sits front row center, doesn't make faces, claps when he can't avoid it. But during the Q&A, he gets up and asks a question that discredits her. (I have the question somewhere in my mounds of research — you gave it to me eons ago.) Dana has a Dan Brown–type following, so there is press at the event, and their public exchange becomes *very* public.

At this point, I don't know what the next beat is. I want to get to a scene between the two of them, but first I want to know what the president and/or provincial would do. They've done everything to him that can be done. What's left to take away?

Perhaps she demands an apology/retraction and they order him to apologize and retract and he says no? Would it make sense that they'd pull Jesuit obedience out of the bag of tricks at that point? It would be great for me if they would because I'd love to establish that in episode 2. I have e-mails where we went back and forth about that, so I think I know what to do at that point. I guess my only question is, would they do it? (I guess I mean would the provincial do it? I think the college president is not going to be a Jesuit. Would it be at all believable that he's an ex-Jesuit, or are we a few years away from that?)

PAUL. It would be highly unlikely for the superior to invoke the vow of obedience as such (not impossible, but eccentric). What is more plausible is that the superior says, "It is my clear *wish* that you retract and apologize" — and, confronted with C's refusal, his next step is "As you know, St. Ignatius says a truly obedient Jesuit doesn't wait for a command but, as soon as he can discern the wishes of his superior, acts on them without being told. My wishes are clear. You're refusing even to countenance them. You're going to be up for reconsideration on readiness for vows in six months. How am I going to give you a positive report unless you show some adaptability?" Thus, he telegraphs to Crae that if he doesn't play ball, he'll get blacklisted.

One other possible scenario (less likely). The superior gets Crae alone one-on-one and says, "You think you're the only real Jesuit in the province. You wear the cassock to show us how authentically Ignatian you are and imply that the rest of us are phonies. So, Mister Ideal Jesuit, give an example of Ignatian obedience, the obedience that obeys absurd or repulsive orders like the command to water a dry stick. I'm commanding you to retract what you said about Dana. You don't have to like it or think it helpful. You vowed to obey. So show us how a real Jesuit does the obedience thing. Or else shut the xxxx up from now on about the glorious Jesuit past. You're no different from anybody else: you obey when you feel like it, and you don't when you don't."

KAREN. So if I do B, Crae's dilemma is clear, but is there a way to make him obey without lying?

PAUL. Not if you mean obeying his superior's command. He'd have to say something like this: "Look, Ignatius took for granted that the superior would be a Catholic with the good of the Church at heart. I can't trust that you are that sort of man. Therefore, I am obliged to ask you to put your command in writing so that I can appeal it — which I will do, all the way up the ladder to the Vatican. If you're willing to defend the justice of your command, you'll write it out for me — but we both know that's not going to happen, don't we? So instead of playing games, why don't you ask yourself if you're following the pope's wishes implicitly, and we'll compare notes on the matter. It would be an interesting conversation, especially if some of our lay benefactors could listen in." At that point, the superior turns purple and begins to talk about hurt feelings.[44]

In answering one of my hypothetical plot questions below, Fr. Paul provided more insight as to why he had written the Pagels article.

KAREN. What would my Fr. Black Sheep say if someone asked him why he took her (fictitious Pagels) seriously enough to be bothered? Is it that she is misleading a flock of groupies, or more that this is what we now call scholarship? Or some combination, or something else I'm not thinking about?

PAUL. He'd say that it's precisely because she doesn't deserve to be taken seriously — and yet is — that her hot-air balloon needed to be punctured, even though it involved the expenditure of a cartridge designed

---

[44] "Three Questions," August 2007.

for nobler game. He might quote Wittgenstein's answer to Maurice Drury's question as to why he tore apart a visiting lecturer so ruthlessly: "A bad philosopher is like a slum landlord. It is my job to put him out of business." W's point was that philosophy is more than a parlor game and that morally destructive choices are made by those captivated by the bogus reasonings of a glib fraud — i.e., he wasn't crushing a young professor who'd made an innocent blunder so as to end his career but was exposing a self-inflated sophist for the fraud he actually was. The damage Pagels does is wider than that to a coterie of groupies. It's true no scholar of Coptic or Gnosticism who reads or cites her, but she's one of those academic figures like Stanley Fish or Carl Sagan that embody an attitude of politically progressive wisdom in the minds of nonacademics, and so function almost as priests of the Leftist Cult of the Masses. Within the closed circle of academic politics, where she's long been treated as a joke (except in the fringe departments like gender studies) Pagels is more or less harmless. But with the huge attention given the *Da Vinci Code* and the Gospel of Judas, and her dozens of interviews in which she gave out nonsense and pretended to know what she was talking about, she became Wittgenstein's slum landlady and needed to be put out of business. She wasn't, of course, but she got her hair mussed a little.[45]

I had been looking forward to multiple seasons of telling Paul's stories, where Paul would be unsilenced by ghostwriting dialogue for me. Sadly, the top brass at AMC changed not long after I'd turned in my script; whereas the first executive had wanted a show about a priest, the guy who took his place said, basically, "A priest protagonist? Are you out of your mind?" And just like that — as is often the case in television — a year's worth of work went up in smoke. And so did my effort to unsilence Paul.

[45] Ibid.

Interlude: Scenes from the *Vows* Pilot

These are two scenes from the *Vows* pilot that Paul helped me write. (I should note that even though the protagonist (Crae) is based on Paul, the sister (Kathy) is not even remotely based on any of Paul's sisters. If anything, she is based on my own sister.)

Scene 1

Int. Kathy Gilchrist's Car — Night

Crae is being driven by his sister, Kathy Gilchrist, who is a couple of years younger. She is trying to get the scoop as Crae stares out the car window at rain falling on dirty snow.

KATHY. Mom will not stop asking me what happened. I keep telling her I don't know, but she thinks I'm holding out on her. [*No answer from Crae.*] Since she knows you always tell me everything.

CRAE. There's nothing to tell.

KATHY. So Tuesday morning, there you were teaching your class and the rector stormed in and said, "Pack your stuff; you're going to the Bronx!"

CRAE. Jesuit superiors don't "storm" into your class. They call you to their office and talk in Valium Voice about impediments to your spiritual growth.

KATHY. Whatever. He said, "We're reassigning you to the Bronx" and you shrugged and said, "Where do we keep the cardboard boxes?"

CRAE. I believe I've explained the obedience thing to you a time or two.

KATHY (*a new thought*). Have you done something to tick somebody off recently?

CRAE. Am I breathing?

Scene 2 — A short while later

Int. Kathy Gilchrist's Car — Night

Kathy is driving. Crae is having trust issues.

CRAE. You're going to turn right —

KATHY. I know.

CRAE. Not this light but the next one.

KATHY. I *know*. [*And then*] Do you realize I'm about to drop you off and you haven't asked a single question about my life?

CRAE. I'm sorry. My brain is still somewhere over the Atlantic. [*And then*] So what's new?

KATHY. Nothing.

CRAE. Was there a specific question you wanted me to ask?

KATHY. No. It's the principle.

CRAE. Okay ... Are you still dating the married guy?

KATHY. See? I knew you were going to bring that up.

CRAE. I wasn't going to bring anything up.

KATHY. He's not married. He's separated. I already explained this.

CRAE. Yes, you have. He's still married but now he has his own apartment, and he can date.

KATHY. You know, you might develop a whole new perspective, now that you've come down off your seven hills. Once you get an eye-level view of what normal people have to claw through these days just to survive.

CRAE. Your very survival depends on sleeping with a married man?

Interlude: Scenes from the Vows Pilot

From the look on Kathy's face, we get the feeling she has suddenly remembered why she doesn't argue with Crae.
KATHY. Let's just not talk about this until you're in a better mood.
Crae looks out the window at the lovely sights of the streets of the Bronx at night.
CRAE. You're safe for a good six months.

Ext. Restaurant — Little Italy — Night
Crae and Kathy exit a restaurant where they've just had dinner and join the other pedestrians.
CRAE. Thanks for dinner.
KATHY. Anytime. Unless I don't make tenure. Again.
CRAE. How's that going?
KATHY. You'll probably make final vows first. Whatever they are.
CRAE. It's effectively the same as tenure. Damocles sheathes his sword.
They walk in silence for a moment. Then:
KATHY. When Dad asked you what you stood to lose if you left, and you said your soul ... did you mean that?
CRAE. I'm so tired of talking about my tribulations. I'd give a kidney for five minutes of trivial banter. From here to the car?
KATHY. I *need* to know.
CRAE. Yes, I meant it.
KATHY. If they make you so miserable that you leave, how is that your fault?
CRAE. If it's my choice, it's my fault.
KATHY. But if they kicked you out, that wouldn't be your fault. And you could still get married and have kids and have a normal life.
CRAE. I'd be released from my vows of poverty and obedience, but I'd still be a priest and I'd still be obligated to perpetual celibacy.
KATHY. Do you really think God would hold you to it?
CRAE. He would, and He'd be right.

The Sound of Silence

KATHY. How can you give up your life for a God who would send you to Hell for making a wrong choice and then realizing it?

CRAE. That isn't what happened. (and then) Kath, I knew what I was saying yes to. I knew I was committing myself — my soul — the salvation or damnation of my soul — to a future that included the possibility that things might not turn out well. It's like marrying a woman who turns out to be schizophrenic: you pray that never happens but if it does, that doesn't change your obligations. And my clueless superiors can no more free my soul from its bond than a crazy wife can free her husband from his — if he believes that his word is his word.

KATHY. Okay, you're noble, I get it. I still think —

CRAE (*won't hear it*). The real measure of a man is how he keeps his most solemn commitments in circumstances where it's difficult and where it's to his advantage to oil out of them. Yes, my life would be more comfortable, more gratifying, more suited to my abilities if I were to bail out. But the person who left to live that life would be someone I would despise, to the extent that I couldn't fall asleep in the same bed with him. I'd be one of the walking dead.

KATHY. And what are you now?

Crae has no answer.[46]

---

[46] Karen Hall, "Out of Order," *Vows* pilot script, AMC, 2006.

8

Enemy at the Gates

I have earned my disillusionment.

— Ani DiFranco

The Benedictine motto regarding hospitality is this: *Hospes venit, Christus venit*. Translation: "When a stranger comes, Christ comes." The extrapolation is "when a stranger comes, Christ comes, welcome him." There is an old joke that the Jesuit version is *Hospes venit, Christus venit, crucifige eum*. "When a stranger comes, Christ comes, crucify him." I used to think that was amusing. But then I lived it.

I had decided to do the research for my show by visiting the scholastics at Loyola University in Chicago and at Saint Louis University.[47] That way, my fictitious community would be a composite rather than based on one specific place. As fate would have it, I had an acquaintance who was a student at Loyola and was also discerning a vocation and spending a lot of time with the scholastics at the Arrupe House. He volunteered to be my temporary personal assistant and arranged for me to visit. In what seemed like no time, he sent me an e-mail of

[47] A "scholastic" is a Jesuit engaged in three years of graduate studies in theology and philosophy in preparation for the priesthood.

The Sound of Silence

my itinerary for the visit. It was amazing. It included a dinner with the university president (a Jesuit), an invitation to a normally cloistered meeting, and even a Cubs game. There were back-to-back events for me for two days. With great optimism, I jetted off to Chicago.

An extra benefit of the trip was that I would have a chance to take Paul out to dinner. We would both be in Chicago the first night of my trip, after which he was off to his annual bass-fishing trip with his parents. I took him, as I always did when I was in Chicago, to the Capital Grille for steaks and martinis. We took along one of his friends (Fr. Matt Gamber, who Paul described as a "fellow leper") so as to avoid scandal, and the three of us had a great time. The only problem was that I had to turn down the scholastics' rector's offer of a welcoming cocktail reception. I apologized and told him that I had already scheduled dinner with a Chicago friend for my first night.

Two things happened while Paul and I were having dinner. The first was that one of the scholastics stumbled upon my blog at the time and thereby discovered that I was — horror of horrors — a conservative. Not only that, but I had mentioned Paul's name in a positive light. My assistant told me that while I was at the restaurant, there was much speculation at the Arrupe House over the identity of my mystery date. Ideas were tossed around, and the parties gathered decided that it was Paul. Much trepidation ensued.

The next morning, my itinerary started with a tour of the campus, given to me by the rector. Let's call him "John." As we were walking, John casually asked me, "Who did you have dinner with last night?" I had a moment of hesitation because I knew that the answer would not please him, but I decided to tell the truth. (As one of my agents used to say, "The truth is a wonderful fallback position.") John had no response, and the tour went on. But in that moment, the tide turned.

For the rest of the day, I sat in on a couple of classes. I can't remember what I did that night. I believe that was the night when I was

Enemy at the Gates

supposed to have had dinner with the president, but that had morphed into a lunch the next day. That didn't surprise me. University presidents are busy people, and I had been surprised that the dinner was on the schedule in the first place.

I woke up the next morning full of vim and vigor and excited about the day's events. I went down to the refectory (Jesuit dining hall) for breakfast. Prior to that breakfast, every time I dined there, the table immediately filled up with Jesuits eager to share their biographies with me. But at this breakfast, no one even made eye contact with me. That seemed bizarre. I went to the coffee stand where I had to wait until a scholastic finished pouring his cup. As he turned around, our eyes met, and I smiled and said, "Good morning!" He said nothing, averted his eyes, and walked away. I returned to my table, where I ate breakfast alone as a room full of scholastics actively avoided me. I realized that I was being shunned.

Almost everything on my itinerary suddenly went away. My dinner with the president, which had turned into a lunch, ended up being five minutes in his office, where he literally met me at the door with "I don't have time for this. What do you want?" I was glad he'd asked, since I hate small talk. After I had talked to him for about five minutes, I could see him relax. I was doing my best Southern belle "what a great city and college y'all have here" routine, and he seemed to fall for it. He then turned on the charm and gave me a little speech about how the young guys were still sorting everything out, so they still had conservative or liberal leanings, and they still liked to discuss all of that stuff, but "after we're ordained, we never even think about that kind of thing anymore." For proof, he turned to his assistant, a white-haired Truman Capote look-alike, and said, "We never talk about conservative-versus-liberal stuff, do we?" Truman Capote assured him (and, more importantly, me) that they did not.

Back at the Arrupe House, the one Jesuit who was allowed to speak to me put me through several rounds of interrogation. He explained

The Sound of Silence

to me that my friend Paul was part of the lunatic fringe and that the Jesuits (even those I deemed liberal) were good men whose hearts are in the right place. I assured him that I had no intention of demonizing anyone but wanted to depict the Society as it was. There were indeed deep divisions, much as with the rest of society. In fact, that was why I thought the show would resonate for the audience, most of whom did not know or care about the infighting of Jesuits.

The visit devolved from warm and inviting to cold and antagonistic. It was Hollywood-level surreal to stay in a house (to which I had been invited!) full of men who had been ordered not to speak to me or even acknowledge my existence. Every time I went to the room to which I had been assigned, I was greeted by a little white sign on the door: "Arrupe House welcomes Karen Hall." I had to love the irony. Paul suggested that I call out "unclean" every eight steps.

After returning to L.A., I got the following e-mail from my assistant:

> I spoke with Fr. XXXX for a very long time tonight and he continues to have *grave* reservations on behalf of the order. He spoke of Jim Martin,[48] and how you had portrayed him as being on board with *Vows* [Note: I did not. I merely said Jim had read the outline and that we had talked about it.] but how Martin said you did not include many of his suggestions. [That is accurate.] Martin also has grave reservations about *Vows*.
>
> Briefly, Fr. XXXX said that the Provincial from Chicago contacted St. Louis and you will not be welcomed to stay on

---

[48] There was a time when I considered both Fr. James Martin, S.J., and Fr. Paul Mankowski, S.J., to be friends. When I sold *Vows*, I sent a copy of the outline to both of them. Fr. Martin had suggestions that I did not take, since the show was to be written from my point of view and not his. He did not tell me that he had "grave reservations" — I assume because he thought his suggestions would mitigate what he perceived to be the problems.

campus there. Also, you won't be able to stay at Chisek and Fr. XXXX regrettably, won't be able to have you in the Chicago community again.[49]

Regarding the latter, an e-mail was sent out from the Jesuit who was Paul's superior. I used to have a copy of it, but, not knowing that I would be writing this book, I deleted it. It came from Paul's superior and went to the greater Chicago community. Paul didn't get it, so it must have been sent only to select members of the greater Chicago community. In it, the scholastics were told not to talk to me or to help me with my research in any way. In addition to Chicago, this order went out to three provinces: St. Louis, Detroit (not sure why), and New York. Also, I was told that the infamous Fr. James Martin had sent out an e-mail to ditto the warnings, wherein he had declared me "a force to be reckoned with." I took that as a great compliment.

Because Paul had been away bass fishing, I had not been able to tell him any of what had transpired. He came back to a pile of e-mails from me, explaining the situation. In one of them, I had asked him what the Jesuits could do to me, since the entire ordeal was feeling quite menacing to me. He wrote back:

> It's all pretty amusing really. These guys can do absolutely nothing to harm you — and precious little to help you, for that matter — and the fact that they feel threatened at all shows just how flimsy their universe is.[50]

Followed an hour later by this:

> I shouldn't be so flippant about your combat; I've written off the lib SJs so long ago that I tend to forget that there are

---

[49] Anonymous, "Photos," e-mail to the author, September 2007.
[50] "Espionage Update," October 2007.

The Sound of Silence

> Christians like you who still care enough about them as human beings as to be worried about their destiny, temporal and eternal. I hope you never change in this respect. In fact, it's almost certainly because they sense your affection for them that they can still be rattled by your criticism. Maybe my "written off" is the wrong word. What I mean is I've come to regard the libs (collectively) as a kind of impersonal vexation, as a soldier might regard the icy water that pours in over the top of his boots and makes his uncomfortable day more uncomfortable still. It's not the water's *fault* that it's cold and muddy, though occasionally it's so unwelcome that the soldier is tempted to attribute an almost personal malice to it. To complain to my superiors about Brokeback Lent and NARAL at Holy Cross is as futile as a buck private's complaining to his colonel about the weather, so I've just given up. Again, I'm glad you haven't forgotten that things can change.[51]

In the end, I decided to make the pilot about a fictitious religious order, so as to escape the wrath of the Jesuits. I never got around to making that change, though, because AMC killed the pilot before I had time.

I was sad to see the show die. I had had high hopes for it because I thought it would be great to do a show where the priest protagonist was not losing his faith, doubting his vocation, or sleeping with his high school girlfriend or male cousin. I wanted to get the show on the air and then, when interviewed about it, say, "This is based on a priest I know." I also saw it as a way to let Paul do some writing. He would have made an excellent television writer. Every now and then, I would send him an e-mail saying, "I need a line to serve as a comeback to XXX,"

---

[51] Ibid.

and he would immediately send me a choice of hysterical possibilities. I always told him that, should I ever get a show on the air, he'd be my first hire. Of course, the Jesuits would never have allowed it. In fact, he asked his superior if he could be an official consultant on *Vows* (per my suggestion) and was met with a resounding no. And that was before they had any idea what the show was about.

Before that trip, I had spent a lot of time praying for the Jesuits and otherwise supporting them. As Paul said, I had high hopes that they would change and return to caring about the salvation of souls instead of a bastardized version of "social justice." I even had the audacity to think that I could help with that change. I thought I had some kind of calling to do what I could (with my writing) to that end. After the week at Arrupe House, that part of me was broken. I gave up on the Jesuits and left them to their fate. I now believe that my "Jesuit calling" was to meet and befriend Paul, a true son of my St. Ignatius, who changed my life. My calling was not to save but to be saved.

Interlude: "You Have to Tell Our Stories"

I have the dubious distinction of having multiple friends who have been chased out of seminaries during the greatest vocation crisis in Church history. One of them said to me, when he learned that I was going to be writing this book, "You have to tell our stories." My good friend and spiritual director, Fr. Sean Raftis, a former Jesuit, agreed. Michael Rose tried to tell their stories in 2015 in his book *Goodbye, Good Men: How Liberals Brought Corruption into the Catholic Church*.[52] The book caused a slight uproar among conservative Catholics, but it did not effect any real change. Eight years later, nothing has changed. In fact, the situation has worsened. So I am going to depart from the narrative long enough to do as I was asked and tell their stories. These three stories represent all the stories that have been told to me. I included Barbara's story to show that this is not a problem just for priests but also for women in religious orders.

At the core of these personal stories, including Paul's, is the war between those who follow the Church's teaching and those who dissent

---

[52] Michael S. Rose, *Goodbye, Good Men: How Liberals Brought Corruption into the Catholic Church* (Washington, D.C.: Regnery Publishing, 2015).

from it, with the latter holding the positions of power. I have four former-Jesuit friends who have different versions of the same story. I have two Jesuit friends who, as novices, came close to not being ordained because they were told that they were "incapable of being happy in the Jesuit order as it is today." God only knows how many men and women have left religious orders (and seminaries) because of similar treatment. All these stories are complicated and nuanced in ways that the scope of this book does not permit me to go into, but even boiled down to their essences, they paint a clear picture of the problem at hand.

Fr. Sean's Story

My spiritual director (and good friend) is a priest named Fr. Sean Raftis. He is a former Jesuit and was a close friend of Paul, who introduced us. Fr. Sean left the Jesuits in 2010 after getting the same kind of treatment that Paul had described to me. As with Paul, Fr. Sean's earliest problems with the Jesuits revolved around their casual attitude about Mass. As Fr. Sean tells it:

> A major variable that led me to know that something was wrong was the cavalier and irreverent way in which Jesuits would celebrate Mass. *Sacrosanctum Concilium*, Vatican II's Dogmatic Constitution on the Liturgy, clearly states that "no one, not even a priest, may on his own authority add, omit, or change anything in the Liturgy" (no. 22).
>
> Examples of overt and intentional violations of this Vatican II directive in the Jesuit world are far too numerous to list here, but abuses included, and probably still include, changing pronouns to gender-neutered pronouns; non-ordained "praying" part of the Eucharistic Prayer; un-ordained giving homilies, under the nomenclature "reflections," homilies which include open hostility to Church teachings on various moral issues and

church disciplines, often critiquing *Humanae Vitae*, advocating for women priests, and using reprobate material like clay cups and glassware, which undermine the reverence due to the Real Presence of Christ in the Eucharist.[53]

Fr. Sean became even more disillusioned during a summer at Regis University, where he and the other men in his class were sent to learn the history of the Jesuits. The (now departed) Jesuit professor Fr. Vincent O'Keefe "expressed his animus for St. John Paul II, including his desire to give the Saint 'the finger' when the papal motorcade would pass by the Jesuit generalate in Rome." At the same time, O'Keefe was singing the praises of the abortion-happy Robert Drinan. Fr. Sean says:

> The lionization of Drinan left me dumbfounded and seeing this very dark side of the Jesuits, many of whom publicly approved of Drinan's vile political career that did incalculable damage to the countless unborn children and mothers who were victimized by the lie of the now (Deo Gratias!) overturned *Roe v. Wade* decision. He also left many Catholics with the illusion that you can be Catholic and pro-choice, which is a theological and logical contradiction.[54]

When Fr. Sean was a theology student, a Jesuit professor at the Gregorian University invited him to Rome for a summer directed-reading course that would allow him to work on his sacred theology licentiate thesis: an amazing opportunity for which he was grateful. But after he got to Rome, the Jesuit professor did nothing to help Sean with his thesis. Instead, he took Sean on daily walks around sites in Rome. Soon Sean became bothered by the dynamic. It seemed to him that the priest just wanted Sean's stay in Rome to be a social event for himself. (Sean

---

[53] Sean Raftis, "Questions," e-mail to the author, December 2022.
[54] Ibid.

is too humble to say this, but my suspicion is that the professor liked being seen around Rome with a handsome younger priest, assuming he was not outright grooming Sean for a future that he envisioned.) After he'd had enough of this, Sean told the professor that he was only willing to meet with him in the parlor of the Jesuit residence or in one of the visitor rooms elsewhere. That did not go over well.

Upon Sean's return to the United Sates, the professor immediately contacted the department in which Sean was studying and Sean's provincial assistant for formation, telling them both that Sean was not very intelligent — a claim that was proven false when his thesis, on St. John Paul II's encyclical *Evangelium Vitae* and the liturgy, was accepted "with distinction." During the months right before Sean left the Jesuits, I remember getting e-mails from him in which he described getting the "icebox" treatment from the members of his community — by the very men who should have been supportive and concerned for him. He agrees with Paul on the Jesuit modus operandi:

> The Jesuits don't kick men out, they "ease" men out, making life so miserable for men by placing them in the worst possible assignments while giving the best assignments to the "golden boys" who shared their leftist political agenda and/or their advocacy of or immersion in the alternative lifestyle culture. If you are straight and orthodox, you are a problem, so they send you to psychiatrists, psychologists, or mental health counselors.[55]

By this point, Sean was trying to decide whether to stay with the Jesuits. His superior gave Sean a last chance to work and play well with other Jesuits by sending him far away to a Jesuit parish in Montana, which had a reputation for being "less political than most." The superior told Sean that there he could make his decision in peace.

---

[55] Ibid.

Interlude: "You Have to Tell Our Stories"

It might have been "less political" by Jesuit standards, but Sean found more of the same. His "welcome" to the community was that the parish priest instructed everyone not to help Sean move any of his things into the residence or the offices. He was told that he could not wear vestments that reflected traditional Roman Catholicism (for instance, a chasuble) and was issued a polyester alb instead. There were numerous nonordained parishioners at the parish who gave the homilies, which were renamed "reflections" at Mass. The tipping point came during Holy Week, when Sean was told to sit in the pews with the parishioners instead of in the sanctuary.

After years of stress, illness, and migraines, Sean asked to become a diocesan priest. He left the Jesuits in 2010 as "Incardinati" — living as a diocesan priest, while still actually a Jesuit. In 2014, he was incardinated into the Diocese of Helena, where he is currently thriving as the priest of two parishes and as president of the deanery. (Not bad for an unintelligent fellow!) After he left the Jesuits, however, he had a near mental breakdown, and today he suffers from post-traumatic stress disorder (PTSD) from his Jesuit years.

Robert's Story

Robert is a friend and former Jesuit whose story started with a tyrannical alcoholic novice master who hated anything remotely conservative or orthodox. Rob was also bothered by the novice master's "particular friendship" with one of the novices, to the point that they took trips together. Compounding his distress was the fact that two other novices were pretty open about their sexual relationship. Rob had never expected to find any of this in the novitiate; he had assumed, reasonably, that men went there to become holier.

When Rob advanced to First Studies, the problems became worse. He was surrounded by gay Jesuits who acted out with inappropriate jokes and constant sexual innuendo, in an atmosphere in which the heterosexual guys were bullied into silence. The rector — the religious superior of all the Jesuits on campus — preyed on students. Rob probably won't mind my saying that he was an exceptionally attractive young man, and that proved to be a big problem. He could tell that the rector was sizing him up as a possible sexual partner, and this was made clear by the rector's asking him out to dinner several times. When Rob politely declined, the rector offered to say Mass for just the two of them. Again, Rob declined. After he had declined a number of times, he was labeled a rigid traditionalist and was dismissed from several campus ministries. The students who accepted the rector's dinner invitations were given plum assignments. When Rob complained to the formation superior, he was told that the rector was a good man and asked why he had such a hard time getting along with people. He said that Rob was the one who had issues.

Rob would lie awake at night, trying to reconcile the ideals of the Society with the abuse and corruption that he was witnessing daily. "The cognitive dissonance I experienced was horrific," he told me.[56]

As his Jesuit career advanced, he experienced more of the same and worse. His years in formation were marred by incidences of sexual harassment, including two occasions on which he awoke to find another Jesuit standing over his bed, staring at him. Whenever he complained, he was told that *he* was the problem.

He finally left the Jesuits, after which he lapsed into a debilitating depression and began to have thoughts of suicide. He found a good (Catholic) therapist, and as they worked together, he realized that he was suffering from PTSD, a result of the sexual and psychological abuse he had suffered, as well as the hypervigilance he had maintained to protect himself physically.

---

[56] Text to the author, January 2023.

Interlude: "You Have to Tell Our Stories"

Rob was finally vindicated when other men came forward to confront his abusers, but that made his PTSD even more severe. "I lost my job and was unemployed for more than a year as I slowly recovered under the care of my excellent therapist," Rob says, but he adds, "The damage has been enormous: it poisoned my relationship with my parents and siblings — and gravely damaged my relationship with my wife. The cost of my therapy is beyond my means, but I cannot function normally without it."

Rob's emotional abuse also made it difficult for his parents and the rest of his family to believe in the Church. He says, "We have been so betrayed, but we soldier on."

As I said, I have heard many, many stories like these. When I was researching *Vows*, I kept a blog on which I wrote about what I was learning about the mistreatment of conservative and heterosexual Jesuits. The responses I got (from Jesuits) were so vicious, I eventually stopped blogging and deleted the blog entirely. I did keep a few choice samples. This one is a prime example. I had shared a link to George Weigel's article "Questions for the Father General," which contained the following paragraph:

> Then there is the third-rail issue in religious orders today: homosexuality. In a letter to the General Congregation, Pope Benedict suggested that there were serious problems with how some Jesuits undertook the pastoral care of persons with homosexual desires. He could have gone farther and addressed this problem within the Society of Jesus itself; it was not that long ago, after all, that the Web site of the Jesuits' California Province featured photos of "Pretty Boy" and "Jabba the Slut" in gay drag at a novices' party.[57]

[57] Quoted in Diogenes, "Weigel on the Jesuits," Catholic Culture, February 21, 2008, https://www.catholicculture.org/commentary/weigel-on-jesuits/.

The Sound of Silence

An unidentified Jesuit made the following comment:

> Upon what evidence is Mr. Weigel basing these grave accusations? Has he spoken with Jesuits around the world and, after exhaustive research and personal conversations with Jesuit priests and brothers, found widespread evidence of their not observing their vows of chastity?[58]

Immediately after that was posted, I received the following in a private message from a close Jesuit friend:

> I could give him *plenty* of evidence of widespread disregard for the kind of chastity Ignatius asked for. He doesn't want that. It is shameful for him to pretend that gay themed cards aren't passed around on birthdays, dildos aren't given as gifts, gay Jesuits don't flock to the same cities to live together or work in the same apostolates, are never heard saying, "I wish there were no straight Jesuits, I just don't see the point in them," there are no movie nights where Brokeback Mountain isn't selected just so the straight guys will leave, no Jesuits died of AIDS from engaging in gay sex, no gay Jesuits get together to go to gay pride parades or that this never clouds their judgment when it comes to thinking with the Church on this issue.[59]

Nothing in that message shocked me. I had already heard it — and worse — from every straight Jesuit I knew.

---

[58] Quoted in Karen Hall, "Anonymous Weighs In," e-mail to Paul Mankowski, February 2008.
[59] Quoted in ibid.

9

Dark Debts

True redemption is when guilt leads to good.

— Khaled Hosseini

When I turned in the first version of my novel *Dark Debts*,[60] I had no idea what the result would be. But as I licked stamps to send the manuscript to my agent (yes, it was *that* long ago), I knew that even if the book never went any farther than my agent's desk, it had been worth the five years I spent writing it. In the process of writing the book, I had brought myself back to Christianity after a fifteen-year self-imposed exile, and I had converted to Catholicism. I knew that was more important than any other result the book could have, no matter how stupendous it might be. The book ended up being successful beyond my wildest dreams, and, having declared myself a writer of theological thrillers, I went to work trying to come up with an idea for a second novel. (It took me two decades, and I still haven't started writing it.)

---

[60] Karen Hall, *Dark Debts* (New York: Random House, 1996).

The Sound of Silence

Dark Debts came out during my Mahony years, before I had met Barbara Nicolosi, let alone Paul Mankowski, and before I had been reunited with Dorothy Walker. My protagonist was a liberal Jesuit (inspired by those I had met) and the editor of a magazine that was based on the Jesuit magazine *America*. There were long passages about (my protagonist) Fr. Michael Kinney's doubts about and disagreements with the Catholic Church, all of which were my own issues at the time. I had joined a Church that, by my estimate at the time, treated women poorly, forced poor couples to have too many babies, made unreasonable demands on priests (the main one being celibacy), and, in general, needed to get with the times. Everything on the modernist playlist. And everything that came to make my skin crawl once I realized that I had fallen victim to modernist heresy and its cult of demonic inversion. Once my eyes were opened, it horrified me that my novel was out there in the world leading people astray.

Dark Debts Redux

For years, I thought about a conversation that I once had with my editor, who thought it would be interesting to let an author rewrite a book a decade or two later, to see how the book changed based on the author's life experience. When *Dark Debts* was approaching its twentieth anniversary, I called my editor, who was by then the president of Simon & Schuster, and asked if I could be the author to carry out that experiment. God bless him, he agreed, and I was thereby given a chance for redemption. The twentieth-anniversary edition came out in 2016, and the biggest change I made was to add a conservative Jesuit character, who could call the liberal Jesuit to repentance. The new character's name was Fr. Gabe Novak, S.J. I probably don't have to tell you that he was Paul Mankowski.

The 1996 version of *Dark Debts* ended with Fr. Michael Kinney, S.J., choosing his girlfriend over the priesthood. The 2016 version ended with the opposite. I did not make him see the light based on a speech or two from Fr. Gabe, but Fr. Gabe called him on the garbage that was Michael's "theology" and made him realize that he needed to rethink a few things. Or maybe everything.

During the process of rewriting the book, Paul aided me greatly. The first thing I asked him was this: "If you were forced to work with a thoroughly modern Jesuit on an intimate level, what would you say to him when you lost your temper?" He supplied the following suggestions:

1. Who's kidding whom? Getting rid of a gadfly is easier than solving a big problem. This is a gutless move masquerading as a charitable one.
2. By your own admission, your view of the Society's mission is a moving target, changing to conform to the times; you can't tell me what you'll believe two weeks from now. Which of us has the problem?
3. In moral and human terms, I regard you all as Styrofoam packing pellets; every breeze of fashion carries you where it wants. You are pro-gay among gays, pro-feminist among feminists, pro-statist among statists. No opinion you hold is worthy of respect because your every opinion is held by the same reasoning you refrain from white slacks after Labor Day.
4. Your biggest liability is that you can't destroy the writings of St. Ignatius or the records of the Jesuit martyrs. If Ignatius or Edmund Campion came back today, would they be applauding the LGBTQ Denim Day at Boston College?
5. You have turned the "Pope's light infantry" into a gay dating service for men who failed as flight attendants. I don't expect you to understand why I want to turn things back, but I would have hoped for some room to maneuver.

6. I'll take my leave if you insist. I see that this summer the Jesuit Liturgical Congress is meeting in Bangkok. I'm afraid I won't be able to join you there.[61]

Cheap Grace

I did not end up using any of those, because he later came up with lines that were more specific to the situation and — in my opinion — better. What follows is an excerpt from the book, where Gabe's dialogue was written by Paul. The two priests are in the middle of an exorcism when the following takes place:

> "God, it is a tribute of Yours to have mercy and to forgive," Gabe prayed. "Hear our prayer, so that this servant of Yours —"
>
> "You're not a skillful confessor, Father Holy Pants. Padre Pio would have known."
>
> Gabe kept praying as Michael could feel his stomach constrict. He hadn't remembered that the demon would blurt out his unconfessed sins.
>
> "He forgot to mention the leggy girlfriend in New York. He goes up there every other week for ... spiritual direction."
>
> Gabe stopped praying and looked at Michael. He handed his *Roman Ritual* to Randa.
>
> "Hold my place," he said.
>
> Gabe headed into the hallway, and Michael followed him, feeling like he was being called to the principal's office.
>
> "You have a *girlfriend*?" Gabe asked.
>
> "You're going to believe a demon?"
>
> "Absolutely not," Gabe said, "which is why I want to hear it from you."

---

[61] "Another Gabe Question," April 2015.

Michael was trapped. To buy some time, he made his way to the library. Gabe followed on his heels.

"Yes," Michael said, figuring the truth was his best defense.

"And you think you can confess, not mention the girlfriend, have me think I have absolved you, and then go exorcise a demon?"

"I don't want to make any major life decisions until this is over."

"You already made a major life decision that precludes this one. Are you deranged?"

"I'm counting on God to be more merciful than you are."

"Mercy is not what you're asking for; it's cheap grace. I believe there's a copy of *The Cost of Discipleship* in the library."

"Do you have one ounce of compassion?"

"Michael, mercy is meaningless without justice. What you are doing is *lying* and inviting God to *share in your lie*. You're asking God to un-God Himself — to give up righteousness to approve of your moral cowardice."

Michael knew, in some recess of his soul, that Gabe was right. But there was nothing he could do about it now, and they couldn't stop in the middle of an exorcism.

"We have to get back in there."

"No," Gabe said. "I'm not playing your game. Pick up the phone *now*, and break up with her *now*, and mean it *now*, and *then* we'll go back in there."

"I'm not going to break up with her on the phone."

It seemed like a no-brainer to Michael, but Gabe's face turned a darker shade of red.

"You're not an idiot. How can you believe in the devil and think you won't end up in Hell for breaking a vow you made to *God*?"

"Gabe, you're a dinosaur," Michael bemoaned. "No one believes what you believe anymore."

"The truth does not become untrue because it's no longer popular," Gabe snapped. "And the fact that it doesn't make sense to you, or to me, or to anyone else, is completely irrelevant to God."

In order to make the dialogue flow, I had to break up the speech that Paul had written, but since the speech was Paul saying what he wanted to say (through a fictitious character), here it is in its entirety:

> Look, you ass — why should I malign asses? — you empty suit, you moral pustule, you ... you *fashionable Jesuit*! Are you deranged? Are you blind? Can you really fail to see that there is no sodomizer of corpses, no terrorist, no atheist, no *Satanist* who is not better off than you? Their sin is to embrace evil under the guise of some good, but you are not only lying but inviting God *to share in your lie*. They see God for who He is and reject him, but you in your act of sacrilege — I mean, in your *insouciance* about your sacrilege — are asking God to un-God Himself. You're asking Him to give up righteousness so as to love your liberal moral cowardice! How does it go in Matthew 12? — "Whoever says a word against the Son of man will be forgiven; but whoever speaks against the Holy Spirit will not be forgiven" — I don't think I ever understood the full meaning of that passage before now. But you and your chums who keep changing God's revelation to suit your convenience have finally brought it home.[62]

---

[62] "Tonight's Question, Should You Have Time," March 2015.

Un-Godding God

Years ago, I came upon the phrase "a God all merciful is a God unjust." I wish I knew to whom to give the credit, because that phrase has been in my mind ever since. The phrase that Paul used in that passage — and used more than once in e-mails when talking about modernist Jesuits — about asking God to un-God Himself is how he felt about the modernist tendency to make God just fine with everything we do. It should go without saying that if God is not righteous, then there is no righteousness. And as a biblical scholar who had read the Bible in all its original languages, Paul knew that God gave us the Ten Commandments and expected that we would keep them, if we loved Him. He also knew that Jesus was, as he put it, "unambiguous about Hell."

My protagonist is one of those Jesuits who, until he comes face-to-face with evil, believes that while there might be a Hell, it is empty save for Hitler and the guy who invented Styrofoam peanuts. With Gabe's (Paul's) help, I was able to confront my protagonist with the harsh realities that he needed to hear. More importantly, I was able to tell the readers that (a) there are two kinds of Jesuits and (b) the modernists' soft view of Hell might be wrong.

Adam and Eve

In the first edition of *Dark Debts,* Fr. Michael tries to answer theological questions put to him by the agnostic female protagonist, Randa. Fr. Kinney did not give Randa serious answers, because he thought Randa was fine with his all-merciful God, no matter what she believed. In the new version, I had Fr. Gabe (Paul) answer Randa's questions. I was, by that time, tired of being pummeled by liberal atheists and agnostics about the stupidity of my believing in "a sky Daddy and a talking snake." I found comfort in knowing that someone as intelligent as Paul could both believe in and defend the most "insane" things in the Bible. So I had Randa ask him about the talking snake, and I let Paul supply the answer. Here is how that went:

> "If God is so good," Randa asked, "why does He allow demons to exist? Or evil, for that matter?"
>
> "Ask him," Gabe said, nodding to Michael. "I'm not a soundbite guy."
>
> "But you're the scholar," Michael said.
>
> "Okay, Adam and Eve," Randa said. She looked at Gabe. "Explain to me how everyone on earth came from two people and we're all being punished because of an apple and a talking snake."
>
> "For starters, the Hebrew story is not about Adam and Eve but 'the man' and 'the woman.' Eve isn't named as such until the story is over, and Adam is 'the man' until chapter 4. Secondly, the account is 'prephilosophical.' It wasn't written in the categories of Greek metaphysics, which didn't exist when it was written."
>
> Randa put up a hand to stop him. "I'm not a scholar. Can you give it to me in crayon?"
>
> Gabe tried again. "The story sets out the key points: that the human race has a single origin, divinely intended. That the man was endowed with rationality and free will, which he could have used righteously or unrighteously; that he used it unrighteously; that the consequences remain with us. It all sounds like bad Bronze Age mythology because the philosophical essay format had not been invented. And to dismiss it as 'mythic' is to make the same kind of mistake that a nine-year-old makes in criticizing the design of a chess set because *real* knights don't look like *that*." The biblical account uses narrative categories to express differences of moral and metaphysical significance, rather than bio-anthropological generation."

"So if it's not meant to be taken literally and it's not meant to be taken as a myth, what does that leave?" Randa asked.

"The truth," Gabe said, without missing a beat. And then he busied himself with clearing the table.[63]

The Unwritten Novel

By 2019 I had an idea that I thought might work as a novel. I had planned to make Paul the protagonist this time, so we'd have a chance to work together again, which had proven to be great fun for both of us. Whenever we would pitch out something that we liked, Paul's response would always be "That was fun." I think he loved writing fiction, and he loved having any outlet for any writing. And I loved having a chance to unsilence him, no matter how slight.

One of the things that I had learned from Paul, much to my dismay, was that there were many priests who had no supernatural faith whatsoever. At present, it is not hard to believe that at all, but this was before it was so glaringly obvious. I wanted to write a character who was a bishop with no supernatural faith who is confronted by an atheist who is in the process of acquiring supernatural faith. I made the protagonist the early-nineties version of me, and, of course, there was a priest who was Paul. This is one of the early exchanges we had about the story:

KAREN. Do you think a bishop (or provincial) would admit to not believing in the supernatural? (In some word-pretzel, Jesuitical way?)
PAUL. I think the bishop would admit disbelief in the supernatural to his friends (lay and clerical) but keep up a patter of pretense of belief for public consumption; of course, that coexists perfectly well with outright hostility to the supernatural in all his official actions.

---

[63] Hall, *Dark Debts*, 370.

The Sound of Silence

Now as to your lay victim ... I think it would be interesting to have a prosperous atheist worldling "gifted" with the stigmata, who is, in fact, more terrified that it might come from God than from the devil (whom she can psychologize away). She is too embarrassed to go to doctors out of fear that they would write her down as a religious nut — either displaying hysterical symptoms or cutting herself to get attention as a mystic; either alternative horrifies her. Here you can ignore the science because no one wants to let science have a look in. She has a Catholic (high school?) friend whom she treats with condescending palsiness, who happens to spot the bleeding and recognize it for what it is. (For dummy names, let's call the victim Vera, the friend Fay, the priest Peter, the bishop Barry).

Maybe Vera is a fashion model, and the bleeding threatens her career as well (ironically, will her stigmata-hiding gloves spark a new trend ... ? nyuk, nyuk).

Let's say the stigmata hits Vera only at certain times, maybe when the name of the Virgin Mary is mentioned, or when Vera thinks of death, or when Gregorian chant is played — whatever (maybe different wounds open at different stimuli). Fay enlists Peter's help (which Vera wants no part of); maybe she arranges a meeting with Peter and Vera and herself in which Peter is in civvies and, without lying, identifies himself only as Fay's friend. In the course of conversation Peter glimpses the bleeding and suspects at least part of the true cause.

Peter feels obligated to notify Barry of the situation. Barry is as horrified as Vera, and for the same reasons, for the most part. At first, he's skeptical about the bleeding and maybe sends an emissary under a pretext to see whether it's true or not. When he gets the bad news, Barry wants Peter to persuade Vera that this is not a divine but a diabolical gift, on the thinking that a hysteric might be cured by the exorcism ritual if she genuinely believed the devil possessed her.

From here there are many ways the plot could diverge. (1) Peter refuses, a liberal priest (Leo) is called in, and Leo gets cured of his liberalism in the very act of disingenuously persuading Vera of the reality of the devil. Or maybe, (2) Peter pretends to play along with Barry and, in teaching Vera about the devil, convinces her about the supernatural in spite of herself.

At this point, maybe, Vera gets a second and even more unwelcome gift — something like the dreams of Jane Studdock in C. S. Lewis's *That Hideous Strength* (do you know that novel?); at night she has dreams that turn out to be visions of things that really happen. Maybe Vera has dreams or visions about Barry that rattle him to suicide or to salvation, depending on how you want to take it. I don't think you'd need any of the scientific elimination of natural-cause stuff such as you get in Blatty's *Exorcist*.

KAREN. Hit me with your best progressive "I believe in God but not in the supernatural" nonsense.

PAUL. "I believe in a God that is beyond all categories, except that of love. My God lives inside me, too deeply inside me to 'come out' of me so as to act in the 'world out there.' The first Christians saw no miracles except the miracle of their own emancipation from myth. To believe that God made the blind see or the lame walk is a kind of slavery, a perpetual childishness. When Jesus said to the apostles, 'I no longer call you slaves but friends,' he announced to them that blindness and lameness — and, yes, sin itself — are conditions we can come to befriend once we have ceased looking for a savior and have accepted the God within, which is to say, when I have accepted my*self*."

KAREN. Wow.

The Sound of Silence

I still plan to write that novel and base the priest on Paul. But without his help, I'm going to have to drop the character's IQ by at least twenty points, and he won't be nearly as witty. Unless Paul wants to help from his present location, in which case I will be thrilled to take dictation.

Interlude: The Planes

I've spent a lot of time and burned a lot of candle wax praying for Paul over the years. I always trusted that God would hear and heed my prayers, but I actually received proof of that. Paul was dreading an upcoming sixteen-hour flight to Australia, so I prayed that he would have "some measure of comfort." I was envisioning a quick trip through security or skinny people sitting on either side of him, or both. God had other ideas. When Paul returned from Australia, he sent me an e-mail in which he asked, "Did you mess with my ticket?" I asked what he meant, and he told me that on the trip over and the trip back, he was "accidentally" assigned to first-class seats. I admitted that yes, I might have had something to do with that. But, I told him, I had only asked for "some measure of comfort." God was the one who had decided that meant first class.

A year went by, and Paul was headed back to Australia. Without saying anything to him, I prayed again for "some measure of comfort." I figured God would come up with something that Paul would find acceptable. Upon his return, I got the following e-mail:

> I had a very, very comfortable trans-Pacific trip, and I thank you for your concern for my comfort, but the gift nearly miscarried.

The Sound of Silence

I knew there was a screw-up when I was given a business-class ticket, and I offered to exchange it for coach class with two fellow passengers whose discomfort was several orders of magnitude greater than my own: an obviously pregnant woman (who preferred to stay with her husband) and a lame old man (whose hip prothesis wouldn't let him climb the stairs to the upper cabin). At that point, I was beginning to attract unwanted attention and decided to bow to fate. I hold in contempt priests who fly upgraded, and it was uncomfortable to find myself in that category myself; this discomfort was only partially relieved by Tanquerey and the inexpressible luxury of flying supine. Somewhere between the Marianas Islands and Hawaii, I began to put two-and-two together and to doubt whether it was a ticketing error after all.

I confessed again.

Another year went by. Paul had another long flight coming up. For the third time, I prayed for him to have some measure of comfort. When he returned, I received the following e-mail:

Somewhere between my check-in at O'Hare and my arrival at the departure gate, my seat was mysteriously reassigned. I detect the remote hand of a benevolent benefactress. Thank you very much! Your generosity is above and beyond the call of graciousness.

But then he added:

May I, however, compound your frustration by pulling another Dalai Lama and asking you not to do me this kindness in the future? Two reasons. First, as the overfed cleric in his roman collar lies stretched out in his huge seat during the boarding process, watching the proletariat squeeze past on their way to coach, he can almost hear their molars grinding, "Vow of poverty, my ass!" Second, being an incurable male chauvinist of the old school, I came very close to offering to swap my business-class berth for the coach seat of an exhausted pregnant woman. In fact, the only thing that stopped me was your imagined voice saying, "Be chivalrous on your *own* nickel, dammit!" Thus the extremely welcome comfort your thoughtfulness provided is compromised by my feeling soiled by traveling less as a (real) Jesuit than a power-lunch cleric of the Georgetown variety. That doesn't make my gratitude the less.

After that, I only prayed for his safety when he had to fly. There were no more seating-assignment "mishaps."

10

The Wilderness Years (2008–2013)

Obedience is a hard profession.
— Pierre Corneille

Paul's first official assignment was to teach ancient Semitic languages at the Pontifical Biblical Institute in Rome. It was an assignment well suited to his skills and abilities and one that he enjoyed, for the most part. I have lost most of the e-mails from that period of time — they were in an old e-mail account — but I remember one in which Paul wrote about his early-morning walks, watching the colors change on the buildings as the sun climbed higher in the sky, and the joy of catching a whiff of baking bread as he walked past the cafés. He also loved his work there. Many of his students were men on their way to becoming priests, which made the work particularly fulfilling. He liked the process of teaching, and once said to me, with a gleam in his eyes, "I am a *hound* with a chalkboard."

He faced two issues while in Rome. He was still much more conservative than most of his Jesuit confreres. And there were no men in his community with whom he had any spiritual companionship. He had a few close friends in Rome, and they met for meals and moral support and to discuss theology and philosophy and such. They called

The Sound of Silence

themselves the White Russians, after the anti-communists activists of the Russian Revolution.

When I visited him in Rome, he took me to see his room because I was writing *Vows* and needed to know how my protagonist lived. I was shocked by the spareness of the room. It was lined on two walls with twelve-foot-high bookshelves, which were completely empty except for his breviary and a Bible. There was a desk and a bed. Over the desk was a picture of the Jesuit martyr St. John Fisher. And that was *it*. He announced that he had something for me, and he reached through some drapes that served as a closet and came out with a small brown leather envelope, which I recognized as a rosary bag. He took out a white pearl rosary — one of several — that Pope St. John Paul II had given him as a thank-you for his work on the *Catechism*'s latest translation. Paul said, "I wanted this to go to someone who understood what they had." I thanked him, and it has been in my purse ever since. (Sixteen years and a lot of purses later, it is still my most treasured possession.)

We were in the room for about three minutes total, lest we start rumors. I took pictures to look at later. As we were heading out, he pointed to his desk and said, "There are nights when there is plaster falling on my keyboard from whatever is going on above me." Then he added, "And that guy has final vows." It was then that I began to understand his anger. He told me many similar stories over the years, and they always ended with "and *he* has final vows."

Paul kept a schedule that helped him avoid most cases of falling plaster. He told me that he tried to be asleep "before the evening nuptials" commenced, and he declared that "nothing good happens after 9 p.m." A nun who inherited his alarm clock says that the alarm was set for 3:37 a.m.[64]

---

[64] Sr. Mary Joseph, Cyber Sea of Galilee, "Remembering Our Friend Fr. Mankowski," Facebook, September 10, 2020, https://www.facebook.com/unsupportedbrowser?v=359482151873695.

The Wilderness Years (2008–2013)

He would get up at that time and spend an hour and a half in prayer and reading his breviary. At 5:00 a.m., he would go downstairs to set up the refectory for community breakfast. Then he would go for his morning walk, after which he would spend a couple of hours on the computer reading the news and his regular sites before going downstairs to clean up from breakfast. He said Mass off campus, usually with a community of nuns. He always did whatever he could to avoid a Jesuit community Mass. He loved a beautiful liturgy, and he detested *any* departure from liturgical norms (one of many things that kept him in trouble with his superiors). He once told me, "If a priest starts Mass in any way other than 'In the name of the Father and the Son and the Holy Spirit,' you are in trouble."

The Plot Thickens

In 2008, the tide started to turn. The Jesuit father general, Peter Hans Kolvenbach, had turned eighty and declared his retirement, and it was time for the Jesuits to hold a General Congregation to elect a new superior general and to set the tone for the next decade of Jesuitdom. This event went largely unnoticed by the rest of the world, but it was a big deal to the Jesuits. For good reasons, Paul had a certain amount of trepidation about it. He said to me, "I'm praying that we get a general who doesn't shave his legs and wear Je Reviens. Is that too much to hope for?"

About a week before he was to get an answer to that question, I received the following e-mail:

> The Rector phoned me this afternoon at 4:30 and asked me to come to his office. A very interesting conversation. He was summoned this morning by Fr. Kolvenbach to come to the Curia, where he met with Kolvenbach and my provincial, XXXX. The subject of the meeting was my future. Kolvenbach said he

wanted to clear things up for his successor. Kolvenbach said there were only two options, dismiss me or give me vows. Kolvenbach identified two sticking points re the latter: Mankowski needs to say, re Drinan, that "he could have done things differently" (K's formulation); secondly, a good Jesuit, said K, does not air the Society's dirty laundry. Kolvenbach said he would leave a memo to this effect for whoever is elected General this Saturday. He said XXXX (whom I've not seen since 2004) should contact me while in Rome and explain the situation to me. The fact that they would interrupt the time given for the "murmuratio" about the new General to deal with this is itself interesting, I think. I don't know where it will go from here.

This made me nervous, so I bugged him for details regarding what this would mean and when he was going to meet with his provincial, to which he replied:

I have no idea when XXXX will get in touch with me — or indeed whether he ever will. Do you remember Kolvenbach's instruction (address to his predecessor)?: "You and [Mankowski's] future provincials should take up this issue each year with him, making him aware that his stand is not 'normal' and cannot last forever." I haven't seen or heard from XXXX since 2004. I'll give him your best, however, if he does make contact.

Said provincial was the man who had banned me in three provinces while I was at Loyola, so there was no love lost between us. He was also someone who hated Paul with a white-hot passion, so I was worried.

At the time, one of our mutual friends instructed me to tell Paul that — in the words of Margaret Thatcher — "now is not the time to go wobbly." That was something that did not worry me in the least. My only fear was that they would kick him out. Our next e-mail exchange on the subject was this:

The Wilderness Years (2008–2013)

> KAREN. Why is everyone acting like they have to hurry and get this problem solved, when all K. is going to do is leave a memo for the new guy? I don't understand the timing. Is it just so they can tell the new guy, "We have issued the ultimatum?" and therefore it's (supposedly) not a mess K. is leaving behind?
>
> PAUL. Yes, I think that's the main reason. As for your question about what will happen, I suspect that things will continue as before. Kolvenbach clearly wants face-saving all around in the Vatican tradition: Mankowski admits he made a mistake, XXXX sobs, "All is forgiven!" and gives Mankowski a big hug and final vows and everybody goes home smiling and drying his eyes. Won't happen.

Looking back, I found little correspondence between us during the period between the "something must be done about Mankowski" conversation and his being brought back to Chicago. We saw each other several times during that time, and we discussed it all in person. In what e-mails I do have, we talked in shorthand. What I knew was that in order to "do something about Mankowski," they had to bring him back to his U.S. province so that the people who were deciding what to do with him could actually get to know him. Paul had a different take on it. He said they were bringing him back for "re-education."

The Jesuits were in a bit of a pickle. Paul had never disobeyed them, had done an exemplary job for them, and had worked with Pope (St.) John Paul II on the official *Catechism of the Catholic Church*, during which the pope had become a fan. Kicking Paul out was not something they could do quietly. It would have caused a commotion, and they had already been read the riot act by Cardinal Franc Rode, the prefect of the Congregation for the Institutes of Consecrated Life and Societies of Apostolic Life.

The Sound of Silence

In a speech to the attendees of the Jesuits' Thirty-Fifth General Congregation, he said:

> With sadness and anxiety, I also see a growing distancing from the Hierarchy. The Ignatian spirituality of apostolic service "under the Roman Pontiff" does not allow for this separation. In the Constitutions which he left you, Ignatius wanted to truly shape your mind and in the book of the Exercises (n 353) he wrote "we must always keep our mind prepared and quick to obey the true Spouse of Christ and our Holy Mother, the Hierarchical Church."[65]

The fact that it would be difficult and require some finesse did not deter the Jesuits from their desire to get rid of Paul. As he explained it to me, they could have dismissed him without cause and without warning. "Until I have final vows," he'd told me, "my superior could simply call me to his office, tell me that I was being dismissed, and ask for my keys." He likened it to the sword of Damocles hanging over his head. It was the main reason he wanted final vows. None of his friends thought he would be dismissed, for the reasons I have stated, but Paul felt that it was a very real threat. He thought that, should it happen, both the Jesuits and the world would get over it in about a week and that, as a former Jesuit, he would have absolutely no voice in the Catholic world. The irony was that he had no voice *as* a Jesuit, but he knew that might change if he were allowed to make final vows.

---

[65] John L. Allen Jr., "Vatican to Jesuits: 'Think with the Church,'" *National Catholic Reporter*, January 7, 2008, https://www.ncronline.org/news/vatican-jesuits-think-church. See also "Cardinal Rode Calls on Jesuits to Restore 'Sense of the Church,'" Catholic News Agency, January 15, 2023, https://www.catholicnewsagency.com/news/11376/cardinal-rode-calls-on-jesuits-to-restore-sense-of-the-church.

The Wilderness Years (2008–2013)

Many (heterosexual) Jesuits, including Paul, have told me that the Jesuit modus operandi is not to kick a guy out but to do things that would make him so miserable that he would make the choice to leave. I watched this happen with my spiritual director, who was made miserable to the point of leaving, and who had a nervous breakdown in the process. It was the choice that his superiors made under the heading of "something must be done about Paul Mankowski."

Paul returned to Chicago in June 2009 and proceeded to meet with a new provincial, a man for whom he had a lot of respect, but a company man, nonetheless. He and Paul were at a stalemate because Paul had no intention of apologizing for the Drinan affair and his provincial couldn't give him formal vows unless he did. There was the added problem that, according to the provincial, there was no job for Paul. And if Paul didn't like working beneath his ability, being unemployed was his idea of torture.

After a few months of going crazy from lack of meaningful labor, he finally was given a job: teaching Latin to high school sophomores at an inner-city school. He was extremely unhappy during that period and came as close to complaining as I ever saw him. In every e-mail he would describe the most recent squabble he'd had with one girl in particular who was driving him nuts. She had no interest in learning Latin (a trait she shared with all his students) and she was very good at faking emergencies and otherwise creatively hitting Paul up for hall passes. None of the students cared that he was a "hound with a chalkboard," and it was a miserable experience for everyone involved.

After a year or two of that, he got a new job. He explained it in an e-mail:

> I've wrangled a part-time job next year at the U of Chicago's extension division: not the major leagues of academe, but it's better than adjudicating bathroom passes.

The Sound of Silence

Later he reported:

> The course there went pretty well — at minimum it was bliss not to have to deal with high school girls shrieking fake-panic requests to go to the washroom.[66]

And then his superior told him that he was going to Jordan. Yes, *that* Jordan. It was in the middle of the "Arab Spring" and during a time when Jordan — and especially its capital city, Amman — was undergoing civilian uprisings that were leaving hundreds of people dead. Navy SEALs had killed Osama bin Laden, and al-Qaeda was vowing revenge. In short, it was not a good time to be going to Jordan. Paul's more cynical friends thought the Jesuits were sending Paul to the Middle East in hopes that he would be blown up, which would solve the problem. I asked my Jesuit friends what they had thought when they'd heard that Paul was being sent to Jordan. One said, "I didn't know what to think. It just seemed like such a curveball. So strange. So off-the-wall." Another said, "I think they were hoping he would disobey."

Jordan

Friends who were much better than I at St. Ignatius's admonition to imagine people's actions in the best possible light accepted the fact that the Jesuits needed to replace a guy in Jordan and Paul was unemployed, so ... I would argue that it made no sense for a man with advanced degrees from Harvard and Oxford and who spoke a dozen languages — none of which was Arabic — to be assigned to a parish in Amman, where the parishioners were almost exclusively the Filipino nannies and housekeepers for wealthy Jordanian families. (Tagalog was also among the languages that Paul did not speak.) What

---

[66] "?," March 2010.

The Wilderness Years (2008–2013)

I remember most from that time was that Paul was often upset about the stories that the Filipino women told him about their lives. Neither their husbands nor their employers treated them well, and in some cases, he felt they were in danger. He worried about them and, other than listening to them and praying with them, there was not much he could do to help them.

Paul observed but never complained during the time he was in Jordan. Here is a typical e-mail:

> Hard to believe I've been here a month already. I'm even getting used to the amplified muezzin who sounds off at 3:35 each morning, doing his imitation of a cat soaked with kerosene and set afire by small boys. As my Arabic improves, I'm able to understand that what they're droning in part is "This call to prayer is sponsored by Diet Dr Pepper and Stay-Free Maxi Pads..."[67]

Paul loved talking about his beliefs, but he rarely discussed his feelings. When he did, he usually started by saying "since you asked," as in this e-mail, in which he remarks on his frustrations concerning his Jesuit status:

> Since you asked, yes, it can be frustrating at times. But I don't really doubt my vocation and (since the time it hit me, late in my senior year of college) I never have. Were Ignatius alive today he'd be fighting like hell for Benedict XVI — that's a no-brainer. It sounds bizarre to say that it's the leadership of the Society that is clueless and Fessio and Koterski and Keefe and I have it right, but that's the case. Any halfway intelligent Jewish dentist — i.e., a man with no dog in this fight — were he to read Ignatius's writings and listen to what the Society is

[67] "Test," July 11, 2011.

up to would agree with us. He may regard what I believe with contempt, but he'd recognize that it's what Ignatius was about.

The main source of personal frustration comes from being isolated from contact with young laypeople who could become recruits (to the Jesuits and to the cause in general), and in being forbidden to give interviews or to publish (except in the field of Semitics). The main source of corporate frustration comes from the lack of integral religious life (kosher liturgy, e.g.) and the sense of opportunity lost: think what our twenty-eight universities could accomplish but for the wrong attitudes of the men who run them.

At bottom, though, the satisfactions outnumber the frustrations, and even if they didn't — well, no one said it was supposed to be fun.

If I were out to build the kind of church my superiors want to build, I would have thrown me out twenty years ago. But since they missed the chance, I have no intention of making life easier for them.[68]

What Has This Guy Done?

Here I digress to tell you a story that is known by very few people. I have a friend (we'll call him David) who is on the board of directors for a Jesuit prep that is run by old-school Jesuits. David also knew Paul and was as unhappy as I was to learn that Paul was headed to the Middle East. I asked David to find out if, by any chance, there was a job for Paul at the prep school. David contacted the principal of the school and explained the situation. We will call this man Fr. Frank, S.J. He had not heard of Paul, but after doing some research, he reported that he would be thrilled to have Paul come to teach at the school, and

---

[68] "Questions," March 30, 2007.

The Wilderness Years (2008–2013)

they happened to be in need of a Latin teacher. I reported this to Paul, who only said, "Let me know what happens."

People say that Paul never complained about being sent to Jordan, and he didn't because he never complained about anything. But I can tell you that he was less than thrilled and really wanted to remain in the States. His elderly parents were in a state of deteriorating health, and he was not happy about being six thousand miles away from them. He also made a lot of jokes about suicide bombers, which let me know that the danger of it was not lost on him.

A week after their first discussion, Fr. Frank called David to report on his progress (or lack thereof), and the first thing he said was, "*What did this guy do?*" When he had asked about hiring Paul, he'd been met by all manner of vitriol and was informed that he did *not* want the likes of Paul Mankowski anywhere near his school. So much for our plan, but it didn't end there. A few weeks later, in the middle of the school year and without a priest to replace him, Fr. Frank was sent to Haiti. He remained there for two years, and David and I deduced that the move was punitive on the part of the Jesuits. They left Fr. Frank there for two years, and I felt horribly guilty, but David said that Fr. Frank returned home (to his old job) in a great mood and almost giddy that he had been allowed to share in the suffering of Jesus. (Now *that* is a Jesuit.)

Much as with my situation at Loyola, Fr. Frank had been punished for little more than saying Paul's name out loud. That is how much they hated Paul.

After Paul had spent two years in Jordan, the Jesuits brought him home. They had tried every trick in the book, and they were still stuck with him.

One afternoon, not long after he had returned to Chicago, I received a long e-mail from Paul that I have, unfortunately, not been able to find. I wish I had it for the details, but I clearly remember the gist of it: a Jesuit superior (perhaps his provincial) had come to Paul's room with what

The Sound of Silence

Paul referred to as "a very nice severance package" and a spiel about how easy the Jesuits would make it for Paul to leave. I do not remember what was included in the package, but as Jesuit severance packages go, it was apparently very sweet. Paul said that the superior was genuinely surprised when Paul informed him that he had no intention of leaving. He had made a vow to live and die a Jesuit, and that was a vow that he was planning to keep. Paul said the guy left in a bit of a stupor of disbelief. He was probably thinking that *he* would have left the Jesuits if he'd been offered that package. (*My* speculation, not Paul's.)

That afternoon, Paul had called the Jesuits' bluff. He'd put them on notice that if they wanted him gone, they were going to have to kick him out. They had been giving him lousy assignments in an attempt to make him disobey or leave, but he would do neither. The Jesuits did not want the onus to be on them, but Paul gave them no out. Not long after that, Paul received permission for his final vows.

Sort of. Final vows come in two forms. The men who are given the higher form are known as the solemnly professed. They outrank the men who are given the second form, known as coadjutors. As a coadjutor, Paul would not be allowed to vote on any official Jesuit business, and he would not be allowed to make the fourth vow to the Holy Father. He told me that it was what he would have asked for. (With the exception of having his picture taken, there was nothing he hated more than mandatory Jesuit meetings.)

While Paul was happy, his friends were not. We *knew* that he was a man St. Ignatius was proud to call a son. We resented the fact that he still was being punished for his faithfulness to Holy Mother Church as well as his objection to a Jesuit who'd paved the way for millions of the innocent unborn to be ripped apart in their mothers' wombs. But it left his martyr status intact, and we knew that it would be counted unto him as righteousness.

11

The Pachamama Years

Proselytism is solemn nonsense. It makes no sense.
— Pope Francis, *National Catholic Reporter* interview, 2013

Proselytize (verb, intransitive): to induce someone to convert to one's faith.
— Merriam-Webster Dictionary

And Jesus came and said to them, "Go therefore and make disciples of all nations, baptizing them in the name of the Father and of the Son and of the Holy Spirit, teaching them to observe all that I have commanded you; and lo, I am with you always, to the close of the age."
— Matthew 28:18–20

Having failed at driving him out, the Jesuits had no choice but to give Paul final vows, which took place in December 2013. I went to Chicago for the occasion, which I almost missed because I had assumed they would take place at the campus church. I sat there for half an hour thinking, "I know he's unpopular, but I thought *someone* would come."

The Sound of Silence

It finally dawned on me that the ceremony was probably happening at the Jesuit residence chapel. By the time I had figured that out, I was guaranteed to be late. I ran to the campus, where I asked a group of students where the Jesuit residence was. None of the students knew what a Jesuit was, much less where they resided, so I was out of luck. I started to walk in what I thought to be the general direction when I ran into a man who knew where I was supposed to go. Bless his heart, he led me most of the way before pointing out a building still in the distance. I took off running and ended up making a breathless entrance during the second reading. The *last* thing I had wanted to do was to make an entrance, and I felt many Jesuit eyes on me as I slipped into a seat near the front. The humiliation left me, though, once I saw the look on Paul's face. He looked greatly relieved to see me. It meant a lot to me to be there for his vows because I had invested so many prayers and an ocean of candle wax in the cause.

I had not met Paul's family until the reception that day, although I had been praying for all of them for years and felt as if I already knew them. When Paul introduced me to his mother, I told her what an enormous help he had been to me over the years, and she said, "Really?" as if she didn't quite believe it. I assured her that it was true. Then Paul introduced me to Jim Mankowski, and I told him the same thing. Without missing a beat, he said, "We just hoped we could keep him out of jail."

I spent some time hanging out with Paul's sisters while he went off to be congratulated by everyone at the reception. While there had been a lot of Jesuits at the Mass, there were only a few at the reception. That certainly didn't surprise me. But the people who loved Paul loved him fiercely, so the room was full of friends who had traveled there for the occasion, including one woman who had flown in all the way from Amman. The atmosphere was quite festive. Most of the people there had, like me, been praying for the occasion for years.

The Pachamama Years

Someone had given Paul a gift certificate — a generous one — to the Capital Grille for the purpose of taking friends there to celebrate. Paul took me and his friend Fr. Paul Shaughnessy, S.J., a military chaplain whose article "The Gay Priest Problem" had won him permanent membership in the Pariah Club. I digress for a moment to point out that the rumor in Jesuitdom was that Paul Mankowski had written the article, since it sounded like him and it came out after he was forbidden to write. I asked them for the truth of it that night, but for the rest of the evening, the Pauls kept ordering martinis for me every time my glass was dry, so by the next day I had no idea what the answer had been, and I never asked again. I do know that Paul Mankowski did not write the article "Are the Jesuits Catholic?"[69] (another Paul Shaughnessy article that Paul Mankowski was accused of writing) because I remember his expressing writer envy over the phrase "semantic lines of retreat" and telling Paul Shaughnessy that he had gotten a lot of use out of it over the years. Beyond that, I have a vague memory of Paul Mankowski saying that he "may have helped a little" with the articles. I don't remember the exact nature of his smirk when he said it, so I don't know to what degree he helped.

After that, things settled down a bit. Paul still had all the usual vexations, but they weren't as bothersome now that the Jesuits could not dismiss him at any given moment. For the next few years, our e-mails were mostly an exchange of "the student who is driving me nuts this semester" stories mixed with family updates and the usual memes and links to particularly outrageous liturgical abuses. And then Pope Benedict XVI resigned.

Again, I don't have many of the e-mails from that time, and I don't remember what we said or thought about that. We prayed and waited

---

[69] Paul Shaughnessy, "Are the Jesuits Catholic?," *Washington Examiner*, August 19, 2018, https://www.washingtonexaminer.com/weekly-standard/are-the-jesuits-catholic.

with a degree of trepidation. I do remember that I had been intrigued by stories of then-Cardinal Bergoglio's humility, especially the part about his riding the bus to work. But there seemed to be so little chance that he would be elected. Paul and I didn't even discuss the fact that a Jesuit was not supposed to become pope. I think Paul assumed that Bergoglio would turn the offer down should it come to him.

And then two strange things happened. The first, which seemed odd at the time but made more sense once we knew all the particulars, was that Bergoglio did indeed get elected. My husband and I owned a bookstore in a mall in Boone, North Carolina, and we had gone to the restaurant next door, along with our then sixteen-year-old son, to watch the announcement on their television. We were all nervous and excited, this being a great moment in Catholic history. When the name was announced, I had a moment of glee. They had elected the humble guy who took a bus to work — surely that was a good sign! Then the second strange thing happened. When I watched the newly minted Pope Francis step out onto the loggia, I got what I can only call a very bad feeling. The only logic that accompanied it was the sudden thought "What if he is a liberal Jesuit like the ones who have made Paul's life hell?" But logic has to do with thinking, and this was much more of a feeling. I stared at the television screen and didn't say anything. My husband and son were staring at me and asking me what was wrong. My son said, "Isn't this the guy you wanted?" I managed to nod. My husband, who knows when there is trouble afoot, asked, "Why aren't you happy?" I answered with a weak "I am." But, as they say in *Star Wars*, I had a very bad feeling about this. I have told this story to many friends, and I have been shocked by the number who had the same experience.

I told Paul about it. In the early days, after the first few awkward press conferences, Paul declared that while Pope Francis was clearly not a Jesuit's Jesuit, he'd surmised from the new pope's remarks that he was "just somebody's doddering uncle." He believed that the pope was merely inarticulate and not likely to cause any real trouble. I disagreed, and for the first time since we'd known each other, I told him that he was wrong. I remember thinking to myself that this was a moment in history — when I was actually smarter than Paul Mankowski! But that was not a lot of consolation. It went back and forth like that for months, with me saying, "This is really scary" and Paul saying, "Now, now." There never came a moment when he said, "I'm sorry, you were right and I was wrong." (He was, after all, a male.) Somewhere along the line, we came to be on the same page. After Pope Francis said, "Who am I to judge?" on a plane ride, I became worried that the Holy Father would change Church doctrine. I asked Paul what would happen if it came to that, and he assured me, in all seriousness, that the pope would be struck down by lightning before that happened. One day, after a particularly egregious airplane press conference, I was in a panic, and Paul and I had the following e-mail exchange:

> KAREN. Remember when you told me that God would strike him with lightning before he did any major damage? You need a new theory.
>
> PAUL. I said (I hope) that God would zap him before he changed doctrine. He's been doing major damage since Day One. That said, I admit I've been gazing skyward longingly and with great concern.[70]

Time went on, and it got worse. After a year and a half of Pope Francis's papacy, Paul and I had the following exchange:

> KAREN. My reflection at the end of Mass tonight was this: I am now only here for the Eucharist, and I don't have to be in a good mood about that.

---

[70] "I have run out of words," October 2019.

The Sound of Silence

PAUL. Sounds right.
KAREN. So it's okay if I'm not in a good mood about it?
PAUL. It would *not* be okay if you *were* in a good mood. Oh, for a fatty embolism ...
KAREN. *Shut up.* You are *not* leaving me here in this mess alone.
PAUL. Now, now. I was making a wish for the arteries of another and better-known clergyman — at least in the first instance.[71]

Our New Year's exchange went like this:

KAREN. Here's to surviving the new decade.
PAUL. Are you sure you want to? The pope's pick Cardinal Tagle is to the episcopacy what Barry Manilow is to the entertainment world. I pray that long before 2030 I'm on the third tier of Purgatory extracting broken arrowheads from my carcass with a grapefruit knife, in reparation for sins of detraction against the editorial staff of *America* — and of sloth.

For all that, I'll respond to your cheers with a good stiff Manhattan this evening — no obligations this evening, no place to drive — and a box of Kraft macaroni and cheese.[72]

In March of 2020, he wrote:

I've started reading Frank Dikötter's *The Cultural Revolution*. This remind you of anyone?

Still, the Chairman prevailed. He was cold and calculating, but also erratic, whimsical and fitful, thriving in willed chaos. He improvised, bending and breaking millions along the way. He may not have been in control, but he

---

[71] "My New Credo," October 2019.
[72] "Happy New Decade!," October 2020.

was always in charge, relishing a game in which he could constantly rewrite the rules. Periodically he stepped in to rescue a loyal follower or, contrariwise, to throw a close colleague to the wolves.[73]

We had many exchanges about the pope, right up until Paul died. On the day that Francis famously swatted at the hand of a woman and (allegedly) called her a "bitch," we had this exchange:

KAREN. It occurs to me that if I spent twenty seconds talking to the pope, he would definitely slap me and call me a bitch.
PAUL. Congratulations (sincerely) on both counts!
KAREN. One of my friends is now calling him Pope Slapamamma.
PAUL. Perfect.[74]

On October 4, 2019, the feast of St. Francis of Assisi, Pope Francis attended an act of idolatrous worship of the pagan goddess Pachamama in the Vatican Gardens. Paul sent me the following email:

I CONFESS I CONFESS I CONFESS MY CRIMES OF IMPERIALIST AGGRESSION AGAINST THE PEACE-LOVING CITIZENS OF THE PEOPLE'S REPUBLIC BUT MAKE IT STOP MAKE

---

[73] "Synodality," March 2020.
[74] "Do Not Cling to Me," December 2019.

IT STOP MAKE IT STOP MAKE IT STOP MAKE IT STOP MAKE IT STOP...![75]

As I write this, four years later, it has not stopped. In fact, Pope Francis has switched to hyperdrive.

Paul voiced his strongest opinion in an e-mail to my spiritual director, who sent it to me after Paul died. In a rare moment of vulnerability, Paul had written:

> I have to say that Pope Francis has single-handedly taken from me all the fun of being a Catholic — not that fun is the point, of course, but it's still a loss. I used to be confident that the Holy See had my back (on doctrine, liturgy, discipline ...), now I never know whether Francis might ordain a woman a deacon on his lunch break or celebrate Mass in a sport-shirt in order to rebuke the "Doctors of the Law." He has too much experience, alas, as a Jesuit superior.[76]

Paul's attitude changed in the last years of his life. E-mails that had once been signed off with "Semper Fi" were now being signed off with "I'm waiting for the asteroid." I wouldn't say that the fight had gone out of him, because he was still fighting the superiors who wanted to keep him from saying Mass for the nuns, but his battles were more localized. I did notice, however, that he had lost hope that the Jesuits could be reformed. In an e-mail he declared:

> I thought there was a chance ten years ago with young guys like XXXX that things (in Jesuitdom) might turn around. Pope

---

[75] "It's Complicated," December 2019.
[76] Paul Mankowski, "Had Enough? Sounds Like Oxford Has!," e-mail to Sean Raftis, April 2016, forwarded to the author on September 8, 2020.

The Pachamama Years

Francis has crushed any hope that this will happen in my lifetime. I feel like a guy married to a wife who went schizophrenic and has been hospitalized for twenty-five years, for whom the hopes of a cure grew more and more plausible for a period and then were dashed. Well, the marriage doesn't end. Just have to soldier on.

He did manage to find a silver lining:

> One advantage to being married to this loon is that I don't even have to pretend to like my in-laws. Good-puppy Jesuits waste hundreds of hours a year at meetings and celebrations and get-togethers doing "brain-storming" sessions and the like, while I stay home alone and fix myself a Manhattan and read Evelyn Waugh in blissful comfort and silence.[77]

One day I came across an article about Pope Francis saying Mass for five thousand immigrants, and I sent the link to Paul with the comment "World's largest first Communion." He replied as follows:

> I trust the Holy Spirit to — pop! — send a friendly aneurysm just before any step into heresy, but of course that leaves a *lot* of real estate insecure in the meantime.[78]

After Paul died, I read that e-mail to my husband, who joked that Jesus' first words to Paul were, "Oops! I thought you were talking about yourself!" I said that Jesus' words were more likely, "I've got an even better idea." It doesn't help the rest of us, though.

---

[77] "Who Are We to Judge?," March 2015.
[78] "New Year's Fun," January 2016.

12

Blindsided

Because of the current global public health emergency, all the Liturgical Celebrations of Holy Week will take place without the physical presence of the faithful.

— Prefecture of the Papal Household, Holy Week 2020

In 2013, the year of his final vows, Paul was finally given a job that suited him. He became the scholar-in-residence at the Lumen Christi Institute (LCI) at the University of Chicago. The LCI's stated mission is this:

> The Lumen Christi Institute's programs enrich academic communities at the University of Chicago, across the nation, and throughout the world with the insights of Catholic thought, in order to engage our secular culture in dialogue and ultimately to renew our civilization by forming leaders for a global society in need of Christian wisdom.

The job was a great fit for Paul, and for the first time since I'd known him, his e-mails contained references to how much he was enjoying his work.

Now that the Jesuits could no longer kick him out, Paul went back to writing, although he mostly limited it to book reviews. He also wrote a chapter for the "five cardinals' book," *Remaining in the Truth of Christ*. His chapter, "Dominical Teaching on Divorce and Remarriage: The Biblical Data," was well within his "area of expertise" as a biblical scholar, so he did not ask for permission to write it. He did not get any blowback from it. What were they going to say — "We disagree with the Church's teaching on marriage"? Paul was happy to be on record for what he knew was sure to be up for debate in the long run. Once again, his motivation was posterity.

In 2017, Paul was allowed to write a review of Fr. James Martin's book *Building a Bridge: How the Catholic Church and the LGBT Community Can Enter into a Relationship of Respect, Compassion, and Sensitivity*.[79] He called the review "Pontifex Minimus," and it famously began with the question "Is sodomy a sin?" He did not back down from there. I regret that I did not get to read the first draft; he told me that there had been a lot of back-and-forth with the Jesuit hierarchy about it and that he had been forced to tone it down a lot. I remain surprised that he was allowed to write it at all.

Life had settled into a relative calm. Our e-mails of any length generally had to do with my complaining about outrageous liturgical abuses at our Novus Ordo church, to which he would usually respond with a simple "We are an Easter people." Sometimes his responses were more colorful:

> KAREN. The deacon had the homily *again*. He made us sing "Jesus Christ is coming to town" (to the tune of "Santa Claus Is Coming to Town") not once, not twice, but three times. (I should say that he made *other people* sing that. I sang not.) When he was done, the congregation applauded and I said, as loudly as I'd say to you during a three-martini dinner in a

---

[79] James Martin, *Building a Bridge: How the Catholic Church and the LGBT Community Can Enter into a Relationship of Respect, Compassion, and Sensitivity* (New York: HarperOne, 2017).

loud restaurant, "We're *clapping*?" Caleb (age sixteen) was mortified, but I swear I had *no* idea that those words were going to fly out of my mouth. I really think that I'm going to skip Purgatory on deacon homilies alone.

PAUL. Promise me this. Should I ever pull that stunt myself — as a result of a partial stroke or dementia, say — you will twist the jagged end of a broken beer bottle in my face four or five times and then shoot me in the midsection with a 12-gauge at short range. It would be a kindness.[80]

Vero Beach

In February 2019, Paul delivered a talk to a group of Catholics in Vero Beach, Florida. My friend (Catholic journalist) Mary Jo Anderson and I picked him up at the Orlando airport and drove him to Vero Beach, where we had a leisurely lunch and a lot of time to talk. The conversation was almost exclusively about the state of the Church and what could be done about it. (Precious little besides prayer, we concluded.) That night, he gave a great talk on the state of the Church, which is included in the appendices here. He concluded by quoting one of his favorite lines from writer Frank Sheed: "I find absolutely no grounds for optimism, and I have every reason for hope."

I was happy that he had been asked to speak to this particular group because it meant that I was now sure to see him once a year. We made plans for him to stay at my house the following year, where he could meet Chris and Caleb and we could all play pool and go bass fishing. But that night we learned that the speaker series was ending this year. So much for that dream.

When we dropped him off at the airport the next day, I asked him how big an audience it would take for him to come back to Florida to

---

[80] "Bless Me, Father, for I Went to Mass," January 2016.

speak again. He laughed. I said, "*Seriously*, how many people do I have to gather for you to come back?" He thought for a long moment and then said, "Four." I asked if he meant it; he swore that he did. I said, "I've already got four. And we *cannot* go this long without seeing each other again." He assured me, "We won't."

The next time I saw him was seven months later when I stood in front of his coffin.

Anno Ab Inferno

In 2020, COVID came, and the entire world changed. But the most important change, for Paul and me, was the shocking way in which the Church reacted. I still find it impossible to believe that the Church hierarchy put up *no* fight when the government decided to close the churches and thereby deny the sacraments to the faithful. At my own parish, the pastor shut down the Adoration chapel, which had been open twenty-four hours a day nonstop for twenty-five years. Even though our governor declared that the lockdown was over, my church remained closed because the bishop declared it so. When it finally reopened, we were not allowed to receive Communion on the tongue for many, many months. This was not a small matter to me, and I wrote to Paul to complain about it.

PAUL. Pope Pius XI would certainly not permit you, much less order you, to receive Communion by hand.

KAREN. Just finished the Pentecost Vigil on TV. I have to tell you, I am hanging on by a thin thread. Asking myself things like, "Was I an idiot to make the Eucharist the most important thing in my life?" Right now it feels that way. I have trouble thinking about anything other than the fact that there is no Eucharist in my future. After half of a year with no Eucharist: Does this count as white martyrdom? Please say yes.

PAUL. Yes. Look at it this way. Our first pope, Peter, denied Christ because he was frightened of arrest and death. Understandable. His successor has nothing to fear but watching a smile from liberal media mavens turn to a frown. Yet for this he has thrown away all the patrimony placed in his hands that to date has been possible for him. Yet we Catholics owe our bishops and pope *obsequium religiosum* — the deference of religious obedience.

I get along by pretending that the year is 1931 and reformulating the directives my superiors give in reality into those their predecessors would have given in the reign of Pius XI. Call it retro engineering. Some maniacs talk to an imaginary friend; this maniac offers his obedience to an imaginary superior.

KAREN. I'm worried about what will happen when there is no longer a dispensation, and we have to go to Mass and, knowing my bishop, there will still be no reception on the tongue. For the safety of all, of course.

PAUL. Well, for starters, the document *Redemptionis Sacramentum*, paras 91–92 makes it clear that you have a right to receive on the tongue, and a 2009 dubium during the Swine Flu epidemic got the answer from the Holy See that not even for sanitary purposes can the faithful be denied Communion on the tongue.

The point to consider is not that the tongue is not "consecrated," but that it is an interior organ, belonging to the inside of the body, such that the Body of Christ is not bounce-passed by the priest but placed directly into the communicant. Communion in the hand makes the communicant an intermediary, usually cooperative, sometimes not. We've all seen sulky or bored teenagers take the Host in hand and start walking away with it at belt level, popping it into their mouths like popcorn ten or twelve steps down the aisle. The Eastern Rite Christians (Catholic and Orthodox) are shocked to see Communion in the hand, and in the Patriarchate of Jerusalem (including Jordan, where I was pastor), Communion in the hand was forbidden precisely out of a concern that the Orthodox not be even further alienated from the Catholic Church. Communion in the hand doesn't have to be casual, but Communion on the tongue can't be casual, and I think everyone realizes the difference at some level. I once made a Communion house call to a dying man; his family also wished to receive. I gave the dying man Communion by breaking off a particle and placing it on his tongue. Then I communicated his adult daughter by placing a Host in her hand. She held it up in one hand like an appetizer and said, "And where are you from, Father?" and then took a nibble. That would be impossible had she received on the tongue.

If I were a layman, I would join those not receiving at all until reception on the tongue was restored. The Missionaries of Charity–Contemplative, for whom I also offer weekday Mass, had the same unhappy experience. At the direction of their regional superior, they asked permission of the auxiliary bishop of Chicago responsible for their vicariate, and he forbade them from having Mass in their chapel from mid-March until last Monday. When he finally permitted the resumption of Mass, he insisted that all sisters receive Communion in the hand, which is contrary to their universal practice. It hurt me to place the Host in their hands, most of which perhaps had never before come in contact with the Blessed Sacrament. They were acting under religious obedience. You don't have any such obligation.

KAREN. I am so disgusted by the fact that so few bishops have asked the question, "How can I get the sacraments to the people?" They just sat back and let the Church be taken from us. I always figured that I could get through anything as long as I had the Eucharist. It never dawned on me that it might be taken away — let alone that it could be taken away by priests and bishops! No one will put up a fight for the Church. They just say, "Oh, well" and go back to fighting for recycling and Pachamama.

PAUL. I was speaking with a UC graduate student who mentioned that she was unsettled not only by the church closures but by the near-total lack of yearning on the part of the bishops to resume the sacramental life. Nothing in their voice indicates that they share the lay hunger for the Eucharist; instead, we hear tetchiness and exasperated and reluctant concession to provide for those annoying layfolk whose docility is so minimal that they *must* have their little wafers, etc.

Most bishops, most priests, most laity see the whole religion thing in the same way that Camp Fire Girls look on the Camp Fire Girls — i.e., it is an occasion to gather 'round the bonfire and bond by singing sweet children's songs. Sure, it also points you to feeding stray kitties and helping old ladies cross the street, but these are only variants on the Happy Clappy theme. Issues like abortion, sodomy, and idolatry are as welcome at the USCCB as they would have been on *Mister Roger's Neighborhood*.

I find it both a matter of distress and of comfort that *all* traditional reservoirs of manhood have gone down the same path. Pro sports and the U.S. Marines and blue-collar workers and the Society of Jesus have all made their truce with Sodom, though with different levels of enthusiasm. That is distressing. But to a certain degree the truce is passive and the effect of indolence. Marines and steelworkers can afford to put up no resistance to the rainbow mafia because, for the most part, it affects them only when they watch TV, by mild or not-so-mild annoyance — nothing that really interferes with hunting or fishing or drinking with their buddies. But sooner or later it is going to interfere, and this is the dram of comfort that I find. The first time someone is actually forced to miss a lunch in defense of or by the imposition of the New Order, then things will get interesting.[81]

On Palm Sunday, when the churches were still closed, I wrote to him to complain about TV Palm Sunday in my living room. I asked what he would be doing for the occasion. He wrote back:

> I think I'll be staring at my own palm for Palm Sunday. To fill you in on things happening on my end: I have had some serious clashes with my house superior on the issue of leaving the house to say Mass. I had been asked by the Dominican sisters who teach at St. Ignatius College Prep (and for whom I say weekday Masses) to celebrate Palm Sunday and the Paschal Triduum, and I accepted. When I told XXX, he refused to let me do this, and I told him I intended to ignore his refusal, and we went back and forth. As I may have mentioned, this is a man who never says Mass nor attends Mass, and I am not about to receive directives on sacramental ministry from him. Finally, I told him I would kick the matter up the ladder. I emailed XXX yesterday but have not heard back. I informed the sisters of the contretemps so they can make back-up arrangements, but it is a first-order vexation at present.[82]

The rest of the e-mail worried me greatly. He wrote:

> Some temporary relief may be in view. Back in February I had already asked for and received enthusiastic permission from

---

[81] "The New World," June 2020.
[82] "Palm Sunday," April 2020.

Blindsided

XXX to volunteer for any corona-related priestly service. This week I got an e-mail from one of the auxiliary bishops of New York with this message:

> Know how grateful I am for your response to be of service in this time of great need. I had two very sobering conference calls yesterday which addressed the present state of the virus' impact and what we can expect in the coming weeks. It is very grim as you can well imagine. We discussed several scenarios and the likelihood of our getting into the hospitals is slim. Thankfully our hospitals have committed chaplains on call, so the patients are covered. We discussed our most pressing need: the morgues. We are daily anticipating large numbers of those who will die. Fr. John Anderson is working with the Office of Emergency Management to coordinate our availability to offer a brief prayer service with the blessing of the bodies before they are taken for cremation. This is all reminiscent of the days following September 11, only more bodies. Providing a service at that moment will hopefully be a consolation to families. The second area of need is being present to medical staff who are staying in area hotels in the city.
>
> We envision perhaps being available in a large room or in the lobby for medical staff to talk. As you know they are dealing with enormous stress and are in great need of counseling, prayer, comfort, and encouragement. We are still working out the particulars for this area of pastoral service. I realize that these two needs are changing every day. If you are still willing to assist in these two areas, please send me a return e-mail. We will then compile a list and you will be contacted when needed. As we

feel the frustration of wanting to do something, please remind yourself that our daily Masses and prayers are among the most important things we can do. Thank you again for your willingness to be of service.

I wrote back asking to be included as a volunteer for this work, but at the moment it seems they're not far enough along in the organizing to make a decision. I hope this works out, but it's obviously tentative. At present I'm wondering how, if the local superior wins, I'm going to make it to Low Sunday. I may end up in Kazakhstan teaching liturgical dance to transitional deacons.[83]

I once again marveled at the goodness of this man, who, like a true priest in *persona Christi*, was willing to lay his life down for complete strangers. While I was extremely worried about the prospect of his going, I was at a point where I needed to see a priest act like a priest, so it was comforting to me. I wrote to him: "I am very proud of you. Terrified, but proud." The next day I received the following e-mail:

Haven't heard from the bishop yet, but this is the number I plan to sing walking up the O'Hare jetway to fly to LaGuardia:

> Start spreadin' the flus
> I'm heavin' today.
> I just can't part with it:
> New York, New York!
>
> Drunk vagabonds — shoo!
> Keep six feet away!
> You're just the start of it:
> New York, New York!

---

[83] Ibid.

Blindsided

I wanna throw up in a city that wouldn't know,
And find I'm stacked in a morgue:
Twelve to the row ...

Those Wuhan bat brews
Just melt me away
I'll make my last infarct of it
In old New York!

Incinerate me there
In HAZMAT underwear
My last a-CHOO!
New York, New York!

I want to break up on a gurney already broke
And find I'm one of a mob, back of the queue,
Waiting my turn, turned into smoke ...

These out-of-town crews
Just get in the way
Take A.O.C. with me
In old New York.

Just vaporize me there,
And I'll help pollute the air:
A new a-CHOO to you, New York, New York.[84]

As it turned out, New York was turning down volunteers from outside the state, so he never got to sing that song.

We did have some typical e-mail exchanges in 2020, though, mostly in the late summer. On August 6, I sent Paul an e-mail from Montana,

---

[84] Ibid.

The Sound of Silence

where Barbara Nicolosi and I had gone to visit Fr. Sean. I had made them go with me on a long trail ride on that day, and I sent Paul pictures of us on our steeds.

> KAREN. We all survived my cowgirl fantasy. It was everything I'd hoped and dreamed, and Barbara and Sean were good sports. I have attached photos. One is us toasting you at dinner around the campfire. Enjoy!
>
> PAUL. Great photos — those are keepers! I do not see any Maker's Mark or Beefeater in the saddle bag, but perhaps the photographer wished to avoid the anachronism. I'm delighted it turned out as you had hoped and was very pleased to be on the receiving end of your toast.[85]

On August 10, he sent me a post from Cardinal Cupich with the following caption: "The real miracle involved in the Eucharist is not just that Jesus makes himself present to us, but that he empowers us to move beyond our tendency to withdraw in moments of suffering and become bread broken and shared to nourish others" — to which Paul had responded:

> Jesus said to them, "Amen, amen, I say to you, unless you eat the flesh of the Son of Man and drink his blood, you do not have life within you. For my flesh is real food, and my blood is real drink." Then many of the Jews quarreled and said, "This saying is hard; who can accept it?" As a result of this, many of his disciples no longer walked with him. Jesus then said to them, "Hold on. Hold on. Hold on. Try this: my presence shall empower you to move beyond your tendency to withdraw in moments of suffering and become bread broken and shared to

---

[85] "Yippee Ki Yay," August 2020.

nourish others." "Now *that*," said the Pharisees, "is a schtick we can *live* with." And they lived happily ever after.[86]

Our last e-mail exchange took place on August 18, the day Joe Biden won the Democratic primary. It was short:

KAREN. Did you catch Joe's acceptance speech? It was two entire sentences. Very touching.
PAUL. No. I can't abide it. Praying for an asteroid.[87]

On the morning of September 2, 2020, I sent him a link (I don't remember what it was — probably a video of some insane liturgical abuse) with the message: "I'm sure you've seen this, but just in case ..." When I checked a few hours later, he had not replied. I was mildly surprised, because he usually answered quickly to something that could be addressed with a witty one-liner. I told myself that he must have had a busy morning. Had we exchanged e-mails the week of his death, I would have known about the dental appointment at which he had collapsed. We always talked about dental appointments, as we shared an extreme lack of fondness for them. But I had been busy and had not written to him that week.

Two hours after wondering why he had not answered my e-mail, I received the worst phone call of my life.

---

[86] "Happy Feast of the Assumption!," August 15, 2020.
[87] "Historic Moment," August 2020.

13

Goodbye, Farewell, and Amen

Love is an engraved invitation to grief.
— Sunshine O'Donnell, *Open Me*

I was sitting in my living room, grading grad-student screenplays — a task akin to being swallowed whole by an irritated squid. I was pleased to see Barbara Nicolosi's name light up on my phone — a chance to procrastinate combined with a chance to talk to my best friend. Excellent! I chirped "hello," eager to vent about people with college degrees and no idea how to use a comma. Barbara's voice was quiet and strange, as she said, "Have you heard about Fr. Mankowski?" And I knew.

She told me that Paul had suffered a massive heart attack and was in a coma. (That was the early report.) She didn't want me to read it on social media. (I have always been grateful that I did not, and that I heard it from my best friend, who was also a friend of Paul.)

I hung up the phone and prayed for a miracle, but I knew. Somehow, I knew I was not going to get that miracle. Still, I was going to do everything within my power. I texted Fr. Sean and told him that we needed to talk. He texted back that he was checking out at the grocery store and would call me when he got to his car. I texted back: NO. NOW. I wanted him praying (and to get everyone else praying) immediately.

A couple of hours later, Sean called to correct what I had heard. Paul had had an aneurysm, not a heart attack. The doctors were keeping him on life support until his family members could arrive. For all intents and purposes, Paul was no longer with us and would never be again.

Everything Everywhere All at Once

I think I went through all seven stages of grief in the space of two seconds. I thought, in one sentence, *"God, how could You do this horrible thing, thank You for getting him out of this hellhole, he has suffered enough."*

In the earliest hours, when Paul was on life support and I was praying for a miracle, I explained to God that this was a very bad time to be taking Paul out of the world, as he was more needed now than he ever had been. I managed to make myself add, "Your will, not mine." But the overwhelming feeling that I had at the time and have had ever since was that God was letting him escape whatever hell is headed our way next. That feeling was reinforced when one of Paul's best friends, Fr. Matt Gamber, S.J., died suddenly about a month after Paul. I had a mental image of Paul tugging on Jesus' tunic and saying, "Don't you think Matt has suffered enough, too?"

In a 2010 e-mail, I had said to Paul, "I dreamed that you died, and I was at your funeral with Fr. Sean." That must have been a precognitive dream, because Fr. Sean and I did make arrangements to attend the funeral together. Between his having been run out of the Jesuits and my having been banned in three provinces, neither of us was looking forward to being in a room full of them. We needn't have worried. I didn't do a head count, but Paul's funeral was not overflowing with his Jesuit brethren. His best friends, all old-school Jesuits, had flown in for the occasion from as far away as Rome, but there were only a handful of Chicago Province Jesuits. That was odd to me, but it fully reflected the years that Paul had spent with them.

Fr. Sean and I and another close (Jesuit) friend of Paul joined the line to the open coffin, where the people were all touching their rosaries to Paul's cassock. I did the same with my rosary, the one that Paul had given to me after it had been given to him by Pope John Paul II. (I now consider that rosary to have been touched by *two* saints.) Paul had spent years showing me (and everyone else) what holiness looks like. He never referred to himself as being holy, and I am sure he would have rebuffed me had I ever suggested it to him. He did, however, tell me that he conducted himself the way he did, in large part, because "people lack the imagination to be holy." He was right about that. In our day and time, *who* is modeling holiness for us? And when we imagine what holiness would look like, we tend to think that a holy person would be the last person anyone would want to be seated next to at a gathering. Paul, on the other hand, was the life of any party. He showed his friends, and anyone else who was paying attention, that a person can be saintly while also loving football and Maker's Mark and even while having a wicked sense of humor. He made me rethink everything.

As Sean and I were leaving the church, I spotted the flower arrangement that I had sent. The card must have been very confusing to the family because I had asked the florist to write on it, "You won." Looking back, I wish I'd written something that a normal person would have written, but I was a tad crazy with grief at the time. It made Sean happy, so there was that. It was what I wanted to say to Paul at the moment: They didn't drive you out. They didn't make you lose your faith. They didn't make you lose your joy, your hope, or even your sense of humor. You just kept fighting for what you knew was right, and now you are safely home. You won.

The Sound of Silence

Computergate

The joke among Jesuits for many years had been that the most coveted item in Jesuitdom was Paul Mankowski's hard drive. So it was no surprise that in the fifteen minutes between the doctor's signing the death certificate and his family members driving from the hospital to his room, Paul's computer disappeared. The family wanted it because it was filled with old family pictures that did not exist anywhere else. They explained this to the Jesuits at Paul's residence, who promised to look into it and get back to them. The family asked again later, when they had heard nothing, with the same result. To this day, Paul's family has not received the computer. One of Paul's close friends told me, "That computer is at the bottom of Lake Michigan."

Sean and I went to Paul's room after the funeral. The family had told us that we could take anything we wanted. I took a first-class relic of St. Ignatius that I had given to him many years before; I felt certain that he would want me to have it. I also took a small book on St. Paul by Ronald Knox and a John le Carré novel; the latter because the last conversation we'd had in person had been about spy novels. Sean took an autographed copy of Paul's published doctoral thesis, *Akkadian Loanwords in Biblical Hebrew*,[88] and was thrilled to have it. I will confess that we did a little bit of snooping. Nothing except a little bit would have been possible, since Paul never owned more than could be put into one medium-sized box for easy packing should he get kicked out or in case of a sudden reassignment. (But mostly because he took his vow of poverty very seriously.) The closet contained exactly what I had expected: three black shirts in various degrees of tatter and two pairs of black pants in similar condition. No shoes, as he had been wearing his only pair. One black cashmere sweater that had been given to him

---

[88] Paul Mankowski, *Akkadian Loanwords in Biblical Hebrew* (Leiden, Netherlands: Brill Publishers, 2000).

as a gift when he had come to Vero Beach to speak. It being early fall, that had never been worn, so Sean took it back to Montana with him. We both felt certain that Paul would approve.

I noted that there was one ballpoint pen lying on his well-made twin bed, and for some reason that got to me. Probably because of the importance I placed on Paul's writing. Sean, a fellow migraine sufferer, noted that there were two empty Imitrex canisters in the trash can, which meant that Paul's last night had been a bad one. We both wished that we had known, but we were both used to Paul's talking about his migraines, so neither of us would have urged him to go to the emergency room. Still, it was an eerie sight.

That night, I took Sean to the Capital Grille, where I had spent many happy hours with Paul over the years. We drank a martini toast to him and congratulated him for having — in the words of St. Paul — run the race. We still talk about what a great dinner it was. Aside from the fact that the restaurant is outstanding and the steaks were mouthwatering, there was also a sense of peace over the evening. We were celebrating a life well lived.

That peace did not last long. The month after the funeral was a horrible time for me. A voice in my head would pipe up, "Paul is dead," and I would shake my head in denial and say "no" out loud. It could not be true. He could not be gone. Nights were the worst because that was typically when I wrote to him. I kept writing "e-mails" that I stuck in a file. It made me feel better, and I was aching for something to make me feel better. Every night I allowed myself two drinks and two (low-cal) ice cream bars. They actually made me feel better, which surprised me.

The anger phase of my grief was initially not overwhelming. I had an irrational anger at Paul for leaving me in the cesspool that the world had become. I knew it was irrational — that the timing of his death was not Paul's choice — and it was quickly smothered by the thought of how happy Paul must be in a place where Truth was not up for debate.

The Sound of Silence

I was angered — and intensely so — by Fr. James Martin, who immediately tweeted about losing a "brother Jesuit." This was followed by a long series of comments — people offering Fr. James Martin their condolences and sympathizing with his (alleged) pain. And worst of all, James Martin accepting the condolences with gratitude. Reading the thread made me furious. James Martin and his merry band of followers had hated Paul and had made his life miserable. At the time I said to myself, "This shall not stand." Not that there was anything I could do about it, with the exception of writing this paragraph.

After about a month of what felt like sheer hell, I had a dream that broke the mourning fever. In the dream, Paul and I were sitting on a large ottoman in what looked like the lobby of an expensive hotel. As the dream began, I had the sense that we had already been talking for a while, but I couldn't remember what we had said. Paul stood up to leave; I clutched at my hair in frustration and said, "No, not yet! There are still things we have to talk about!" He said nothing, but gave me a look that said, "It will be fine," and then he winked at me and walked away.

I believe that this encounter was more than just a dream. From then on, I was much calmer about the idea of having to hang on to my faith without him. And he was right. It has been fine. After all of those years of friendship, I have internalized his voice to the point that if I need to "talk" to him, I know what he would say. And thanks to those years of friendship, my faith is solid and unshakable. With the exception of my husband and my children and grandchildren, Paul's friendship was the greatest gift God ever gave me.

I spent months rereading every e-mail exchange with Paul. When I got to the 2020 e-mails, I came across one that had really struck me the first time I had read it; Paul's tone was decidedly different from that of any e-mail I had ever received from him. As I reread it after his death, I realized that — unbeknownst to both of us — it had been a goodbye letter. He had written it in June, three months before he died. I will end with it, as I could not possibly top it:

> Today is the 33rd anniversary of my ordination; as I am 66 this means I've lived half my life as a priest. There must be many young guys receiving their own ordination today in various dioceses; I wonder what the state of the Church will be on their 33rd anniversary.
>
> What moved me to write was to express renewed thanks for your extraordinary gift of the relic of St. Ignatius Loyola, which beams at me from its reliquary on my bookcase as I type this, and which has provided much encouragement and consolation over the years — as indeed have your own prayers and support.
>
> Don't let the bastards grind you down. Amen.[89]

Dear Paul: I won't.
Requiescat in pace.

---

[89] "Vigil of Corpus Christi," June 2020.

Appendix

More Mankowski

Paul on ...

These are some of my favorite quotes from the e-mails: some serious, some funny, and some just plain silly.

Paul on wokeness

Don't be rattled by your daughter's denunciation. Wokeness is not a moral or political crusade but a fashion statement, and your daughter's horror at your bigotries is little different from your sister's lying down in the car (great story!) so that no one would see her in the ugly Pontiac on the way to school. Two years from now the media will generate a new set of fashions and most, not all, of her imprecations will be withdrawn. Keep on keeping on. ("Research Question," July 2020)

Paul on teenagers

Regarding teenagers: God makes them act that way so that, as adults, they can look back with shame and mortification at their own adolescence and prepare their souls for the humility that is an opening to grace. I think Hell (or at least Purgatory) will include being forced to watch a repeated video of the things I did in the seventh grade to impress girls. ("The Oft-Discussed Montepulciano," June 2007)

The Sound of Silence

Paul on his superior at the time

KAREN. So am I correct in assuming that the letter was written as much (or more) for the higher-ups than it was for you? Was it a CYA letter? And does he wish you'd just keep your mouth shut and have a nice life?

PAUL. Yes, yes, and emphatically, yes. ("Canonical Warning Letter," May 2007)

Paul on that one verse in Leviticus

[In response to "Why shouldn't we put to death people who eat shellfish or wear mixed-fiber fabrics, as it says in the Bible?"]

Human life is put together in such a way that certain questions — simply by the fact of their being asked — break open the character of the people who ask them. When someone travels out to the further suburbs of the Old Testament to sniff around for grotesque antiques, it's clear they're not looking for the truth. Their problem is that the truth is all too plain. Confronted with Jesus, they can't squirm out of the truth that Granny and Pope Pius XI and every wholesome eleven-year-old know right and wrong and know that God knows that they know. Facing this fact means giving up a lifetime of cherished wickedness — especially hard if it's cherished in secret. It takes guts. Rather than face up to the humiliation of repentance, many, perhaps most, take the easy route of burrowing into the lives of Christians to expose hidden sins, or they search the Scriptures for hypocrisy. It doesn't really answer anything, but it duct-tapes the mouth of Jesus, and that helps soothe the conscience for a while. ("Leviticus," March 2015)

Paul on the Catholic church in Helmville, Montana,
which has a stained-glass clown window

I like the clown window especially. It puts us all in mind of John Wayne Gacy — clown, child molester, and serial killer, who buried his victims

Paul on ...

under the crawl space of his house in suburban Chicago. Making children laugh is a beautiful gift, a special kind of priesthood, even though Gacy's moral theology may have been closer to Jim Martin's than that of Alphonsus Liguori. There is a sanctity in the giggles of kiddies that deserves a stained-glass window, even if their butchered and sodomized bodies have been known to provoke judgmental and even *homophobic* reactions among Catholics uncomfortable with persons exploring non-binary sexualities. Ours is a both/and church. ("St. Thomas the Apostle," e-mail to Fr. Sean Raftis, August 2020)

Paul on the pope's proposal to change the Our Father
Yes, the Our Father really says "lead us not into temptation." God does not *cause* us to sin; He does put us (as Jesus was led *by the Spirit* into the wilderness) into occasions of temptation. ("Question," May 2019)

Paul on bishops
1. The task of a bishop is to protect from damnation the souls of those confided to his pastoral care. All other episcopal responsibilities are trivial beside this. Indeed, he has no other responsibilities that are not wholly subordinated to this end. A bishop who does not accept this description of his job should resign....

2. The gravity of his responsibility means that a bishop is at much greater risk of damnation than non-bishops. His salvation is contingent not only on his own metanoia and regeneration but on the spiritual life of other persons, his flock.

3. A bishop can do no greater disservice to his flock than to lie; lying is immeasurably more destructive than scandal given by sexual turpitude, jobbery, or peculation. Any lie, regardless of gravity or occasion, gives his hearers reason to believe that the apostles lied about Christ and that the Church is lying when she claims to be a reliable transmitter of divine teaching. ("Oldie," August 2018)

The Sound of Silence

Paul on the Novus Ordo and Sedevacantism

KAREN. I suddenly have all these traddie friends (we've bonded over being horrified by the pope), and some of them are trying to convince me that no Novus Ordo Mass is valid and that their bread is bread. Why do they think that? (I'd rather ask you than them.)

PAUL. I don't know why they think that. Even the pre-Conciliar Eucharistic theology held that a validly ordained priest who pronounced the words of consecration over wheaten bread with the intention of consecrating did so validly. Is this sincere on their part or just a way of provoking you? Do these folks refuse to genuflect before the tabernacle in an ordinary Catholic church? Would they feed my Hosts to the birds?

I have sympathies for the return to the Latin Mass, but Sedevacantism is just plain loopy. ("Another Thing," April 2015)

Paul on a postcard that I had sent him

Did some follow-up research on that card you sent. A rare find. It appears it was recently discovered in a beaver-skin satchel buried five-feet deep in peat in Carrefours, Quebec, dated Noel 1635, signed by Fathers Jean de Brebeuf, S.J., and Isaac Jogues, S.J., and their friend "Puffy." ("Aw shucks ... well ... [rubs nose with sleeve] ... CONGRATULATIONS to Jon M Sweeney ... !," December 2019)

Paul on his sixty-sixth birthday

Thanks for your good wishes and for the toast yet to be toasted! Wine.com informed me a bottle is on the way, so thanks in advance for that as well. My Jesuit brothers left a dozen white roses and a bottle of Dom Pérignon outside my door. Also a severed horse's head. ("Happy Birthday!," November 2019)

Paul on ...

Paul on giving up wine for Advent

Many, many thanks for the bottles bottles bottles of red red wine! As you may remember, I go off the ethanol for Advent and so greatly look forward to that first slosh sliding down my throat and gently detonating on hitting bottom. I will point myself East South East and hoist a glass in your direction on The Eve. ("Rec'd," December 2015)

Paul on NASCAR

You don't have to tell me what NASCAR is. When I was a boy, Richard Petty's 426 hemi was as familiar to me as my night prayers. ("Suppertime," January 2008)

Paul on fishing and NASCAR

Had a good time fishing. Very quiet, very soothing to be off the Internet and away from North Korea, Francis, James Martin, and Chelsea Manning. Glad to see that NASCAR has — so far — resisted *Amoris Laetitia*. (untitled e-mail to the author, September 2017)

Paul on Hollywood

I suspect the only persons for whom Hollywood would not be destructive are lawn maintenance personnel and morticians. (untitled e-mail to the author, April 2015)

Paul on Jephthah and his daughter

I see her with her castanets and harem pants, weighing 240 pounds, and Jephthah making a great show of slapping his brow and saying, "Oh *shucks*, princess! I made the *stupidest* vow yesterday! Don't know what I could have been *thinking*. Well anyway, listen to this ..." ("You Can't Un-See This, I Tried," April 2015)

Paul on judging

KAREN. I'm being taken to task for "judging." It seems to me that the world is a cesspool from the "thou shalt not judge" of it all. I've always said that this does not mean "thou shalt not discern." But now I'm wondering, is that the best I can do? I remember reading somewhere that "thou shalt not judge" meant not to condemn the person to damnation and therefore give up on him or her. Can you offer any clarification?

PAUL. My take is that "thou shalt not judge" is the negative corollary of the petition of the Lord's Prayer: "Forgive us our trespasses, as we forgive those..." That's to say, we are forbidden to come to the judgment that someone by his sin has put himself "beyond forgiveness" — whether the forgiveness due comes from us or from another injured party. Therefore, if one makes it clear to a gay-pride zealot that, by renouncing sodomy (and any other sins), he can regain the state of grace, one is not contravening the "judge not" command. Does that help? ("In Need of Biblical Scholarship," April 2015)

Paul on Matrimony

KAREN. An idiot in a comment box has said this to me:

> Matrimony wasn't even a sacrament for the first 1100 years. There is also an inherent bias in matrimony laws that privileges clergy. Priests can leave the priesthood and the sacramental vows they took, marry, and still receive communion. So much for vows for life to the Bride of Christ.

Could I borrow a smackdown? Then I will leave him alone.

PAUL. A Catholic believes that all seven sacraments were instituted by Christ during His earthly ministry, even though the word

Paul on ...

"sacrament" was not on His lips. To argue that matrimony only became a sacrament when declared by the Council of Verona is like denying that the Eucharist is a sacrament because Jesus didn't have His picture taken with St. Peter after his First Communion (both, you remember, had other business that night). As for vows, it's true that they can be dispensed; true, too, that those who enjoy being scandalized will find plenty to amuse themselves in that realm. ("Need Help with an Idiot," April 2015)

Paul on David and Bathsheba

KAREN. I'm still stewing over David and Bathsheba. This guy killed a woman's husband while having an adulterous affair, and God still loved him. What is the point? We should all go and do likewise?
PAUL. Now, now. David's third, fifth, eleventh, and sixteenth wives were exemplary multitasking caregivers and serve as models for the upcoming synod. ("Seriously...," April 2015)

Paul on divisiveness

Last Monday I was at St. Louis University giving a talk on Flannery O'Connor. The Jesuit organizer got this e-mail from one of the unhappy students:

> While I am grateful for Fr. Mankowski's willingness to come without honorarium and for much of the wisdom he shared on Flannery O'Connor, I am incredibly upset and downright angry at his intentional divisiveness through a one-dimensional characterization of James Martin, coupled with his extreme example. I think he did much to damage the Church through his words, and I would like to share my perspective with him in hopes that he would be more careful in the future.

The Sound of Silence

Sadly, the priest I was critiquing was not James Martin. I can't even be divisive without being divisive!" ("We'll Always Have Japan," September 2019)

Paul on Thanksgiving 2019

I will be not be overeating, as I am in the middle of a twenty-one-day bread-and-water fast (in reparation for the sins of priests, bishops, popes...). I'll drop by my niece's house to say hello to family and then slip out into the darkness. Happy Thanksgiving!" ("Happy Thanksgiving!," November 2019)

Papers and Talks

Author's note: This section is filled with papers and talks on a variety of subjects, for a variety of audiences, over many years. I recommend that you do not try to read straight through all of them. Take them slowly so you may receive their full benefit.

Truth Himself Speaks Truly

An address to the Conference on the Christian Worldview and the Academy, sponsored by the Witherspoon Institute, Princeton University, November 10, 2007

by Paul Mankowski, S.J.
Pontifical Biblical Institute, Rome

*Credo quidquid dixit Dei Filius
Nil hoc Verbo veritatis verius.*[90]

Christian faith is often spoken of as if it were a stop-gap measure — a kind of epistemological duct tape — used to patch over defects in our rational grasp of the assertions made by our religion. St. Thomas Aquinas, in his Eucharistic hymn I just quoted, suffers no such bashfulness. Here is Gerard Manley Hopkins's rendering:

> What God's Son has told me, take for truth I do;
> Truth himself speaks truly, or there's nothing true.

Truth himself speaks truly: this is a conviction, I contend, that the Christian brings to his reading of the Bible — better, to his hearing of

[90] This from St. Thomas Aquinas's hymn "Adoro Te Devote."

the Bible — not a conclusion that his study of Scripture must inductively supply. That's to say, the Scriptures are addressed to the man antecedently convinced that, precisely because their ultimate author is God, they are trustworthy.[91] What I want to attempt this morning is a brief exercise in apologetics, taking to heart Josef Pieper's dictum that the task of the Christian apologist is "not to prove his belief but to defend it." I want to argue that, in accepting the Bible as trustworthy *a priori*, the Christian does not sin against reason. Further, I want to persuade you that this can be done without a tumble into fideism. Finally, I want to put forward some considerations — not proofs, suasions — for thinking our predicament is not as dire as it is often made out to be.

Mark Twain's schoolboy famously said, "Faith is believing what you know ain't so," and perhaps the characteristic of Sacred Scripture that most embarrasses the educated Christian is that the Bible records miracles, and belief in the inerrancy of the Bible entails belief that the miracles recorded really happened. So, in claiming that the Christian reads the Scriptures as a text that has God as its author, am I claiming that he believes the truth of every Old Testament extravagance: in Aaron's rod-turned-serpent? Balaam's talking donkey? Elijah's unfailing flour jar? Well, yes, that's exactly what I'm claiming. In fact, I'd go still further and contend that the defensive maneuverings by which some theologians explain away such texts not only fuels the skepticism they pretend to diminish but are wrongheaded from the get-go,

---

[91] See the *Catechism of the Catholic Church* §156: "*Motivum* credendi id non est quod veritates revelatae lumini nostrae rationis naturalis tamquam verae et intelligibiles appareant. Credimus 'propter auctoritatem Ipsius Dei revelantis, qui nec falli nec fallere potest'" (citing *Dei Filius* 3:DS 3008). See also Thomas Aquinas, *ST* IIaIIae 2 ad 9: "Ipsum autem credere est actus intellectus assentientis veritati divinae ex imperio voluntatis a Deo motae per gratiam."

Truth Himself Speaks Truly

the product of a misplaced philosophical timidity. Our repugnance at assenting to miracles is, for most of us, a by-product of our natural and common reliance on inductive reasoning — whence comes the bumptiousness of Twain's schoolboy — yet it is induction whose logical credentials are shonky, and it's the nay-sayers of miracles from whom a little epistemic queasiness ought to be forthcoming. You'll remember the challenge thrown down by David Hume in his *Enquiry concerning Human Understanding*:

> These two propositions [says Hume] are far from being the same: *I have found that such an object has always been attended with such an effect,* and *I foresee, that other objects, which are, in appearance, similar, will be attended with similar effects.* I shall allow, if you please, that the one proposition may justly be inferred from the other; I know, in fact, that it always is inferred. But if you insist that the inference is made by a chain of reasoning, I desire you to produce that reasoning.[92]

The "objects of human reason" Hume sees in play in these propositions are what he calls Matters of Fact, sharply distinguished from the objects he calls Relations of Ideas, propositions "discoverable by mere operation of thought" — such as are discovered by mathematics — and whose truth is demonstrably certain. Matters of fact, by contrast, borrow their elements from our experience of the world. Thus, whereas negating a Relation of Ideas (say, that the whole is equal to the sum of its parts) is unthinkable,

> the contrary of every matter of fact [Hume writes] is still possible, because it can never imply a contradiction, and is

---

[92] David Hume, *Enquiries concerning Human Understanding and concerning the Principles of Morals,* ed. L. A. Selby-Bigge, 3rd ed. edited by P. H. Nidditch (Oxford: Clarendon, 1992), 34.

conceived by the mind with the same facility and distinctness, as if ever so conformable to reality. That *the sun will not rise tomorrow* is no less intelligible a proposition, and implies no more contradiction, than the affirmation, that it will rise. We should in vain, therefore, attempt to demonstrate its falsehood. Were it demonstratively false, it would imply a contradiction, and could never be distinctly conceived by the mind.[93]

Therefore, while the notion of a squared circle dissolves into unintelligibility, an assertion contrary to our experience of cause and effect is perfectly intelligible in itself and entails no contradiction.

Now, it should be obvious that all the miracles of the New and Old Testaments belong in this latter category: however grossly repellent to our inductively cozened instincts, they are intelligible, they involve no deductive misstep. We know what it means for water to turn into wine, and we know what it means for a man to be carried three days in the belly of a fish: if they occurred in our presence, we'd be able to recognize these events for what they were. To prove that such things *couldn't* happen, the skeptic needs to answer Hume's challenge and produce the "chain of reasoning" that links cause and effect; in default of such a link, the Christian who extends credit to the biblical account is, *eo ipso*, guilty of no irrationality. Are all miracle claims immune to falsifiability? They are not. My favorite counterexample comes from the autobiography of the seventeenth-century French mystic Jeanne Marie Guyon. In a chapter in which she expounds the details of her pieties, her housekeeping, her open-handedness, and her mother-in-law's resentment, Madame Guyon tells us that her husband demanded that she keep accounts lest her

---

[93] Ibid., 25.

lavish disbursements to charity bring the household to ruin. She does the accounting though omits to deduct what she has given away in alms, and her books balance all the same — "not a farthing more nor less," she exclaims, "an admirable instance, my God, of thy providence."[94] A little too admirable, my dear.

We're right to accept the biblical narratives with the same serenity with which we reject Madame Guyon's squaring of the circle. And the more clearly we see what faith commits us to and what it doesn't, the better armed we are *against* fideism — by which I mean truculent credulity reinforced by a programmatic avoidance of hostile argument: the intellectual equivalent of stuffing one's fingers into one's ears. We should engage the counterclaims readily and treat them with full seriousness. What we have no grounds for, and what I'd like to see put behind us, is the habit of apologizing for divine intervention in the Bible as for the presence of some eccentric great aunt in one's apartment. The God who, in sovereign freedom, created the universe and all its array, and who ceaselessly sustains its existence, ought to be able to visit His handiwork without affront to the credulity or the metaphysics of its transient houseguests.

A more straightforwardly logical challenge is presented by internal contradictions in the Bible — at least, *prima facie* contradictions — such as those posed by the two creation accounts in Genesis,

---

[94] "Avant la mort de mon mari, ma belle-mère lui ayant dit che je le ruinerais par mes charités ... il me dit qu'il voulait absolument que j'écrivisse toute la dépense de la maison, tout ce que je faisais acheter afin qu'il jugeât de ce que je donnais au pauvres.... Je m'y soumis pourtant sans rien retrancher de mes charités; chose admirable de votre Providence, ô mon Dieu, je n'écrivais aucune de mes aumônes, et ma dépense se trouva juste, sans un sol de plus ou de moins." Jeanne Marie Guyon, *La vie par elle-même: et autres écrits biographiques*, Sources Classiques 29, ed. Dominique Trone (Paris: Honoré, 2001), 406.

or the divergent genealogies of Joseph given in Matthew and Luke. Since contradictory assertions cannot both be true, the Church must understand the putative conflict as either not contradictory or as not involving two assertions. Here it is not a case of the reader's intuitions of reality clashing with the reality presented by the text; rather it is the Bible itself, by its inclusion of the apparent contradictories, that demands that we read them along different axes of interpretation. Take the two accounts of divine creation. In Genesis 1, the animals are created before man, and man is to be their ruler; in Genesis 2, the beasts come after. In Genesis 1, man is to have dominion over the earth (1:28); in Genesis 2, he is to serve the earth (2:5, 15). In Genesis 1, male and female are created together; in Genesis 2, they are formed sequentially, and so forth. Note that these accounts are given in adjacent chapters and their contrasts are stated *en clair*, no Higher Criticism is required to identify the discrepancies, which were as obvious in the sixth century BC as they are to us. It is not some queasy modernist exegete; it is the Sacred Text itself that is shouting at us: "What you are meant to learn from my narrative is not the chronology of the development of the material order."

To pick up on another problem from the same narrative, one that mistakenly vexes creationists and mistakenly consoles their adversaries. In Genesis 1, the event of creation is presented as occurring in six "days" — *yamim*, in Hebrew. I needn't rehearse for you the dispute over the scientific plausibility of the timeline. The point at issue is: What does the book of Genesis mean by *yom*? Our initial operating assumption will be that *yom* means what English speakers mean by "day" — i.e., the course of the sun in the sky from one dawn (or dusk) to the next. But according to the creation narrative there was no earth at all until the third *yom* and the sun was created in the *yom* after that; thus, four *yamim* had passed before the measure we call a day was even thinkable. The naiveté, once again, does not belong to the science of the sacred author, but to the hermeneutics of the reader — whether defiant creationist or gleeful Darwinist — who insinuates his own alien meaning into the Hebrew text and then, like a magician yanking a rabbit out of a hat, confronts us with the meaning he claims to have found there. By contrast, reading Hebrew *yom* as a nontemporal reality is not some makeshift interpretation fetched from afar but is demanded by the ancient narrative on its own terms.

There is an alternative explanation of such contradictions: namely, that the writers — or, if you prefer, compilers — of the Hebrew Bible failed to notice the discrepancies in the texts and left them in out of ignorance, inattention, or sloth. This hypothesis overtaxes my own credulity by postulating a gratuitous miracle — inasmuch as it attributes to the sacred author an obtuseness beyond the capacity of unaided human imbecility. I can believe a lot of things, but I can't believe that.

Now, even if certain interpretations of the biblical narrative are interdicted by the Bible itself, the correct interpretation of a disputed passage does not always fall out once the erroneous ones are eliminated. And this brings us up against the much larger problem of hermeneutics. The Dogmatic Constitution *Dei Verbum* of the Second Vatican Council sets out the issue concisely:

> Since everything asserted by the inspired authors ... must be held to be asserted by the Holy Spirit, it follows that the books of Scripture must be acknowledged as teaching solidly, faithfully and without error that truth which God wanted put into the sacred writings for the sake of our salvation.[95]

The question that follows is: How do we identify an assertion of the Holy Spirit as an assertion? A statement may have an assertoric form

---

[95] *Dei Verbum* §11.

while lacking assertoric intent,[96] and even a close scrutiny of a biblical narrative can fail to find in it "that truth which God wanted put into the sacred writings for the sake of our salvation," and to which inerrancy attaches. A simple example: some of Jesus' statements are identified by the evangelists as parables, and even though some of the propositions will have a logically assertoric form ("a sower went out to sow...") we're clearly not invited to assent to the concrete historicity of the statement. Yet other narratives recounted by Jesus are not explicitly identified as parables and yet partake of the same literary form; for example, the pericope commonly known as the *Parable* of the Good Samaritan (Luke 10:30–37) simply begins, "A man was going down from Jerusalem to Jericho, and he fell among robbers." Though its thrust is obviously didactic, the account is naturalistic in detail and narrative in form and could, indeed, describe an event that actually happened. Yet no Christian doctrine hinges on the facticity of the event described, and to be mistaken about the historical assertory value of the account does not implicate one in doctrinal error.

---

[96] E.g., when embedded in a quotation, or when used ironically. For the jargon here employed, see Jürgen Habermas, *Between Facts and Norms: Contributions to a Discourse Theory of Law and Democracy*, trans. W. Rehg (Cambridge, MA: MIT Press, 1996), 14: " 'Real' is what can be represented in true statements, whereas 'true' can be explained in turn by reference to the claim one person raises before others by asserting a proposition. With the assertoric sense of her statement, a speaker raises a criticizable claim to the validity of the asserted proposition, and because no one has direct access to uninterpreted conditions of validity, 'validity' (*Gültigkeit*) must be understood in epistemic terms as 'validity (*Geltung*) proven for us.' A justified truth claim should allow its proponent to defend it with reasons against the objections of possible opponent; in the end she should be able to gain the rationally motivated agreement of the interpretation community as a whole."

A third case we might take up concerns Luke 16:19–31, Jesus' account of the rich man and the beggar Lazarus. Here, too, the evangelist does not identify the story as a parable, and the overlap with the parable form is only partial. Yet the facticity of the narrative is not an idle question because Jesus gives us a conversation between the rich man, damned in his place of torment, and Abraham, in the abode of the blessed. Are we to understand the rich man and Lazarus as real persons or as fictive? Is Jesus asserting that communication takes place between the damned and the blessed, or does the narrated conservation simply reflect a midrashic figure of speech? Within the terms of the story, Hell is not an empty place, and the damned retain intellect, will, memory, and some mode of perception. Are we to understand these inferences as asserted by Holy Scripture or not? It matters to our convictions about eschatology how we respond to such questions, yet exegetes ancient and modern fail to agree on the answers.

Our problem here is no different from the dilemma of the Ethiopian eunuch whom St. Philip encounters in the Acts of the Apostles (8:26–39), and the solution to his quandary is the solution to ours. You remember that the eunuch, while on his way to Jerusalem, is reading the book of the prophet Isaiah. "Do you understand what you are reading?" asks Philip. "How can I," responds the hermeneutically deficient Ethiopian, "unless there is someone to guide me?" and he points to Isaiah 53:7: "As a sheep led to the slaughter or a lamb before its shearer is dumb, so he opens not his mouth." Thereupon he asks Philip, "About whom, pray, does the prophet say this, about himself or about some one else?" In our jargon, the eunuch is asking what proposition is being asserted by the text, and thus proposed for the assent of faith; in the language of *Dei Verbum*, he is asking for "that truth which God wanted put into the sacred writings for the sake of [his] salvation." Acts 8:35 reads: "Then Philip opened his mouth, and began at the same scripture, and preached unto him Jesus (ευηγγελισατο τον Ιησουν)." There wasn't a written New Testament in existence at this point, whence the biblical exegesis Philip offers in response is itself — importantly — extra-biblical.

My claim then is that, where the assertory value of biblical texts is disputed, the ultimate referee will be the continuing community that authoritatively assembled the Bible in the first place: that's to say, the Church. I haven't attempted to prove this claim here (though I think it is provable); for the nonce I'm just nailing my colors to the mast; nor am I using "Church" as code to mean the Roman Catholic Church in a juridical sense. Rather I'm pointing to that fact that there was a Church — an *ekklesia* — before there was a Bible, and that the Bible is itself a dogmatic construct. While the individual books of Sacred Scripture had an independent history, the decision to treat them as parts of a unity — viz., the Christian Bible — was the consequence of dogmatic convictions, i.e., antecedent beliefs about God and the Church. Whence it seems performatively consistent that the authority that assembled the Bible by rejecting *those* texts and accepting *these* may be trusted to judge the assertoric value of the propositions the accepted texts contain — propositions that contradict or that accord with the dogmatic convictions that guided the assembly in the first place. If this assertion appears dangerously anti-intellectual, I'd suggest that at least some of the disquiet comes from the fact that we've all been influenced by the Enlightenment project of emancipating the Bible from the Church by using extra-ecclesial criteria of authenticity. Yet this project, as I contend, is self-defeating. For the Bible — on these terms — is an unbiblical notion: it needs a table of contents, and that table of contents can't be found in its pages.

At this point in my remarks it may be well to confess what I should perhaps have made clear earlier, that my academic training is in philology rather than exegesis and that am I addressing you not as a professional theologian but as a fellow believer. That said, I do spend the greater part of my time entangled in the Bible, largely in the bottom fifth of the sacred page, in amongst the compost of variant readings in the *apparatus criticus*, from which vantage point I bring a maggot's-eye view to the problems of revelation (in the narrowest sense) and of biblical theology (in its widest). Having spoken (albeit elliptically) about the discursive content of the Bible, let me briefly touch on the reliability of its transmission.

The Church was vouchsafed no scriptural book in autograph: that's to say, she doesn't have any original text directly from the hand of the sacred author. We have copies of copies, copies of copies of translations, copies of copies of compilations, and so forth. Is this a handicap? Well, it would be, if we believed the Holy Spirit's contribution began and ended with the dictation of the original text, whereat He retired to gaze upon the process of transmission like a nervous batting coach watching the action at the plate from the dugout. But it's reasonable to believe that the same Spirit who aided, say, the prophet Hosea in his prophesying continues to assist the Church in her reception of the prophecy in its written mode, and that the vicissitudes of textual transmission — at least up to such time as the Church has accepted the book in a recognized form (or forms) — are no more accidental than the primitive inspiration was accidental. Even if the Church never comes to possess the original text from the fist of Hosea, she has the texts God wants her to have.

The same consideration, I believe, puts in their right perspective concerns about the authenticity of the canonical texts raised in response to theories about ideological tampering. One of the questions submitted to me in preparation for this conference was "Did the kings edit scripture when it was copied to suit their political agendas?" Well, there's no shortage of scholarly arguments in support of this hypothesis — and it is, remember, a hypothesis — that the redaction or "guided editing" of Old Testament books was carried out in various times and places in the service of political ends. Yet even if we concede the possibility of political tampering in any given case, it doesn't follow that to falsify a text is to state a falsehood, and viewed through the lens of canonical reception the tampering simply becomes one of the unexpected tools by which the developing text takes its shape, the shape in which the Church will ultimately make it her own. There's an unseemly aspect to the transaction, I grant you, but no more unseemly or unexpected than the fact that Moab, born of the incestuous union of Lot and his elder daughter, should become an ancestor of David through David's great-grandmother Ruth; no more unseemly or unexpected than the circumstances by which the brothers of Joseph sold him into slavery, only to meet him in Pharaoh's palace and be assured by him, "God sent me before you to preserve for you a remnant on earth.... So it was not you who sent me here, but God" (Gen. 45:7f). If treachery and incest can be turned by God into means to rescue the progeny of Abraham from extinction, we shouldn't be unduly shocked if unscrupulous editors and venal scribes (equally unconscious of their role) have a hand in the preservation of the books they dishonored.

I have not, of course, demonstrated, or attempted to demonstrate, the truth of any particular assertion made by Sacred Scripture, and after all, these assertions are proposed by the Scriptures themselves as truths to be apprehended by faith. It may seem dismaying to you to realize that your faith commits you to a lifetime of arguing in its defense, and that all your battles will be rearguard battles, fought to regain the turf lost to your opponent's offensive. But, in fact, it couldn't be otherwise. The contested affirmations and points of doctrine will be chosen not by those who find them satisfactory but by those who don't, and their skepticism or antipathy will have given them a head start in their preparations. You'll find, moreover, that by the time you've prepared a counteroffensive the locus of conflict has often shifted elsewhere, since the aspects of the Christian proposition regarded as incredible or repellent changes with the changing preoccupations of the hour. Our great-grandparents were hard-pressed to explain Methuselah's 969 years and the double death of Goliath; our own generation is called to account for the moral teachings of Leviticus and St. Paul; what controversies will summon our great-grandchildren (*your* great-grandchildren) to the battlements no one can say. The only thing we can be certain of is that they will feel as ill-prepared as we do. It's in the nature of the dialectic.

Truth himself speaks truly, or there's nothing true. A Christian is a person who believes the Good News: in briefest terms, the good news concerning one specific miracle: He who was slain for our sins, lives. Whence it's worth remembering that, in making an act of faith in the word of God, the Christian is primarily not committing himself to a book but to a Person: the Word made flesh — in order that (in the words of *Dei Verbum*) "man might in the Holy Spirit have access to the Father and come to share in the divine nature."

> This plan of revelation [*Dei Verbum* continues] is realized by deeds and words having an inner unity: the deeds wrought by God in the history of salvation manifest and confirm the teaching and realities signified by the words, while the words proclaim the deeds and clarify the mystery contained in them. By this revelation then, the deepest truth about God and the salvation of man shines out for our sake in Christ, who is both the mediator and the fullness of all revelation.[97]

God's definitive self-revelation is in His Son, not in texts about His Son. And those texts are illumined not only by study but by the life lived in a continually deepening relationship to their subject. "Think not," says St. Bonaventure, "that reading will suffice without fervor,

---

[97] *Dei Verbum* §2.

speculation without devotion, investigation without admiration, observation without exaltation, industry without piety, knowledge without love, understanding without humility, and study without divine grace."[98] This is a challenge for any Christian, considerably daunting to those of us who make primary contact with Holy Writ in the larval form of Semitic philologists, and yet it keeps us alert to the paradoxical tension of divine revelation.

In Genesis 11, we're told that in the beginning all the earth had the same words and pronounced them the same way. Then God, coming down to destroy the pretensions of the builders of the Tower of Babel, confused their language — all language, no exception being made for Hebrew. This means that, on the Bible's own terms, Hebrew is itself a corrupt and secondary language — and not the language God spoke to Adam and Eve in the Garden. We were not given a Qur'an or a Book of Mormon in which God's mind is "mainlined" into ours. St. Paul assures us there is one mediator between God and man, the man Christ Jesus (1 Tim. 2:5), yet not even Jesus' words are unmediated. Jesus spoke in Aramaic, yet apart from half a dozen transliterated vocables, we have no *ipsissima verba*. Clearly we were not meant to mistake the shell for the kernel by directing our worship at God's utterance instead of Himself. As George MacDonald wrote, God saw to it that the letter, as it could not give life, "should not be throned with the power to kill."[99] It isn't.

---

[98] St. Bonaventura, *Itinerarium mentis in Deum*, prologue, no. 4, in *Opera Omnia*, V (Quaracchi, 1891), 296: "(Nemo) credat quod sibi sufficiat lectio sine unctione, speculatio sine devotione, investigatio sine admiratione, circumspectio sine exsultatione, industria sine pietate, scientia sine charitate, intelligentia sine humilitate, studium absque divina gratia, speculum absque sapientia divinitus inspirata."

[99] George MacDonald, *Unspoken Sermons, Third Series: The Creation in Christ*.

Recent Work on the Patterning of Open-Syllable Vowel-Shifts in Pre-Masoretic Hebrew

An Address on the Occasion of the Thirtieth Anniversary of the Founding of Thomas Aquinas College

by Paul Mankowski, S.J.
Pontifical Biblical Institute
September 21, 2001

When you invite a Semitic philologist to address you after dinner, the inference, unlikely as it may be on its own terms, is that you have a post-prandial appetite for Semitic philology. This is not, as it happens, an appetite I share, but it is not the part of a guest to disoblige his hosts, and accordingly for this evening I have chosen as my title "Recent Work on the Patterning of Open-Syllable Vowel-Shifts in Pre-Masoretic Hebrew." As you are doubtless aware, the pioneering study on the subject of non-Masoretic phonology was done by Einar Brønno in his celebrated monograph *Studien über hebräische Morphologie und Vokalismus* published in Leipzig in 1943.[100]

[100] Einar Brønno, *Studien über hebräische Morphologie und Vokalismus auf Grundlage der mercatische Fragmente der zweiten Kolumne der Hexapla des Origenes* (Leipzig: Deutsche Morgenländische Gesellschaft, 1943).

The Sound of Silence

In 1943. An extraordinary year, when you stop to think about it. What kind of reasoning would have given Brønno the liberty — or the nerve — to pursue a pathetically impractical academic enterprise at a moment when civilization was in the process of dismembering itself, when the outcome of the struggle was sickeningly uncertain, and when the terms of the conflict had an apocalyptic moral urgency?

The question is larger than Brønno, of course. Isn't it obvious that, at a time of national crisis, pursuits such as philosophy and theology and the other abstract disciplines are a grotesquely irresponsible self-indulgence, that we should put aside these mind games and apply ourselves to the practical tasks that face us? Or, even if we should decide to linger in the academy, doesn't common sense tell us that it is metallurgy, not metaphysics, by which we do our part?

C. S. Lewis targeted this problem in a lecture addressed to Christian students at Oxford called "Learning in War-Time." It was given in 1939. He did not comfort his hearers with any sententious remarks about the ennobling effects of learning on the individual. He did not argue that good scholars make good infantry leaders, good citizens, or even good men. Rather, he asked how a Christian could be so cavalier toward his duties as to engage in study at *any* time, in *any* circumstances:

> How is it right [he asks], or even psychologically possible, for creatures who are every moment advancing either to Heaven or to hell to spend any fraction of the little time allowed them in this world on such comparative trivialities as literature or art, mathematics or biology?

Lewis saw that it is futile to ask whether a course of action is good or bad unless one has a clear idea of the end that it is meant to serve. In this case, the end is our salvation and the salvation of our fellow men. He answers: "Human culture has always had to exist under the shadow of something infinitely more important than itself," and he argues, "if men had postponed the search for knowledge and beauty until they were secure, the search would never have begun.... [Men are different from other species in that] they propound mathematical theorems in beleaguered cities, conduct metaphysical arguments in condemned cells, make jokes on scaffolds, discuss the last new poem while advancing to the walls of Quebec, and comb their hair at Thermopylae."

Not all such activities are of equal dignity. Nor should they be. The sublimity they share is not intrinsic nobility but a sublime disinterestedness. They have a tang of holy disobedience about them; they are pursued in defiance of the powers that would urge a man to look exclusively to his animal needs and debase himself to any extent in order to fill his stomach or preserve his life. Such intimidation may be diffuse and unprompted; it may be concrete and malicious — but the mathematical theorem and the joke on the scaffold exhibit their kinship precisely in their defiant detachment from the world of mammalian well-being, a world in which all of us are drones and slaves. Vladimir Nabokov professed to find in all true literature a radically seditious message, corrosive of any despotism.

> The twinkle in the author's eye as he notes the imbecile drooping of the murderer's underlip or watches the stumpy forefinger of the professional tyrant exploring a profitable nostril in the solitude of his sumptuous bedroom, this twinkle is what punishes your man more surely than the pistol of a tiptoeing conspirator. And inversely, there is nothing dictators hate so much as that unassailable, eternally elusive, eternally provoking gleam.[101]

When arts become truly liberal arts, they become liberating as well; they are subversive because they have refused the bribe offered

---

[101] [Vladimir Nabokov, *Lectures on Literature*, ed. Fredson Bowers (San Diego: Harcourt, 1980), 376.]

The Sound of Silence

to and accepted by the servile culture at large. The despot may or may not despise propositional logic, or astrophysics, or the music of Bach. He may be President for Life of Romania, or he may serve on the accreditation board of the Western Association of Schools and Colleges. But what infuriates him is radical spiritual freedom, what Nabokov calls the "eternally provoking gleam" displayed by those who pursue logic or physics or Bach — precisely in their unconcern for the opinions of others and indeed for their own comfort, safety, or success.

These activities of defiant detachment are not our ultimate human end, or *telos*. They may serve our damnation as easily as our deliverance. But they resemble our ultimate end in that they are pursued for their own sake and not for the sake of some ulterior good. It's a risky business, of course. The man who gets a Ph.D. in theology and for whom God becomes not an end but a means will go to Hell; his brother who gets a diploma in refrigerator repair, if he instrumentalizes his learning, will go to Oxnard. Still, most of us are willing to concede the principle that *corruptio optimi pessima* and to admit that, even though the search for knowledge often ends in failure, it is a great thing that it can be pursued at all.

"Human culture," says Lewis, "has always had to exist under the shadow of something infinitely more important than itself." This is true, but incomplete. For that which is of supreme importance not only overshadows human culture but is a necessary condition of its existence. Just as spirituality only bestows itself on those who are interested in something other than spirituality, so, in the long run, disinterested learning can only remain disinterested, the liberal arts can only remain liberal, to the extent that the resemblance they have to the ultimate human end is not taken for the real thing.

A quiz. See if you can place the following quotation:

> Divine Revelation ... frees the faithful Christian from those specious and yet absurd notions of freedom which because

they are false and subvert the life of reason, deceitfully enslave all who believe in them. In particular, it teaches that self-rule is not the same as independence, but rather that the assertion of complete independence destroys the capacity for self-rule. For to say that a man governs himself is to say that he has within him the principle which governs him.

It comes from the founding document of this institution, which I nicked off the TAC website. I have three comments to make: First, I want to thank the person responsible for calling it a founding document and avoiding the imbecile usage whereby an institution comes up with a "mission statement" containing a mission it gives itself, as if an ensign should say "aye, aye, sir!" in response to his own commands. Second, I wish to express the hope that you recognize that my remarks this evening are little more than a footnote to the passage just quoted. Third, I want to underscore the point that freedom itself can only survive — can only fail to corrupt — where truth is understood to be superior to freedom. It is a question of putting first things first.

The notion of self-rule advanced in the founding document should be placed in contrast to the role played by control — or power — in the postmodernist critique of liberal education. According to this account, education is essentially a tool of social coercion by which the dominant classes seek to extend their monopoly of power-over-the-marginalized by restricting the mode of academic discourse and by restricting the curriculum to a canon of "classics" chosen with malice aforethought — with the ideological aim of indoctrinating the pupil that the prejudices and self-serving myths of the powerful are to be embraced as universal and immutable truths.

Now, it is likely that most of us, at one point or another in our lives, have had a teacher whose interest was not in discovering or transmitting the truth but in making disciples, in forming a little coterie of

The Sound of Silence

admirers. But by the same token, we can see that such teachers are not the rule but the exception and that liberal education — more than any other education — is, in fact, a *forfeiture* of power, entailing a progressive surrender of the advantage that the teacher has over his student. Look at it this way: If I know Latin and you don't, I hold all the aces in my hand. Your knowledge of what authors and works exist, the translations by which you have access to them, the final word on the interpretation of difficult passages — all this is entirely in my power. But — if I teach you Latin, I put an end to my monopoly; I relinquish my control. You become free to read the works you choose to read, to translate them as you deem right, to propound and defend your own interpretation: Latin letters become a vast estate in which you and I walk as free and equal citizens.

Of course, this is true not just of Latin but of the liberal arts in general, whose aim is expressed in the words of the Renaissance aphorism "The pupil who does not surpass his master fails his master." The teacher's vocation is oriented, so to speak, at unemployment; his goal with respect to his pupil is to render himself superfluous. And you students will know that Thomas Aquinas College has succeeded in its purpose by this measure: if you can return to campus five or ten years after leaving, seek out your former tutors, and, from the bottom of your heart, say, "Dr. Kolbeck, Dr. Dillon, Dr. Guskin — you're *useless*." No teacher can receive a higher accolade; no compliment comes better from an ex-pupil.

Once we are made heirs of the patrimony of human culture, will it edify us or corrupt us? The answer is: both. While liberal arts liberate, they are indifferent as to whether the freedom they provide will be used for good or ill. There is even a sense in which they are impotent to decide between truth and error, provided their own procedural canons are followed. To take a trivial example from the trivium (grammar), the Fourth Lateran Council in 1215 issued a decree called *Omnes utriusque sexus*, which prescribes that all persons of both sexes are obliged to go to confession once a year. It was interpreted by a fourteenth-century monk named William of Newcastle such that the obligation of annual confession applied only to hermaphrodites — *Omnes utriusque sexus*. Notice: Brother William's Latin is flawless; the problem with his reading is that it is insane.

"A clean heart create within me, O Lord, and a steadfast spirit renew within me." Liberty without self-rule is useless — worse than useless — and self-rule requires a clean heart and a steadfast spirit: for us sinful men, constant cleansing, continually renewed resolve. I would propose two indications by which you might gauge how your time here is profiting you in this regard. (To employ Wittgenstein's distinction between a criterion and a symptom, these are symptoms of spiritual health and not criteria of it). First, that at the end of four years, you find adoration of the Blessed Sacrament more fascinating — fascinating in the pedantic sense in which it "binds to itself" your imagination and your intellect in mysterious ways — than it did before. Second, that each year you make better confessions than you did the year previously. For almost all of us, making a better confession will mean confessing more sins, not fewer sins, as it means that we discover and repent of truths about ourselves to which we were blind before, working hopefully toward the time in which the whole mass is leavened. Self-knowledge, though painful, is a necessary precondition of self-rule, putting first things first.

There are many respects in which the anxieties faced by the incoming class of TAC students are novel — at least with regard to the previous thirty years. But in the ultimate terms, the points on the compass have not changed. And thirty years from now, the children of the class of 2005 will themselves be of military age, facing God knows what adversity. Like all men, they will be called upon to put first things first: in the words of the catechism, to know, love, and serve God in this world so as to be infinitely happy with Him in the next.

The Sound of Silence

The responsibility is grave. But the execution of the task need not be. Notice the asymmetry here. Where first principles are missing or askew, even a man's amusements carry with them something of the odor of the tomb. But where first principles are in order, they can assimilate to their sacred purposes occasions of little consequence or none at all. Because his holy defiance rests on a deeper obedience, because he knows, as Socrates knew, that no ultimate harm can befall him, the just man is made free of the world. Baseball has its place. Banquets have their place. Jests can be made on the scaffold. He can read Dante while under bombardment and Ezekiel in the Dodgers' bullpen. And even when the civilization that nursed him seems to be dissolving before his eyes, he can give himself cheerfully to Padre Pio, and Weird Al Yankovic, and Semitic philology. In respect to which, regarding the problem of labialized vowels in open syllables in the pre-Masoretic manuscript tradition, let me leave you with this thought: that I regret my time is up. Thank you.

The Priest as Evangelical Witness

*Paper presented at the 2007 annual conference of the
Australian Confraternity of Catholic Clergy*[102]

I have titled today's talk "The Priest as Evangelical Witness" and, in doing so, am picking up on a point made the last time I addressed the ACCC. In the course of that lecture five years ago, I quoted a line from the former Archbishop of Paris, Emmanuel Suhard, in a retreat given to his own clergy in the 1940s. Cardinal Suhard singled out the priest's duty to serve as a witness and said:

> To be a witness does not consist in engaging in propaganda, nor even in stirring people up, but in being a living mystery. It means to live in such a way that one's life would not make sense if God did not exist.

Heathendom, of course, is perfectly comfortable with self-interest, and the heathen ordinarily shrewd in spying it in operation among other men. "If you love those who love you," asks our Lord, "what reward have

---

[102] Paul Mankowski, S.J., "The Priest as Evangelical Witness," Australian Confraternity of Catholic Clergy, Melbourne, Australia, November 2007, https://www.clergy.asn.au/the-priest-as-evangelical-witness/.

you? Do not even the tax collectors do the same? And if you greet only your brethren, what more are you doing than others? Do not even the Gentiles do the same?" It makes sense to seek one's own satisfaction, one's own comfort, one's own advantages — assuming, of course, that we live in a world in which there is no true reason for nobility, or selflessness, or disinterested love, a world in which we will never be called to account for our choices, a world in which there is no God. Conversely, to be a living mystery, to act in a way that cannot be understood except as a response to imperatives greater than the self, is to direct the minds of others toward the source of those imperatives. It is to be a witness.

Witness of Celibacy

Perhaps the way in which the mystery of which Suhard speaks is most strikingly evidenced is by way of the evangelical counsels of poverty, chastity, and obedience. It's noteworthy that, in Vatican II's Dogmatic Constitution on the Church, *Lumen Gentium*, these counsels first find mention not in the chapter on the religious state but in the prior chapter on the Church's Universal Vocation to Holiness. The practice of the counsels, under the impulsion of the Holy Spirit, undertaken by many Christians, either privately or in a Church-approved condition or state of life, gives and must give in the world an outstanding witness and example of [the holiness of the Church] (LG 39).

Not all clergy, obviously, are constrained by vows to live according to these evangelical counsels, yet I'd contend [that] any priest, whether diocesan or religious, who is sincerely striving for holiness permits the counsels to shape his life in a way congruent with his circumstances. They constitute three axes, as it were, in which we understand the project of the imitation of Christ.

Celibate chastity, without question, is the most dramatic witness borne in ordinary circumstances by the priest today, for the obvious reason that chastity is the aspect of priestly life most dramatically at variance with the obsessive preoccupation with sexual gratification by which our culture is marked. Among all the heathen, among most non-Catholic Christians and many Catholics as well, priestly chastity is uniquely perplexing, and consequently, uniquely eloquent testimony to Him for whose sake the satisfactions of the flesh are renounced. It's hard to overstate the force of that testimony. Even priests manifestly defective in other respects — men who are lazy, choleric, untruthful, or coarse — are viewed by the faithful (and not only the faithful) with the recognition that there is a mystery of love deeper than their patent deficiencies, a mystery tied to their celibacy. It makes no sense if God does not exist. It makes no sense, unless God is lovable even to human unloveliness.

We've all been told that mandatory priestly celibacy is not irreversible and that in the future the requirement may be abrogated. I don't believe it will happen, but if it did, it's clear that the non-celibate priesthood would be diminished in mystery — not less pious, necessarily, but tamer, more task-oriented, more "bourgeois" (by which I mean partaking of the pedestrian concerns and fashions of the life of the mid-level bureaucrat). The atheist or half-Christian would see a married priesthood as a sensible innovation, and the very things that make it reasonable in their eyes deprive it of witness value.

Chastity as Spiritual Chastity

I would enter two words of caution here. First, not a few priests of my acquaintance are, perhaps, overly impressed by the sacrifice they make as celibates. Some are led to permit themselves any other indulgence by way of compensation for their celibacy. Such indulgences not only weaken the testimony given by chastity, but they tend to weaken a man's capacity to remain chaste (after all, there's a single will choosing to renounce or to succumb). Of this more later. Second, it sometimes happens that a priest views his celibacy as requiring no more than sexual abstinence, and he feels himself at liberty to involve himself in romantic friendships — often, deplorably, under a spiritual pretense — provided no embraces or sexual congress take place. This is self-delusion. I've known priests who, as the woman in question was married and her husband uninterested in religion, had awarded themselves a kind of Pauline privilege, ostensibly supplying the spiritual companionship she wanted from her husband and did not receive. When, as sometimes happens, Father's *amitié amoureuse* alienates his companion from her husband, he is offending against the integrity of a marriage, even if physically chaste. The witness such a man gives to the husband in this situation does not bear thinking about.

That said, in spite of the manifest failings of the Catholic clergy in matters of chastity, that chastity remains a living mystery, paradoxically fascinating even to those secularists who reject it. This was evident on one level from the preoccupation of secular media with the sexual dimensions of the Vatican's criteria for seminary admission, and it's evident on another level in those aspects of clerical life that scoffers hold up for ridicule. When partygoers garb themselves in fancy dress as a priest or a nun, which of the evangelical counsels is to the fore in their mockery? Exactly.

Obedience as Witness

The evangelical counsel of obedience is usually less dramatic in its impact, but not without effect. The demeanor a priest exhibits in accepting an uncongenial post, for example, can speak a lot to those around him about the place of God in his life. Here the contrast with lay and heathen life is not so sharp (almost everyone is subject to some vexing authority in various aspects of his life), but again it is the gratuitousness of the priest's donation of self that can make the difference.

I was recently told of a book in which a woman describes her fixing brunch for a monk whom she had invited to her house. She asked him,

"How do you like your eggs?" and the brief tilt of his head and look of incomprehension told her, incontrovertibly, that he'd never had a way he liked his eggs. He'd simply eaten what was put in front of him. The incident lasted only an instant, but it made a deep impression on her, regarding the texture and meaning of a life lived so differently from her own. The occasion may be trivial, but the sign value is not. Not only monks but every priest has forfeited areas of discretion in his life that the people around him take for granted. The point is that people are watching, people are measuring a priest's renunciations and indulgences against his stated commitments by way of trying to understand what makes him tick. Freely offered obedience serves not only to edify, but to strengthen the faithful in their own obligations.

To make use of an analogy from another walk of life, military officers often receive unwelcome orders from their own superiors and must pass them on to their troops. The troops will almost always be able to tell whether their officers find the orders congenial or not, yet the key factor is not whether the commands are welcome to those officers but the alacrity with which they are received as commands. Any inflection of sarcasm or dismay or contempt that creeps into an officer's manner in relaying commands from above will, in effect, give his troops permission to tailor their obedience to their own convenience. By the same token, a priest's alacrity in carrying out assignments to his disadvantage communicates the presence of a supernatural order of grace according to which he sets his priorities and makes his decisions. It exemplifies the death to self that John the Baptist exemplified as necessary to the coming of Christ: he must increase, John said, but I must decrease.

Poverty as Witness

The evangelical counsel of poverty is one of the pivotal issues of priestly discipleship and one of the most difficult to talk about in concrete terms. My own experience of religious life is that community discussion of "poverty issues" is exceptionlessly ugly — partly because almost everyone feels vulnerable to criticism in some aspect or other of his life, partly because there's an unspoken recognition that poverty and chastity issues are not entirely unrelated. Today's questions of religious poverty, moreover, are detached from the classic ascetical Christian tradition in a way that the other evangelical counsels are not. We sense a certain cultural continuity in reading what Augustine or Alphonsus Liguori has to say about chastity and obedience, because for the relevant purposes we continue to live in their world. But social and economic changes have made it the case [that] every clergyman and religious in the First World enjoy a degree of physical comfort and security impossible for all but the very wealthiest nobles prior to the nineteenth century — and this irrespective of the severity of his chosen austerities. In fact, bashfulness about using the word "poverty" of our renunciation of ownership of property has brought it about that many religious communities speak about "simplicity of life" instead.

Granted all this, the way we priests eat, dress, recreate; the vehicles we use and the way we furnish our living quarters, such things are subject to the same ceaseless scrutiny by the world. "To be a witness," says Cardinal Suhard, "means to live in such a way that one's life would not make sense if God did not exist." Well, what do our elected comforts and discomforts witness to?

There are two equal and opposite errors to be avoided here. One is a pharisaical rigorism that finds any superfluity (a cigarette, a novel, a second glass of wine) to be a cause of disedification that delegitimizes one's priestly life. This path, unless carefully signposted by living saints, leads to madness. Its contrary is a self-administered moral anesthetic that excuses any priestly indulgence on the grounds that the laborer is worthy of his hire. As I mentioned earlier, there is a tendency for priests to think that the sacrifices made in the order of chastity justify compensation in the form of any and all carnal refreshment, provided it's nonsexual, whence it's easy to tumble into a life of pleasure-seeking bachelordom, collecting the usual boy-toys, watching the movies and frequenting the bars and overlapping, to some extent, the recreations of the young professional bronco. Too often, as we know, the overlap becomes total. But more importantly, there comes a point at which the witness we give in other aspects of our life is impaired by concern for personal comforts — and this not by pharisaical envy but by honest dismay given to the good-willed faithful. (One bonus of the Catholic-interest blogs — for those familiar with this world — is that it lets us hear the candid and uncensored opinions of layfolk about us their clergy: opinions that are overwhelmingly, almost miraculously, charitable in the main but also include the blunt observation that, when excess or luxury in food, drink, or comfort is used as a substitute for sex, it's hard to see the resultant chastity as a spiritual renunciation at all.)

Adhering to What Befits the Clerical State

I make no distinction between diocesan and religious clergy in these matters. On the one hand, any vowed religious who really wants to can, in my experience, find a way to obviate his obligations of poverty by shrewd exploitation of prosperous lay friends and the perquisites of his own job. A Jesuit so inclined can live as sumptuously as a diocesan priest who enjoys a large private income. On the other hand, Canon 282 §1 — "Clerics are to follow a simple way of life and avoid anything which smacks of worldliness" — applies to diocesans as much as to religious, and the same is true of Canon 285 §1: "Clerics are to shun completely everything that is unbecoming to their state," and §2: "Clerics are to avoid whatever is foreign to their state, even when it is not unseemly."

While we're on the subject, another equilaterally operable Canon is 284: "Clerics are to wear suitable ecclesiastical dress, in accordance with the norms established by the Episcopal Conference and legitimate local custom." It's obvious to me that local custom is somewhat different in the USA and Australia regarding clerical garb, and I'm not in a strong position to say whether or not it's legitimate local custom. But one of the advantages of giving a drive-by harangue of the present kind is that I can light a fuse to a powder-keg of ecclesiastical controversy, secure in the knowledge that I'll be out of harm's way when the detonation takes place.

So here goes. My own conviction is that most priests most of the time are consulting personal convenience rather than apostolic impact on occasions when they choose to put off the Roman collar and dress in mufti. God knows I am not insensible to those conveniences. Further, there are some unpredictably urgent tasks for which clerical attire is ill-suited, such as painting the ceiling of the presbytery or changing the transmission fluid on the parish van. In April of 1999, during a tertianship experiment, I found myself in central New South Wales helping with pregnancy testing on a beef herd, shoulder-deep into a bemused heifer, and I admit that I permitted myself a derogation from Canon 284 in favor of the loin of the non-baptized party. There are circumstances in which even Pius XII would lay aside his clergy stock *ad majorem Dei gloriam*. That said, such circumstances are rarer than commonly acknowledged. I generally apply what I call a "two-ring test."

External Signs of State of Life

We all know of married men who yank the wedding ring off their finger before leaving on their "boys' night out," and it's sometimes the case that priests put off the external signs of their priesthood for analogous reasons. Mufti lets a priest go to the kind of bars and restaurants and movie theaters that a man in clerics would be shy of entering. It lets the priest stare at skirts (etc.) that cross his path without provoking more than the usual indignation. It lets a priest buy the kind of reading material that would raise eyebrows otherwise. It frees the priest from the public pressure to edify — or at least not to be disedifying. In mufti the priest can flip off people who cut him off in traffic and deal brusquely with panhandlers and quarrel with salespeople and waiters and airline personnel — all the while emancipated from the duty to uphold an institutional reputation.

Living with the inconveniences of a public state of life. The second ring derives from Tolkien's famous trilogy. This is a ring not removed but rather worn in circumstances of need. Its property is to render the wearer invisible. Mufti, as we all know, gives the priest the ability to reveal his priesthood to those he wants and withhold it from those he wants. He can run with the hares or hunt with the hounds as the advantages of the particular social situations dictate. In the USA, a few years ago at any rate, the detestation directed at priests at the height of the clerical abuse scandal moved some priests to wear civvies as a kind of camouflage. Less dramatically, most of us have faced the prospect of a long plane flight in which we longed to be free of the importunities of fellow travelers and to journey instead as Mr. Average Passenger. However, turning oneself into Mr. Average Passenger — for a priest — is like Bilbo Baggins putting on the Ring in order to avoid his cousin Lobelia. It's a sneaky way out that makes him a tiny bit more cowardly every time he takes it. Many resort to the expedient; few take pride in it. Summing up, I'd contend that, on those occasions when removing one's collar is not yanking off a wedding ring and when donning mufti is not slipping-on Tolkien's ring, then it's a responsible choice — neither an instance of taking the easy way out nor of laying aside one's duty.

To repeat: the Canons that touch on priestly worldliness, as well as the spiritual dispositions that give them force, apply equally to religious and diocesan clergy. As underlined by the cry of John the Baptist mentioned above, the point of these cautions against profane indulgences is that noisy self be eclipsed by the person of Christ. With the exception of priests who are strictly cloistered monks, we're all in the same boat.

Asceticism as Witness

Yet the mention of monks is not wholly beside the point. One of the huge post-conciliar losses to the priestly life generally has been the sea change in the model of contemplative life: a life once aimed at mortification — a death to self through asceticism — now aimed at self-actualization. The "self" has taken center stage. This change is important because, in spite of fifty-plus years of propaganda to the contrary, the monastic ideal remains a potent icon in any priest's self-understanding. Obedience, simplicity of life, and fidelity to prayer have different orientations in the case of a canon, a friar, and a diocesan priest, obviously, but they are all monastic in transmission and all essential to the clerical life. Where monastic life is healthy, it builds up even non-monastic parts of the Church; including and in particular the lives of priests in the active apostolate. Where monastic life is corrupt or lax, the loss extends to the larger Church as well — it's as if a railing were missing on one side of a balcony. When I was preparing for priesthood, my teachers lamented what they called the "monastic" character of pre-conciliar seminaries and houses of formation (fixed times for common prayer, silence, reading at meals, etc.), complaining that such disciplines were ill-suited to their lives because they were destined not to be monks but pastors, missionaries, and scholars. But looking at the lives of my contemporaries, one of the things I find most obviously lacking is an appetite for prayer created by good habits of prayer — habits that are usually the product of a discipline we never had. The same is true of asceticism and self-denial generally. When laypersons enter a priest's living quarters, for example, they don't necessarily have to be shocked by the austerity, but they ought to walk away with the impression that the man who lives there is good at saying no to himself. And monks are, or used to be, our masters at saying no to the self.

Shifting the Focus to the One to Whom We Witness

It is not my purpose to erect some kind of mental tribunal in which each priest brings evidence against himself. The point of Cardinal Suhard's dictum was not that his priests should exculpate themselves of worldliness but that they should shift the focus off themselves entirely to give witness to God. They do this by being a living mystery, and that means to live and move and have one's being in a universe opaque to the worldly.

This opacity of spiritual goods to the eyes of the ungodly has been wittily expressed by C. S. Lewis in his spiritual classic *The Screwtape Letters*. It takes the form of a fictional correspondence in which a senior demon coaches a junior in the damnation of a human soul assigned as his target. At one point, Screwtape takes a step back from concrete advice to vent his exasperation at the impossibility of understanding God's motives. God, in this correspondence, is simply called "the Enemy":

> The truth is [writes Screwtape] I slipped by mere carelessness into saying that the Enemy really loves the humans. That, of course, is an impossibility. He is one being, they are distinct from Him. Their good cannot be His. All His talk about Love must be a disguise for something else — He must have some real motive for creating them and taking so much trouble about them. The reason one comes to talk as if He really had this impossible Love is our utter failure to find out that real motive. What does He stand to make out of them? That is the insoluble question.... We know that He cannot really love: nobody can: it doesn't make sense. If we could only find out

what He is really up to! Hypothesis after hypothesis has been tried, and still we can't find out.

Of its nature, love is incomprehensible to Screwtape (at one point, he writes of a Christian household, "We are certain [it is a matter of first principles] that each member of the family must in some way be making capital out of the others — but we can't find out how"); by the same token, the fact that there is no capital to be made out of our poverty, chastity, and obedience is nonsense to the dogmatic atheist.

Indispensability of Truthfulness

The gist of what I have to say can be put quite simply. Christians believe Christ rose from the dead because they believe the witnesses who said Christ rose from the dead. They believe that the Church, and in a particular way the apostles, told the truth about Jesus. Moreover, the constant fidelity of the faithful, their acceptance of the authority of the Church in matters of doctrine, sacraments, and prayer, finds its taproot in the conviction of the radical reliability of the apostles. Truthfulness is thus an indispensable quality of a bishop, and of the priests and deacons who share his ministry.[103] When a churchman tells a lie, he weakens the faith of the faithful, weakens their conviction that the apostles were not lying when they confessed the Resurrection, the gift of the Holy Spirit, and the assurance that the Church had the mind of Christ.

---

[103] Henceforth, unless otherwise indicated, I use the word "priest" to mean any man in Holy Orders, inasmuch as he shares the episcopal function of witnessing to the truth: "The function of the bishops' ministry was handed over in a subordinate degree to priests so that they might be appointed in the order of the priesthood and be co-workers of the episcopal order for the proper fulfilment of the apostolic mission that had been entrusted to it by Christ" (*Presbyterorum Ordinis* 2 §2).

Sin against the Eighth Commandment

Now, it is my conviction that in our own time the sins most characteristic of clergy are sins against not the Sixth but the Eighth Commandment. Any sin, obviously, is a serious matter for the sinner, but since the faith of Christians is connected in a particularly intimate way to the trustworthiness of the Church's ministers, offenses against truth committed by the clergy are especially troublesome. In fact, I believe that most of the woes that beset the clerical life today can be traced to this sin. Attempt at reform, accordingly, should aim to restore integrity, in the fullest sense, to the life of the priest.

Giving One's Word

Let's start with the positive case, the connection between integrity and truth that can be discerned in our most solemn undertakings. When one man says to another, "I give you my word," he is saying more than "I give you my mind on the matter" or even "I give you my personal assurance." In saying, "I give you my word," he says, "I give you the truth about myself." Notice that the expression "I give you my word" belongs to the class of utterances philosophers call "performative locutions" — phrases that enact, that bring into being, the very thing they express. "I promise," "I pronounce you man and wife," "I hereby excommunicate you" — all these are examples of performative locutions. You will notice that there is a certain sacramental quality to them; like a sacrament, they effect what they signify.

What is brought into being by the act of saying, "I give you my word" is a bond, a unilateral obligation on the part of the giver to give the truth about himself, and only the truth, to the receiver. Thus, the characteristic expression of protest when the undertaking is violated is, "But you *broke* your word!" — that is, you broke the bond you established with me; what you offered as the truth about yourself turns out to be no truth at all.

The Sound of Silence

But what is the purpose of such an undertaking in the first place? What is to be gained, for example, by saying, "I give you my word that I never touched the petty-cash box," as opposed to saying simply, "I never touched the petty-cash box"? Well, there is a sense in which the receiver (he who accepts someone's word) is indemnified against deceit. If I say to my boss, "I give you my word, I give you the truth about myself, that I never touched the petty-cash box," and my boss accepts my word, and then it turns out after all that I did pilfer money from the box, then my boss is free to deny me any human good that hinges on my worthiness and — this is important — he has my permission to deny me this good always. To give a man your word is to attach a default clause, so to speak, to the contract: if I fail to deliver the truth I promise you, then you are free to despise me, now and as long as I shall live.

May God Do to Me ...

We can find ghostly remnants of this "default clause" in the language of the Old Testament, looking at the oaths and solemn undertakings various persons make. In the moving passage where Ruth swears she will not abandon her mother-in-law, Naomi ("Where you go I will go, and where you lodge I will lodge; your people shall be my people, and your God shall be my God"), she concludes, "May the Lord do so to me and more also if even death parts me from you" (Ruth 1:17). Or again, after the treacherous death of Abner, when his courtiers come to persuade David to cease his fast of mourning, David swears, "God do so to me and more also, if I taste bread or anything else till the sun goes down!" (2 Sam. 3:35). Originally, along with the pronouncement of the oath formula — God do so to me and more also — a gesture was performed, a hand drawn across the throat, or fists clenched and pulled apart to mimic the rending of garments, which served as a kind of ritual shorthand: "May God cut my throat in this manner, and more also, if I fail to do what I now undertake, may the Lord rip me in two in this manner, and more also, if I fail to deliver on my promise!" That is to say, may God annihilate me, may God bring me to naught, if I speak not the truth.

On the purely natural level, if I give my word that I never touched the petty cash and it turns out that I lied, the value of my word becomes nil, nonexistent. I indemnified my creditor, as it were, by means of my reputation for veracity. Once the indemnity — that reputation — is revealed as valueless, it is pointless to offer it as security in another transaction, and it is just as absurd to accept it. For this reason, I find it baffling (and wryly amusing) when a man goes to the matrimonial altar for the second or third or sixth time in ten years and pledges fidelity to his bride. What is exchanged? What could be exchanged? What do the parties imagine is exchanged? Perhaps all this is obvious. I wonder if you will say the same about my next contention. In recent months it has become embarrassingly public knowledge that several prominent ecclesiastics have violated their solemn promises of chastity. Immediately following the revelations was a chorus of admonition inveighing against the sin of morose delectation, of taking pleasure in their disgrace. As far as it goes, that is quite proper. On the other hand, if a man freely and publicly makes a solemn commitment and then betrays it, in deriding him we do him no injustice. We have his own permission to do so. He has invited us to despise him as clearly as the ancient Hebrew who takes a vow invites God to cut his throat if he backslides. Prudential concern for the common good may urge us to temper our derision or restrict it to discreet expression. But even where contempt for the defaulter is intemperate and public, it is not *his* person that has been thereby wronged.

Promises, Oaths, Vows

Now, if I give another person my word, it is to him, another human being, that I extend the liberty of contempt if I default, if the word I give is false. In more solemn undertakings it is God who is invoked as avenger. The language of canon law, which in this matter marches closely with ordinary speech, distinguishes between promises, oaths, and vows. A promise (*iusiurandum promissorium*) is an undertaking exchanged between one person and another (cf. CIC 1201 §1). An oath is the invocation of God as witness to the truth, that is, the truth asserted to other persons (CIC 1199 §1).[104] A vow is a promise made to God (CIC 1191 §1).[105] I wonder how often those who take oaths and vows realize just what it is they are offering, what they are putting on the line, and how gravely, in fact, they are pulling their hands across their throats, so to speak, in addressing their promises to God or invoking the Divine Name as witness to their undertakings.

Let me offer as typical, and for general consideration, the Jesuit vow formula:

> Almighty and eternal God, I N., though altogether unworthy in Thy divine sight, yet relying on Thy infinite goodness and mercy and moved with a desire of serving Thee, in the presence of the most Holy Virgin Mary and Thy whole heavenly court, I vow to Thy Divine Majesty perpetual poverty, chastity, and obedience in the Society of Jesus; and I promise that I shall enter that same Society in order to lead my entire life in it, understanding all these things according to its Constitutions. Therefore, I suppliantly beg Thy Immense Goodness and Clemency, through the blood of Jesus Christ, to deign to receive this holocaust in an order of sweetness; and that just as Thou gavest me the grace to desire and offer this, so Thou wilt also bestow abundant grace to fulfill it.

---

[104] Iusiurandum, idest invocatio Nominis divini in testem veritatis, praestari nequit, nisi in veritate, in iudicio et in iustitia.
[105] Votum, idest promissio deliberata ac libera Deo facta de bono possibili et meliore, ex virtute religionis impleri debet.

The Priest as Evangelical Witness

The phrasing will vary somewhat between the formula required by one religious institute and other, but the essential point will be the same. And the essential point is that the vow, though *received* by a religious superior, is *addressed* to almighty God, with all the angels and saints invoked as witnesses. God does not change. God does not die. God does not fade away. If God was ever part of the ritual, God will be always part of it, and the promises made will be eternally fresh. Now, what, in the order of things, has changed by virtue of the vow? If we take the example of the Jesuit formula, before pronouncing the vow the man does no wrong by disobeying his superior's command; by making the vow he freely says, "Henceforward let it be a mortal sin for me to disobey." In making a vow a man offers his very self, his soul, as collateral, so to speak. (In the biblical Hebrew and Aramaic the words for "self" and "soul" are the same.) That means that the penalty for default is *I never knew you!*

Taking a vow is a risky business. Vows always involve undertakings that are difficult — at least potentially difficult — to keep. No one makes a promise to eat when hungry or to sleep when tired. Everyone recognizes there is something noble about making a vow or an oath, about freely putting oneself under an obligation. Everyone recognizes that the stakes are large, nothing less than a man's very self: "What shall a man give in exchange for his soul?" (Matt. 16:26). Everyone recognizes that the creditor will not and cannot weaken or forget, that he is "the same yesterday, today, and forever" (Heb. 13:8). When a man takes a vow, he gives God his word; he gives God the truth about himself. That is why *this* word is infinitely more perilous to break. Who of us that are priests and have made solemn undertakings can listen without a shudder to Jesus' saying in the Gospel of Matthew: "On that day many will say to me, 'Lord, Lord, did we not prophesy in your name, and cast out demons in your name, and do many mighty works in your name?' And then will I declare to them, 'I never knew you; depart from me, you evildoers'" (7:22–23)?

The Sound of Silence

"I never knew you." As I read these words, they are not a mere verbal gesture — a kind of cold shoulder — but they state the stark facts of the matter. Think of a wife whose husband cheated on her by a liaison with another woman, then covered his sin with a lie, then propped up the first lie with half a dozen new lies, then supported each of the secondary lies with a dozen others, on and on, year after year, erecting a scaffold of deceit underneath him. And when it collapsed, and his betrayal became patent, the wife might well say to her husband, "You're not the same person I married. The 'you,' the self, you offered to me turns out to be no one at all. *I never knew you!*" How can the debt be paid? What shall a man give in exchange for his very self? Having given his word, and broken it, with what can he make good the loss? "You're not the same priest who vowed fidelity to me. You're not the same priest who prophesied in my name. I never knew *you*."

St. Thomas More's Case

Let me focus on a concrete and instructive example.

In April of 1534, Sir Thomas More, Lord Chancellor of England, was summoned to Lambeth Palace and required to take an oath by which he would undertake to uphold the Act of Succession, which declared that the marriage of King Henry VIII and Catherine of Aragon was void and invalid. More refused to swear the oath, thus incurring the automatic penalty of life imprisonment and forfeiture of all his property. Why did More refuse to take the oath, knowing, as he did, that most clergy (then Catholic clergy, remember) and all but one bishop (then Catholic bishops, remember) tailored their convictions quite handily to the political reality and professed their loyalty to the new order? Here I quote Professor John Finnis:

> To take the Oath would be to swear that he, More, maintained the marriage to be invalid, when in his own mind he maintained

it to be valid. Thus, taking the Oath would be, for him, asserting publicly, and with God as his witness before men, a deliberate falsehood, intended to deceive others about the state of his own belief — in short, it would be to lie. So: More went to the Tower on a point of morality, the absoluteness, the unconditional truth and force, of the quite ordinary and universal (though specific) moral norm which excludes lying, most clearly lying on oath.

It goes without saying that Thomas More's refusal was a courageous act. Yet it was not an act of bravado, not an instance of political agitprop, but the result of careful deliberation about the moral and spiritual goods at stake, as More explained to the commissioners who were appointed to administer the Oath. He wrote to his daughter Margaret, "I showed unto them that my purpose was not to put any fault either in the Act or any man that made it, or in the oath or any man that swore it, nor to condemn the conscience of any other man. But as for myself, in good faith my conscience so moved me in the matter ... that I could not swear without the jeopardizing of my soul to perpetual damnation."

Notice, More did not say that any and every honest man must refuse to swear the Oath; he did not say any and every man who swore would commit a mortal sin. Rather, he realized that, in calling God to witness, by professing to believe what he did not believe, by offering as the truth about himself what he knew to be false, he would forfeit his immortal soul forever.

A Man Whom I Know...

Let me give another concrete case, one of which I have more direct knowledge. I know a man who, the week before he was ordained a deacon, was assembled [with the other ordinands] by his superior in the parlor beneath his office and presented, for the first time, with the formula of the Act of Faith. You know the formula to which I refer: it consists of recitation of the Nicene Creed plus the undertaking to "firmly embrace and accept all and everything concerning the doctrine of faith and morals which has either been defined by the Church's solemn deliberation or affirmed and declared by its ordinary magisterium," and so forth. Having given the theologate time to read through the text, the superior then said, "I know this moment may be very difficult for you. I invite you, however, to allow the Holy Spirit, who has brought you this far in the journey, to carry you through to next Saturday." There was no doubt whatever what his words meant. My informant believes that each man in the room knew that he was being invited (and, given the timing and circumstances of the occasion, urged) to perjure himself. The invocation of the Holy Spirit was an added blasphemy that, though shocking, did not alter the facts in any material way whatever.

Every ordinand in the room made the Act of Faith. My informant has excellent reason to believe that several did so in good faith; he is just as convinced that several men did not embrace and accept the Church's doctrine on faith and morals and, accordingly, that they solemnly perjured themselves that evening.

Such a man would hope that he is wrong. He would hope that the heresy voiced by some was not really *ex animo* dissent but unreflective conformity to the atmosphere of theological Whiggery then in fashion; he would hope that others followed the superior's suggestion simply because it came from him, blindly, mechanically, without attending to his words or to the issues at stake.

Moral eunuchs. But my informant's relations with some of these men were changed forever, for either they are incapable of swearing an oath, and thus moral eunuchs, or else capable of swearing, and thus perjurers. Neither alternative is gratifying; a third possibility is not evident. In some important way, their manhood, as well as their priesthood, was permanently mutilated. After all, the occasions on which human beings solemnly profess who we are and what we believe are rare. We don't have that many opportunities. For the most part, our daily lives are spent in a welter of courtesies, compromises, acts of diplomatic evasion, not to mention tactical silences; all of these may be innocent, and all are certainly necessary to civilized community, but they say little or nothing about the ultimate meaning and purpose of our lives. It is by our most important commitments, vows and oaths and promises, that we plant a flag in the sand, so to speak, that we tell the world the truth about ourselves, about the deepest allegiances of our souls.

Motions of Civility

We might well pity men who are moral eunuchs, and, though it requires a greater effort, we might pity men who are perjurers. But I submit that it is impossible to *respect* them. This is not so much an observation about human psychology as an entailment of the logic of giving one's word; perjurers and moral eunuchs have denied us a view of the true self to respect. In a philosophically important way, there is "nothing there" to respect. As a consequence, all one's dealings with these men become necessarily superficial. Mutual wariness and suspicion become inevitable. Trust is nonexistent, not because it is a good deliberately withheld, but because it is a good not in one's gift. We share dwellings and tables amicably enough, we go through the motions of civility, but only as actors feeding each other lines in a script written for a religious life that belongs to someone else.

If all this sounds like moral swaggering on my part, let me add that I make no claim to the courage of St. Thomas More; except by occasional trifling vexations, I have never paid a price for my beliefs. I don't know if I could face what St. Thomas More faced without folding at the knees. But there's a difference between the man who embarks on an undertaking and finds the difficulties greater than anticipated, and the man who never engages the difficulties in the first place. We can feel compassion for those men who, being weaker than Thomas More and trapped in a dilemma not of their own making, succumbed under force to the threat of imprisonment and destitution and swore an oath they didn't believe: an ugly failure, but an understandable one. But what do we make of men who — under no external compulsion whatsoever — forswear themselves and whose castration is a self-inflicted wound?

Isolation of Faithful Priests

The moral landscape in which faithful priests operate today makes inevitable some level of emotional isolation. True communion, union of minds and hearts, is only possible among men who are in agreement on first principles, who recognize the same goods as governing their lives. In the absence of such communion — indicated, as I have argued, by the alacrity with which one's peers and superiors forswear themselves on matters of prime importance — a priest frequently finds himself inclined to cynicism. By "cynicism" I mean not a habit of sardonic comment on the seeming triumph of hypocrisy, but rather the kind of despair that tempts one to measure triumph and failure in purely this-worldly terms, to make one's own, that is, the values of those who have prospered by cunning and deceit. Difficult though it is to resist, to succumb to this kind of cynicism is to start down a road from which few men return. The alternative is to take our vows, oaths, and promises seriously, trusting that God will vindicate His word, the word He sent among us, the Word made flesh. In the interim, a certain amount of heartbreak is the inescapable price to be paid for integrity; nobody ever said it would be easy. The priest who tells the truth about himself, who lives the truth about himself, is bound to collide with, and be worsted by, the *realpolitik* of the world he inhabits. Whence, as G. K. Chesterton has written, his true victories will be those of his apparent defeats:

The Priest as Evangelical Witness

Look in what other face for understanding,
But hers that bore the child that brought the Sword,
Hang in what other house, trophy and tribute,
The broken heart and the unbroken word?

One Flesh: Reflections on the Biblical Meaning of Marriage

Harman Lecture 2003[106]

Paul Mankowski, S.J.
Pontifical Biblical Institute

"There's a f***ing head in the refrigerator!"

On July 22, 1991, when the Milwaukee, Wisconsin, police finally entered the apartment of gay serial killer Jeffrey Dahmer, they found parts of several dismembered bodies stashed in various parts of his living quarters. A friend of mine who was once an FBI agent told me that the discovery was more shocking than it was unexpected; that street cops, when they find a murder victim whose body has been mutilated, surmise, and are usually right in the surmise, that the killer is a deranged homosexual male.

"The body," says Pope John Paul II, "and it alone, is capable of making visible what is invisible, the spiritual and divine. It was created to transfer into the visible reality of the world, the invisible mystery

---

[106] The Harman Lecture is an annual event at the John Paul II Institute for Marriage and Family in Melbourne, Australia.

hidden in God from time immemorial, and thus to be a sign of it."[107] The street wisdom of American homicide detectives, I venture to say, has intellectual tributaries different from those of the pope's theology of the body; but their gaze is trained on a single reality, a single truth. In their respective ways, both theological reflection on the original endowment of the created order and empirical study of the murkiest recesses of pathology attest to one and the same human nature. What I wish to do this evening is to examine the biblical teaching about this nature, especially that which concerns what the pope calls the nuptial meaning of the body. I want to argue that the Bible instructs us about our sexual nature in a way that is at once entirely unsentimental and at the same time invested with an elemental moral beauty. It is my hope that by attention to the biblical narrative, we can arrive at a deeper understanding of the sacramentality of marriage, and a more profound grasp of the reason why the severed head of Cardinal Angelo Sodano will not appear in the papal icebox.

The book of Genesis gives us two accounts of the coming-into-being of things that are, somewhat misleadingly called by scholars the two accounts of creation. In spite of their differences, I believe they are complementary rather than contradictory accounts, meant to engage different aspects of human cognition. The first version is presented in chapter 1 of Genesis. Here the Creator is referred to throughout as "God" (Hebrew *Elohim*); the Hebrew verb of production is *barah*, which means "create" in the strict sense. *Barah* always refers to something new, always entails absolute causality and the unconditioned operation of the agent — that is, you never *barah* something "out of" preexisting material. Most importantly, the verb *barah* is used exclusively of God. No creature ever *barah*s anything. "In the beginning, God created [*barah Elohim*] the heavens and the earth." Notice that

---

[107] Audience address, February 20, 1980.

One Flesh: Reflections on the Biblical Meaning of Marriage

the heavens, the realm of divine activity, is mentioned first, and earth, the realm of human endeavor, is in the second place. The act of creation is divided into six "days," on the last of which "God *created* man in His own image, in the image of God he created him; male and female he created them." These verses are familiar to us all, and I trust you'll forgive me if I underline some obvious points possibly dulled by familiarity. First, man is here a distinct creation. Second, man is *ha'adam*; the Hebrew word means "human being" in the generic sense, like the Greek *anthropos* or Latin *homo*. Third, this *adam* is at once male and female. Fourth, and most mysteriously, this *adam* is somehow formed in the image and likeness of God. Why is this mysterious? Because the words "image" and "likeness" point to something that can be seen or touched, whereas God is invisible and intangible. Where, then, does the likeness take hold? The sacred text does not tell us.

Let us now pass to the second account of the coming-into-being of things that are, which spans Genesis chapters 2 and 3. In this account the invariable name for the maker is the Lord God, Hebrew *YHWH Elohim* — the proper name is added to the word "God." We are told not that the Lord God creates but that He makes — the more common verb of making has none of the restrictions of the creation verb *barah*. Moreover, the Lord God makes not the heavens and the earth but the earth and the heavens: the place of honor in this account is the realm of human activity. At Genesis 2:7 we read, "The Lord God formed man" — *yatsar*; the verb is used of modeling with clay — "The Lord God formed man of dust from the ground and breathed into his nostrils the breath of life [*nishmat hayyim*], and man became a living being." Notice how this departs in two respects from the first account: first, man is formed out of something that exists already (dust); second, God breathes His own breath into his "product" in order to bring him to life.

The first account of creation is, so to speak, more philosophical, even metaphysical; it is interested in the clearest possible distinctions between

The Sound of Silence

God and His creation and between the several orders of creation themselves. As we have seen, in the one place in which it mentions similarity, man's being created in the image of God, it leaves obscure the nature of the resemblance. The second account is more "historical" — by which I mean not that it has better scientific credentials than the first but that it is interested in the connections between things that come to be and the cause that brought them into being. We're told that God formed or modeled man from dust and, moreover, that He breathed some of His own breath into him. Continuities, rather than discontinuities, are to the fore.

It's important to remember that, at this point, male and female are not yet part of the picture. The living being is simply *ha'adam*, the man. And notice how the origin of the sexes is narrated. First, the LORD God plants a garden in Eden and puts the man there. Second, The LORD God gives man a command: "You may freely eat of every tree of the garden; but of the tree of the knowledge of good and evil you shall not eat, for in the day that you eat of it you shall die." Death, something not yet part of human or indeed of any creature's experience, is set before man as a consequence of disobedience. Third, the LORD God says, "It is not good that the man should be alone; I will make him a helper fit for him."

Next God forms (*yatsar*) all the animals and brings them to the man to see what he will call them. The text reads, "The man gave names to all cattle, and to the birds of the air, and to every beast of the field; but for the man there was not found a helper fit for him." Man's naming God's creatures, in a mysterious way, puts them in their place; it determines their relationship to him. They may be useful to him in many ways, but clearly none is the helper fit for him; none cures the situation the LORD God pronounced "not good" — viz., man's being alone.

A word about the creature called the man, *ha'adam*. The Hebrew text calls *ha'adam* a "he" — that is, *ha'adam* is masculine in some sense, but apparently not yet a male. Of course, we can think of other examples

One Flesh: Reflections on the Biblical Meaning of Marriage

of sexual ambiguity — androgyny, for instance, or the epicene qualities of pre-pubertal children — but the text gives us no reason to think that either of these conditions is before us. All we know is that he is capable of speech and of naming (and to that extent rational); that he is capable of receiving and being bound to a command (and to that extent morally responsible); that he belongs in a fruit orchard with dominion over the beasts he shares it with; and that he is a "he." This brings us to Genesis 2:21-24:

> So the LORD God caused a deep sleep to fall upon the man, and while he slept took one of his ribs and closed up its place with flesh; and the rib which the LORD God had taken from the man he made into a woman and brought her to the man. Then the man said, "This at last is bone of my bones and flesh of my flesh; she shall be called Woman, because she was taken out of Man." Therefore a man leaves his father and his mother and cleaves to his wife, and they become one flesh.

A few points deserve mention. The Hebrew text says not that the LORD God *made* the rib into a woman, but that he built it (*banah*) into a woman. The building verb extends the verbs of creating, making, and forming that have expressed other aspects of divine activity. In this Genesis account, the woman is fitted together from material that preexisted in the unitary creature, *ha'adam*, the creature Pope John Paul calls the "two-in-one." Note, too, that the man does not simply wake from his trance and find the woman next to him; the LORD God brings the woman to the man; God presents her to him. And in this act of presentation the man expresses both his delighted recognition of fittingness and deep kinship — "This at last is bone of my bones and flesh of my flesh" — and the recognition that he is now a male: "She shall be called Woman [Hebrew *ishshah*] because she was taken out of Man [Hebrew *ish*]."

But of course this isn't entirely true. In choosing to name the woman by reference to himself *post-surgery*, the man and his masculine self-love may have sailed out ahead of the facts. And — skipping ahead a chapter — it is no accident that, in the curse God pronounces on the man in banishing him from the Garden, He reminds him of his humble human origin by pointedly rubbing his nose in his generic name: man — *adam* — came from the slime of the earth — *adamah*: "In the sweat of your face you shall eat bread till you return to the ground [*adamah*], for out of it you were taken; you are dust, and to dust you shall return."

But all that is to anticipate. In the original situation, God brings the woman as a gift to man, and in this encounter they find the possibility of becoming a gift to one another, precisely in their embodied sexuality. This is the key to the pope's reflection on the nuptial meaning of the body. Here I quote Christopher West:

> The body has a "nuptial meaning" because it reveals man and woman's call to become a gift for one another, a gift fully realized in their "one flesh" union. The body also has a "generative meaning" that (God willing) brings a "third" into the world through their communion. In this way, marriage constitutes a "primordial sacrament" understood as a sign that truly communicates the mystery of God's Trinitarian life and love to husband and wife — and through them to their children, and through the family to the whole world.[108]

Of course, as the *Catechism* points out, this does not mean that God is "sexual." God "is pure spirit in which there is no place for the difference

---

[108] Christopher West, "The Theology of the Body: An Education in Being Human," Internet Archive, https://www3.nd.edu/~afreddos/courses/264/west2.htm.

One Flesh: Reflections on the Biblical Meaning of Marriage

between the sexes. But the respective 'perfections' of man and woman reflect something of the infinite perfection of God" (CCC 370). This is why the pope speaks of sexuality precisely as a sign of God's mystery. Following the Scriptures, he uses the man and woman's union as an analogy by which to understand something of the divine mystery. God's "mystery remains transcendent in regard to this analogy as in regard to any other analogy, whereby we seek to express it in human language. At the same time, however, this analogy offers the possibility of a certain ... 'penetration' into the very essence of the mystery."[109]

"Therefore a man leaves his father and his mother and cleaves to his wife, and they become one flesh." Hebrew *baśar*, here translated "flesh," has a fairly wide range of significance. It can mean simply "meat," that is, the flesh of animals; it can mean organic kinship (as in English we speak about "blood relations," Israelites spoke of people sharing the same flesh); it can also refer to the genital organs, both male and female. And finally, it often means simply the body, for which Hebrew has no special word. Some scholars want to isolate one of the definitions of *baśar* to the exclusion of others in understanding this passage, but I think all the shades of meaning are in play.

In modern jargon, we say that sexuality has an integrating function; that is, when it does not miscarry, it integrates or puts into a harmonious unity diverse aspects of our personhood: our emotions, our intellect, our corporeal drives or instincts, our qualities of character and religious convictions, and, of course, our longings and affections. The Bible expresses this integrating function in pointing to the "one flesh" — the man leaves his father and his mother and cleaves to his wife — clearly pointing to sexual congress and to marriage — and they become one flesh — again, the "one flesh" includes and celebrates sexual union but also includes all the aspects of personhood latent in Hebrew *baśar*.

---

[109] Pope St. John Paul II, General Audience, September 29, 1982.

The Sound of Silence

Readers of Plato's *Symposium* may remember the story of the origin of love given by the comic playwright Aristophanes: human beings were created in spherical shape and truly hermaphroditic — each having two heads, four arms and four legs, and both male and female genitals. Each sphere was sliced down the middle, forming two ordinary persons, whence each person erotically strives to find and rejoin his original matching half in order to recover the bliss of the primordial union. This isn't the way of the biblical account. The aloneness of the original unitary creature was pronounced "not good." The cleaving of man to woman is not a matter of fusion to restore pristine androgyny; it is an exchange of selves, a mutual giving of gifts. We are made whole by giving, and by being able to receive, the gift of self. The component selves of the union are not obliterated (as in the myth of Aristophanes) by this sacramental embrace but [are] brought to the final fruition of their individuality.

The final verse of Genesis 2 is especially moving: "And the man and his wife were both naked and were not ashamed." The Hebrew text says, "The man and his *woman* were both naked," but the translation "wife" is undoubtedly correct. They belong to one another and have found themselves in one another, and the lust that sees the other as a tool of gratification rather than a gift has not yet made its appearance — hence each feels no shame in the presence of his spouse. Pope John Paul has focused on this passage with particular care:

> Prior to the rupture of body and soul caused by sin, the body enabled them to see and know each other "with all the peace of the interior gaze, which creates ... the fullness of the intimacy of persons" (Jan 2, 1980). Living in complete accord with the nuptial meaning of their bodies, the experience of original nakedness was untainted by shame.[110]

---

[110] West, "The Theology of the Body."

One Flesh: Reflections on the Biblical Meaning of Marriage

I think it's important to remember that our prudery in approaching the biblical text can lead us astray in two contrary directions, often simultaneously. We shouldn't blink from the truth that the one-flesh union spoken of in Genesis is realized in sexual intercourse: it is nakedness that reveals the nuptial meaning of the body. Yet this meaning points not only to a union of bodies but to a communion of persons brought about through the body. As Pope John Paul teaches, this *communio personarum* in "one flesh" reflects the inner life of the Trinity. This reflection attains an iconic status in the embrace of man and wife, but we shouldn't forget that it is also realized in any sexual congress between any man and any woman, as St. Paul teaches in 1 Corinthians 6:15-17:

> Do you not know that your bodies are members of Christ? Shall I therefore take the members of Christ and make them members of a prostitute? Never! Do you not know that he who joins himself to a prostitute becomes one body with her? For, as it is written, "The two shall become one flesh." But he who is united to the Lord becomes one spirit with him.

This is important. St. Paul is instructing us that a purely emotional bond between two persons, no matter how exalted, does not and cannot form the "one flesh." Sexual union is necessary. On the other hand, the sexual embrace is so momentous that the "one flesh" union is achieved even in degraded and transitory sexual encounters. A man's brief liaison with a prostitute may be forgotten by both parties the next day, yet it is invested with eternal significance because of the nuptial meaning of the two bodies that became one.

We can see then that Genesis and St. Paul jointly and severally eliminate sodomy, bestiality, and masturbation from the sphere of conscientious human action. None of these actions can be meaningful choices because each makes nonsense out of the nuptial and generative meanings of the body. The American moral theologian Germain

Grisez and his disciples give the name "pseudo-sex" to these actions because they are inherently deprived of sexual significance. Look at it this way. When we speak of racial relations we mean *inter*-racial relations, the dealings between one race and another. In the same way, sexual intercourse means "inter-sexual" intercourse, intercourse between a person of one sex and a person of the opposite. To speak of "homosexual intercourse" is as vacuous as saying that a set of twins enjoys good racial relations. Why do we speak of two men having sex? Why don't we say they "have species"? Well, obviously, we all have recourse to the language of *sexual* relations between two men or between two women, and we speak this way because the activities involve the sexual organs of the actors. But notice how once again language leads us back to confront the falsehood. Why call a certain bit of tissue a *sexual* organ? Only because it has a role in inter-sexual congress. Why call it a *genital* or *generative* organ? Only because it has a role in the transmission of life through fecundation — i.e., fecundation of the female by the male. In sodomy and masturbation and masturbatory expedients like coitus interruptus, the genital organs may be stimulated, but the purpose or goal of their arousal cannot, however remotely, be called sexual or genital or generative. As Cardinal Arinze said recently, such actions are a mockery or parody of sex. They mock and distort the meaning of the bodies they manipulate. Once again, completed sexual intercourse between a man and a woman, however degraded the circumstances, honors the nuptial meaning. Erotic contact between two men or two women, however exalted the intertwining of their souls, is pseudo-sex.

Of course, a man and a woman also may be drawn to one another romantically and still fail to become one flesh by failing to exchange the gift of self in sexual intercourse. This is the reason why the Church insists that sterile individuals are perfectly free to marry while she insists that impotence is a diriment impediment — an impediment,

One Flesh: Reflections on the Biblical Meaning of Marriage

that is, which can never be dispensed for any reason and under any circumstances. For the marriage to be consummated, i.e., brought to completion, sexual union must take place; there must be one flesh; the meaning of the body must be honored.

The legal recognition of same-sex marriages is a hot topic today. It will be clear that the very concept of a marriage between persons of the same sex can only come about by ignoring the role of the body. For this reason alone, same-sex marriage can never be reconciled with the biblical teaching and will never be countenanced by those churches that hold the Bible as sacred. Yet even within the sphere of civil society it can be seen that there is no *public* reason, no reason pertinent to the common good, to privilege the performance of pseudo-sex. Ironically, the same-sex marriage proposal is only possible once sex is abstracted from the picture and marriage is viewed as a pure act of will between individuals; for a marriage of minds, or wills, there's no reason indeed why they should ever meet, ever be in the same country. Nor is there the slightest reason why "they" should be limited to two. Drew and Jason cannot be a couple in the same way that Beth and Mark are a couple, so why not add Matthew to the ménage of Drew and Jason, and Sam and Julio as well? Once the decision has been made to ignore the nuptial meaning of the body, traditional terms like "marriage" and "spouse" can never be more than a bad pun. Paradoxically, in the same-sex union controversy, it is the Church that vindicates the human body and its sexual meaning, while the proponents of unrestricted sexual license are forced to exploit an entirely abstract, disembodied, and fleshless notion of "soul-mating" in order to advance their agenda.

We left the first man and first woman back in the Garden of Eden gazing without shame at one another in their bodily glory. Yet they were under a command, and this command they disobeyed. "Then the eyes of both were opened," reads verse 7 of chapter 3, "and they knew that they were naked; and they sewed fig leaves together and made themselves loincloths." With the loss of original innocence comes the opportunity of lust, that is, of erotic desire that seeks its own good and not the good of the other. The sexuality that was once an unproblematic exchange of gifts now becomes a highly problematic realm of selfishness, where exploitation, and the fear or suspicion of exploitation, has tainted the original dignity of sexuality. Shame enters the picture, and the loincloths are necessary to hide the constant reminder of shame. Then come the judgments of God. For the woman: pain in childbirth, and the ambiguous announcement that "your desire shall be for your husband, and he shall rule over you." For the man: a life of toil and struggle earning his bread by the sweat of his brow.

Man's immediate response to God's pronouncement is reported in one of the most beautiful and moving sentences in the whole of the entire Old Testament: "And the man called his wife's name Eve [*Havah*], because she was the mother of all living [*Hai*]." Here I want to quote from Leon Kass's superb book on Genesis:

> The man hears the prophecy of hardship and trouble and death, the evils that he unwittingly purchased with his enlightenment, but he does not despair. Despite having his nose rubbed in the truth that he can achieve no more than a return to his earthy and dusty beginnings, the man looks instead to a promising future. Guided by one glimmer in God's speech to the woman, the soul-saving passion of *hope* fixes his mind on the singular piece of good news: "My God! She is going to bear children!" Woman alone carries the antidote to disaster — the prospect of life, ever renewable. With revelational clarity, the man sees the woman in yet another new light, this time truly: not just as flesh to be joined, not just as another to impress and admire, but as a generous, generating, and creative being, with powers he can only look up to in awe, gratitude, and, very likely, a good dose

One Flesh: Reflections on the Biblical Meaning of Marriage

of envy.... Despite the forecast of doom, man's soul is lifted by the redemptive and overflowing powers of woman. He names her anew, this time with no reference to himself: only now, at last, is she known as Eve, source of life and hope.[111]

The original harmony has been shattered, but not all has been lost. Adam and Eve are now exiles and aliens, forced to gouge a living out of a hostile earth, but they do so cognizant of the generative, as well as the nuptial, meaning of the body: husband and wife are potentially father and mother.

As the history of Adam's descendants gives way to the patriarchal narrative, we see God's chosen people holding fast to the blessings of generativity in the midst of nations that are indifferent or hostile to it in several ways. (In this respect, they resemble the rearguard battles of Catholics in secular democratic societies like our own.) The pagans give themselves over to sodomy, incest, onanism, bestiality, ritual infanticide, ritual castration — all of which is confronted and rejected by the emergent People of God. And it must be said that, for Israel, the generative had to some extent eclipsed the nuptial. Broadly speaking, the Old Testament does not concern itself with the reflexive consequences of sex, i.e., the effects of sexual arousal or of the moral choice to engage in sexual activity upon the character of the actor. Or, to use the jargon of personalist philosophy, the Old Testament is interested in the transitivity, as opposed to the intransitivity, of sexual congress. The prime focus of the patriarchal sexual morality of the Old Testament was that the "curriculum of fecundity" not miscarry — that a man's seed be implanted into the fertile parts of a woman, the man and woman being so related that the resulting birth serves to strengthen the overall well-being of the pertinent family, clan, and nation. In pre-exilic Israel

---

[111] Leon Kass, *The Beginning of Wisdom: Reading Genesis* (New York: Free Press, 2003), 117.

this excluded adultery and incest but under certain conditions (e.g., those of patriarchal bedouinism) permitted concubinage and polygamy. On the other hand, it should be stressed that sexual arousal in itself is irrelevant to the picture. For example, female homosexual activities do not change fertility conditions and do not cause the curriculum of fecundity to miscarry; in the Israelite view of sexual transitivity, they are simply beside the point.

When I spoke earlier of the integrating function of sexuality, I mentioned that it has two aspects: first, it brings the diverse components of human personhood together into a harmonious unity; second, it permits the individual to make a gift of self to another and receive the gift from another person — a "one flesh" integration in which the body has a nuptial and generative meaning. Pseudo-sex, on the other hand, is dis-integrating. It breaks apart the unity of the body and isolates organs for its own purposes. In this way it dis-integrates the perpetrator, divides him against himself, as his erotic desire is split off from the rest of the acting person, and it dis-integrates the perpetrator's target (I can't bring myself to say "partner") since lust detaches body parts from the whole person to whom they belong and from his good.

The dis-integration brought about by pseudo-sex is often psychical. But not always. Pseudo-sex comes to hate integrity, to war against unity of the body, precisely because the body has meanings that stand in judgment of pseudo-sex. You may remember the grisly story in Judges 19, where the Benjaminites implore the Ephraimite who lives in their village to hand over his Levite houseguest so that they might rape him. The Ephraimite refuses, whereupon they seize the Levite's concubine and sodomize her to death on the doorstep. The next morning the Levite chops the concubine into twelve pieces with his cleaver and sends a piece to each of the tribes of Israel. In doing so, he was symbolically effecting the butchery perpetrated by

One Flesh: Reflections on the Biblical Meaning of Marriage

the sodomy of the Benjaminites. Jeffrey Dahmer, the gay serial killer of Milwaukee whom I mentioned at the outset, is the spiritual descendent of these men. Pseudo-sex is butchery: sometimes it is the psyche that is fractured; sometimes the meat and bones and sinews as well. Pseudo-sex is at war with the "one flesh" — and its hostility takes the form of dis-memberment, in the full etymological sense of the word. In these terms, the media barrage of fury and outrage trained on the Catholic Church after the Vatican's recent instruction on same-sex marriages is entirely predictable. A head in the icebox is simply a trophy signifying the triumph of dis-integrating, dis-membering passion over the unity of one person's body. But the war is being waged on a much broader front, by well-dressed, well-spoken, well-educated citizens who, perhaps, cannot themselves account for the strength of their antipathy to the teaching Church.

"The body," says Pope John Paul II, "and it alone, is capable of making visible what is invisible, the spiritual and divine. It was created to transfer into the visible reality of the world the invisible mystery hidden in God from time immemorial, and thus to be a sign of it." Many commentators have noted the irony that it should be the pope, in his encyclical *Fides et Ratio*, who should come to the defense of human reason in the face of the many secularists who have lost their trust in it. There is an analogous irony in the fact that, in an age deeply in the grip of sensual pleasure-seeking, it should be the pope who should vindicate the goodness of the body against modern Manichees. Perhaps it's not an accident either that the vindicator should be a celibate — that an exceptionally holy man, who has made his body into a pleasing sacrifice to God, should be given the vision to see the full worth of what he has placed in God's hands. Perhaps, too, his contemplative gaze on the creative virginity of Mary has taught him the motto of his pontificate — Be Not Afraid! — the conviction that Christ, born of a Virgin, can deliver us from the wrath of our enemies. So writes G. K. Chesterton, addressing the (contracepting) Manichees of his own day:

> That Christ from this creative purity
> Came forth your sterile appetites to scorn.
> Lo: in her house life without lust was born,
> So in your house lust without life shall die.[112]

---

[112] G. K. Chesterton, "An Agreement."

Betrayal: Fr. Jason's Double Life

by Paul Mankowski, S.J.

[The following (fictitious) account is composite. The names encode no real individuals, no specific institutions. The priestly life here sketched straddles that of religious orders and diocesan seminaries, and the resultant solecisms are deliberate. No element, however, has been contrived without actual parallel in the current formation of American priests.]

As did his two older sisters, Jason went to the Catholic college that his father had attended, back in the forties, on the GI Bill. Jason viewed the "Catholic angle" of the place with neither warmth nor rancor; he regarded his religion much as he did the ethnicity of his last name: an inherited trait that he might be called upon to defend against occasional detractors but that imposed no other burden of sentiment or duty.

He was a good student and an extraordinarily gifted actor; most of his free time was spent with undergraduate theater groups. Although he was good-looking and popular with women, Jason found that his affections never quite matched those of the women he dated, like a tennis player whose racket didn't meet the ball squarely. When he returned to school in August to begin his senior year, Jason admitted to himself that he would never marry.

To discuss his homosexuality with his parents was out of the question — not because he couldn't face their wrath but because he couldn't face their compassion. A shouting match, disowning, expulsion, the quivering finger pointed out the door — all that he could handle. But none of it would happen. Instead, he knew, his mother would begin a novena to the Little Flower for his "conversion," and his father would withdraw into a world of sorrow and self-blame. Fury he could deflect; but even the thought of his parents' love burned Jason like hot oil.

Coming clean was unthinkable, yet that didn't make life any easier. Already he noticed that his mother began to aim her questions about the "girls in his life" a little more pointedly, obviously eager for information about the woman who would become a daughter-in-law. The prospect of facing those questions month after month, year after year, questions that probed deeper and deeper while he made progressively fewer convincing excuses and evasions, the ingenuity and shame with which his mother would explain his bachelorhood to curious relatives — all this he viewed with a kind of numb horror. The future held nothing but loneliness, and a loneliness maintained by a wall of increasingly elaborate deceit.

One day in the same autumn, the answer to all Jason's miseries came to him — so quickly, so clearly, so much of a piece that he laughed out loud that a solution as obvious and uncomplicated as a two-by-four could have eluded him for so long. He would become a priest.

He had gone to Mass on campus one Sunday night, not out of habit or interest but simply to accompany a rather homely girl in the drama club whom he liked and felt sorry for. Halfway through the Eucharistic Prayer she noticed Jason begin to shake with laughter; she even giggled herself in sympathy, imagining that some gaffe on the part of the chaplain had set him off. But he was laughing with happiness and relief as, one by one, the astonishing advantages of the priestly life dropped like ripe fruit into his hand.

To begin with, celibacy was self-explanatory. No archly worded questions from relatives, no breast-beating on the part of his father. No raised eyebrows at class reunions or random meetings with friends. No more painfully planned evenings with women at restaurants or movies that he needed for cover but that filled him with shame and confusion. Priests usually lived with other priests, and the terror of a lifetime of solitude seemed much more remote. Moreover, not only was the priesthood an honorable profession, but his mother would be elated about her son, Fr. Jason.

The question of whether he had a vocation never really entered Jason's mind. This is not because he entertained any cynicism about the notion; the simple fact of the matter is that, until the idea of priesthood came to him, he never had any interest in theology or in the Catholic life at all. He had no feelings — positive or negative — toward the Church, and as he had encountered them almost exclusively at Mass, he had no strong opinions about priests as a group beyond a vague dissatisfaction with their skill at ceremony. If anyone had asked him whether he had a vocation, Jason would probably have answered yes, not because he was sure it was God who summoned him but because the suddenness with which the rightness of priestly life came upon him sounded very much like the notion of "divine calling" he had gotten from books and movies. Yet, for Jason, the idea of Being a Priest was everything, the only real thing; the notion of a Church that this priesthood was meant to serve had no part at all in his thoughts.

Throughout the remainder of his senior year, Jason began to spend a lot of time at the chaplaincy. He went to Mass two or three times a week, introduced himself to the chaplains, made himself useful with his considerable abilities at music and production. Gently he intimated to one of the priests that he was not repelled by the prospect of a clerical

The Sound of Silence

life. The man had been impressed by Jason's interest in the chaplaincy, and soon they were discussing the vocation question as a live possibility.

Jason was an excellent actor; so good, in fact, that he could assume a role unconsciously. This worked greatly in his favor in the next few months. In the first place, he was very alert to what the priests wanted to hear; he quickly learned, for example, that they were suspicious of a vocational path that was too neat; they looked for some evidence of conflict. So, without deliberately lying, he began to invent a tale of spiritual ups and downs that he knew his listeners would find edifying. He knew, too, that they wanted to believe that he had dated seriously, and he was able, truthfully, to point to relationships with several women whom the chaplains knew themselves. The fact that he both oversimplified and overelaborated certain aspects of these encounters was not one the priests were likely to discover. Moreover, Jason was convincing. His audience liked him and so were predisposed to believe. The story he told was told so well that he began, for the most part, to believe it himself.

In the fall after he graduated from college, Jason entered the seminary. His first years were uneventful. He found most of his fellow seminarians companionable, and the enthusiasm nearly everyone brought to the program was infectious enough that his sexuality was never much of an issue. He felt the spiritual formation to be tedious but not offensive. Most of the training was centered on ministry, and this was understood principally as social and political concern for disadvantaged people. Jason warmed very quickly to this notion, not because of any theological convictions in its favor but because the shame he associated with his own homosexuality gave him a spontaneous sympathy for other outsiders of any stripe. He had been apolitical before, but he gradually became distinctly left of center. For the first time in his life, the idea of "not fitting in" became associated with that of righteousness, and it was an intoxicating feeling. The pleasure of sanctimoniousness is hard for anyone to handle, but for those who have cursed themselves most of their lives, it goes right to the head. Jason was drunk on Justice.

Most of his mentors took this newfound commitment, not without reason, as a sign of maturity. They were concerned to wean young men of prosperous suburban backgrounds from a callow materialism and to show them that understanding the demands of the Gospel necessitated an awareness of people generally forgotten, generally ignored. The enthusiasms of the Left were neither an end in themselves nor even a necessary means to this goal, but they were ordinarily taken as evidence that the process was working, change of heart was underway. Jason saw this and rejoiced in it.

Because he was especially alert to the nuances of the likes and dislikes of his superiors, and because he was more than usually anxious to please, Jason was a kind of model seminarian in the early part of his formation. I had entered the seminary the year prior to Jason and could watch, at a distance, as he won the reputation among our instructors of "a man who really understands what we're trying to do." As long as he knew he was being sized up, he played the part expected of him. Gradually, though, the hard scrutiny passed. He sensed he was "in," and as the pressures came off, so did the frequent congratulations and encouragements of his relatives and family. Jason had taken vows of poverty, chastity, and obedience. At first, while he was still aglow with admiration at his own generosity; these vows seemed only too easy to keep. When it came to be that he was no longer in anyone's spotlight, they began to rankle.

Poverty was the first to go — not drastically, of course, but step by step. When the ordinariness of his life began to take its toll, Jason would console himself with little pleasures, trivial acts of self-indulgence: an extra Manhattan, an expensive dinner, a night at the theater or the movies. He acquired, partly by gift and partly by redirecting money meant for books, an unusually elaborate stereo system. All of his wardrobe was nice and most of it unnecessary. He accepted the offers of friends to use their beach condos for vacations, and he could always find someone to lend him a car or a credit card in a pinch. During this time, his devotion to the cause of the oppressed intensified rather than slackened, and the seeming contradiction caused little comment among his superiors — among those whose opinion counted, at any rate. There were two reasons for this. In the first place, the practice of priestly abnegation was generally viewed as part and parcel of an older style of religious life, of a piece with an entire fabric of tradition and sentiment that was certainly provincial and often harmful. Personal austerity was thus regarded as a regression, a return to the mentality of the Catholic ghetto, not as an element of spiritual growth. Secondly, there was an unspoken but clear message given by his contemporaries that a certain kind of naughtiness was becoming in a priest and even added to his effectiveness. The ground was uncertain here, and it was, of course, never put into words, but Jason correctly surmised that some kinds of inconsistency were prized because it was assumed that the real unity must occur at a deeper, more spiritual level; moreover, a priest who discreetly evidenced a disregard for some rules could be relied upon not to be doctrinaire about others, not to be a pedant. He was a sound man, a man not of the Letter but of the Spirit.

Jason now began the study of theology that, after four years, would culminate in his ordination. Although the discipline was mild, he found even minimal restrictions more and more irksome, like pieces of sharp gravel lodged in his shoes. Even a request that he notify someone of overnight absences seemed an unreasonable and gratuitous insult. In addition, for the first time in his life, Jason was brought face-to-face with the teachings of the Catholic Church. He was appalled by what he found. One might ask how Jason could have gone so far in the program without having made such a discovery earlier, but it must be remembered that it was his imagination, not his intellect, by which he made his way into

Betrayal: Fr. Jason's Double Life

the seminary, and this imagination was fascinated by a picture of the life of a priest for which the Church was merely a backdrop — red paint and gilt pillars — with no history or reality of its own.

Concomitant with the shock of meeting the Church for the first time, "terrible as an army with banners," a Church whose mass and inertia seemed entirely contrary to the anti-authoritarian ideals on which his notions of ministry were based, Jason encountered an equally unsettling fact: his homosexuality was no longer a dead letter. I have misled you if you have gotten the idea that Jason had been at any time unchaste. Neither in high school, nor in college, nor again in the seminary had he stumbled. Even when he finally admitted his tendencies to himself, he never seriously contemplated the possibility of acting on them. But things changed. Several of his classmates were open about their own homosexuality, and openly contemptuous of anyone who found it incompatible with priesthood; for the first time in his life, Jason was taken to a gay bar, and, though he did nothing but drink and joke, and had no idea what he was leaving and what he was entering, he felt he had crossed a kind of Rubicon. The slow erosion of his vow of poverty had worked in two ways to make the problem more acute: a habit of voluptuousness, of ever-so-slyly illicit pleasure, had borne him gently but surely from the sensualities of alcohol and sunbathing and the Jacuzzi to the threshold of sex. Moreover, because he had learned to live in defiance of one of his vows without calling down the wrath of Heaven or his superiors, there was no longer any horror of oath-breaking that stood between Jason and his appetite. The only question was what he could get away with.

To do him justice, Jason was frightened at his own predicament. There had been no conscious duplicity or fraud on his part when he decided to become a priest, but now he realized with peculiar clarity that there was never any renunciation in his decision, no severing of the umbilical cord that bound him to the World. On entering the seminary, he had left behind no riches, real or imagined — nothing, in fact, but the mental picture of distressed parents and an empty apartment. What was worse, he understood just as clearly that there was no turning back; he was no more capable of telling the seminary rector than his family the real basis of his vocation.

Meanwhile, the more he learned about the Church, the more it was obvious to Jason that Catholic doctrine and the moral authority that flowed from it formed the two greatest obstacles to the fulfillment of the sexual promptings and political schemes that burned insistently inside him. Jason was no fool. He understood perfectly well that the "life of gay abandon" (as one of his friends expressed it) could not coexist with Catholicism. One or the other would have to be sacrificed. Earlier he had simply assumed that it was his sexual inclinations that were to be trammeled, or at least deflected. Now, under the influence of politicized gay acquaintances, he began to think differently. The rhetoric of conspicuous compassion and the political dogmas that had formed his mind over the years made the next step so obvious that he was unaware when it was taken: the problem (he decided) isn't with me, but with the Authority that won't recognize who I am. Unconsciously Jason was baptized into the churchlet of the Self, that coziest of all congregations, as he wryly mouthed a parody of an earlier Baptist: "The Church must decrease, that I might increase."

Jason was adept at handling the vocabulary of oppression and liberation, and he began to shift the focus of his passions for social justice from the familiar capitalists and generalissimos and trained them instead on the Church itself — or rather, on the hierarchical Church. He developed a profound hatred for the Masculine, an idea that in the heat of his disgust took on an extraordinary solidity, an idea that comprised everything rough, male, unyielding, unanswerable, aggressive, black-and-white, naysaying. The fevers of indignation and lust brought out the histrionic side of Jason, and in his imagination, the

Betrayal: Fr. Jason's Double Life

pope and bishops were not only tainted by the hated Masculine but were its archetype, its caricature, its Platonic ideal. Yet Jason did not become a gay activist or even "come out." Instead, he took up the causes of women's ordination and repeal of the prohibition of contraception.

His motives for championing these two causes were varied and operated on different levels. Jason's political canniness told him that both issues struck near the heart of the teaching Church; that is, they called into question the basis of authority full stop; he told himself, "Cut the carotid artery, and the whole Magisterium is dead meat." But in a more elemental way, he understood that if the connections between maleness and priesthood and between sex and fertility could be shown to be arbitrary (and then severed), an enormous weight would be lifted from his own shoulders. So, in his seminary classes and in the high school Confirmation lessons he gave on weekends, he cast himself in the role of women's advocate, arguing that in sexual matters they were victims of cruel and obtuse male hierarchs. Once again, the seminary faculty viewed his enthusiasm with satisfaction, as a sign of intellectual independence. Almost all of them, for various reasons, were of the same mind as Jason on the Big Issues, though they were generally more discreet in expressing themselves. Jason was by no means out of the ideological mainstream of his contemporaries, and when the time came, he was unanimously approved for ordination by the evaluation board.

Ironically, the ordination ceremony itself was the lowest point of Jason's career. As he lay prostrate on the marble floor of the cathedral, listening to the names of the martyrs and saints winging overhead, he felt for the first time in his life the weight of the ancientness, the appallingly heavy *majesty* of the Church, and it nearly crushed him. He hated the Church for its solidity; he hated himself for his flimsiness and duplicity. He cursed his parents, his professors, his classmates. He envied the simplicity of the man stretched out next to him; he envied him the possibility of taking it all seriously, of not having to be jokey or flippant or camp, of being able, if only for a few moments, to accept the Sacred at face value. Most of all, he envied him the chance to find in all this weight a Rock to cling to or a Temple to serve, instead of a hostile flattening pressure that squeezed out the breath until one suffocated.

It was largely because of his own ordination ceremony that Jason decided to become a liturgist. Jason was an excellent actor; he felt both the power and the limitation of symbols. He was no longer under any doubt as to what he was up to; it was imperative for him to "trans-value" the entire symbolic structure of the Church — imperative not politically but personally — it had become a question of survival.

Jason needed ambiguity; he needed it not as some men need alcohol but as all men need oxygen. Sharp boundaries, clear distinctions, univocal meanings — all such things were for Jason devices of asphyxiation. Clarity was the prime bogey, the Enemy Number One. Clarity divided the world into a chessboard, and Jason hated the white squares yet couldn't bring himself to stand in the black. He thrived on the greyness in which his homosexuality and his priesthood could coexist, nuzzle each other, tease each other, without ever having to make a final reckoning, a definitive choice. A stray line of Ronald Knox, muttered in sarcasm by one of the "unreconstructed" faculty members, had pierced Jason to the core:

> *What matter whether two and two be four,*
> *So long as none account them to be more?*
> *What matter whether black be black or white,*
> *If no officious hand turn on the light?*

That verse gave Jason the program of his campaign as a liturgist. The key was not to turn on the light, to make sure that the right questions were not asked, to blur every boundary and cloud every distinction; this, and only this, would give him the air he needed to breathe.

Betrayal: Fr. Jason's Double Life

Jason was under no illusion that he could simply replace the doctrines and symbols themselves (his ordination had convinced him of their endurance), but he knew, by pumping a multiplicity of meanings into the words and gestures that made up the tapestry of the Church's life, that he could effectively geld them of their impact — in the first place by sowing doubt as to whether a "right" meaning existed, and in the second place by gently foregrounding a more expedient meaning as the most basic or fundamental one. Jason noted with satisfaction that this was precisely the course taken by other gay priests who worked in moral or dogmatic theology. The game was to say, first, "Nobody really knows what doctrine X means." Next, "Whatever X means, it can't mean Y (what you always thought it meant)." Then, "If it means anything at all, it would have to be Z." And finally a whisper after hours to the interested few, "Just between us, Z is what the real theologians would have been saying all along if they were free to ..." If the battle cry of the older theologians had been "*Distinguo!*" the murmur of the moderns was "*Confundam.*"

It must not be imagined that Jason was in any sense conspicuous, either for his beliefs or his behavior. He had not announced publicly that he was gay, and the mildly effeminate mannerisms he exhibited were scarcely distinguishable from the affectation of tenderness that passed for sensitivity among his clerical colleagues. Further, inasmuch as making his views clear was the very opposite of his intention, in the rare instances when someone raised an eyebrow over a position he took, Jason was provided with plenty of orthodox cover into which he could retreat: the high grass of deliberate double entendre. Of course, most important of all was the fact that no one, and least of all his bishop, wanted to ask closely about doctrine, even when it was suspected that a priest might be sailing too near the wind. The chancery shuddered at the prospect of enforcing doctrinal discipline even more than the faculty feared to be its victim; and so, paradoxically, the strategy of maximum ambiguity worked to the advantage of both. Jason was able to operate well within the accepted bounds of creativity.

The strategy of ambiguity took several forms in Jason's campaign. Perhaps the simplest was the linguistic trick of always substituting a generic term for the specific, so that, for example, the Mass was always a "liturgy," and the celebrant was always a "presider." In the first place, no one could say the general terms weren't true, but more to the point was the fact that the use of the vaguer and less familiar word abetted the process of unmooring the traditional meanings that Catholics connected with the specific one. Thus, once "presiding at liturgy" came to mean both what a priest does at Mass and what a nun might do at a prayer service, the semantic shock of a woman presiding at the (Eucharistic) liturgy will have been reduced to naught. Further, the feeling of arbitrary injustice in the Church's allowing women to preside at some kinds of liturgy and not others could be greatly intensified. "Blur," Jason said to himself as he started Mass, "obfuscate, nuance, mystify…"

Jason's First Law of Liturgy (confessed to no one but himself) was, Just So It Ain't by the Book. Initially Jason deviated by "shocking the bourgeoisie" — importing dancers in leotards to present the offertory, inventing rituals out of whole cloth to enact on the altar, dealing throughout with maximum informality. It worked, but it provoked some complaints. Later he decided on a subtler, more effective approach. He stuck fairly close to the traditional forms of piety, but he exaggerated them, and used them to interrupt the anticipated course of the Eucharist. Once he pulled a rosary out of an empty chalice just before the Consecration and invited the worshippers to join him in praying a decade "for the marginalized." Many people were vaguely upset, but who could object to the Rosary, or to his fervor? "Game. Set. Match," Jason chuckled to himself as he tripped down the aisle for the recessional.

Betrayal: Fr. Jason's Double Life

Jason was especially shrewd at exploiting the fact that, in the minds of most Catholics, the notion of "priest" was inextricable from that of "sound Church teaching," so much so that the priest was often granted an almost oracular reverence, as if he were not the servant of doctrine but its source; nor was Jason blind to the irony that he for whom the teaching of the Church meant nothing at all until it began to interfere with his life should turn this sentiment to its destruction. In his most solemn and didactic voice, he would explain to his classes and congregations that his deviations, his ever-so-subtle adjustments of meanings, were expressive of a "good theology," in a way that made it perfectly clear that the older usages were not. So, for example, he might wear the green chasuble of ordinary time on the feast of a martyr, explaining that green, the color of life, stood for the value of human life that the martyr embodied. A positive sign, he would stress, not a negative one. Or again, just to keep others off-balance, he would bow profoundly before the tabernacle on some occasions, and utterly ignore it at others. To do it always in one way would edify, to do it always in another would get him written off; the trick was to keep God's people guessing, to keep meanings in flux. "If thou hast been unfaithful in small things," he reasoned, "yet shalt thou be unfaithful in great." And so, little by little, a millimeter at a time, edging, doubling back, making strategic retreats and cautious advances, he ensured that the vision of the Faith was always just slightly murkier after Mass than it was before. Jason was pleased with himself. He could breathe again.

Then one day he returned from Mass to find a message slip on his desk. A friend from earlier days, a man who had left the seminary before ordination, was ill. Could Jason visit? With a sickening sense of foreboding, he drove to the hospital and asked his way to the ward. As he made for the door pointed out to him at the nursing station, Jason tried to "switch on" his customary bedside sunniness, but as he stepped into the room his breath seemed to be punched out of his lungs by the

The Sound of Silence

sight before him. He stood in silence for some moments, trying to find in the patient's eyes, unnaturally large over the hollowness and pallor of his cheeks, some resemblance to the exuberant, dandified wag with whom he had crawled the bars and lampooned the bishop. While he struggled to find words of greeting a nurse hurried into the room; the look with which she took in both patient and visitor pierced Jason more deeply than anything she could have said. She gave a strained smile and chirped (just a little too cheerfully, Jason thought, for Jason was an excellent actor), "Good afternoon, *Father*" and turned to her patient.

In an instant, in the twinkling of an eye, Jason's world was unmade. He had the sensation of a man who has spent his entire life looking through what he believed to be a telescope, only to find to his horror that he was the specimen under a microscope instead. He wanted to shake the nurse and ask her, "What did you *mean* by that?" He wanted answers; he wanted ... clarity. But he merely stood by dumbly and watched her find a vein in his friend's arm, insert a thin steel shaft, and then fill a plastic tube with dark blood while she chatted about the weather. As Jason saw the nurse push a wad of cotton against the vein while she withdrew the needle, he noticed she was wearing rubber gloves. "Well, that can mean more than one thing," he said to himself.

❖ ❖ ❖

Four years later, I concelebrated at Jason's funeral Mass. One of the Scripture texts was mine to read: "Go, and learn the meaning of the words, 'It is mercy I desire, and not sacrifice!' " I tried to keep my mind on the readings and the homily, but my eyes, against every effort to the contrary, kept straying back to Jason's family in the front pew. His sisters wore identical masks of controlled disgust, as if they were doing unavoidable business with a public official whom they knew to be corrupt. His father looked simply stunned; his lower lip still dangled slightly in shock, and his eyes, every few minutes, would detach their gaze from the casket and wander over the sanctuary — a man looking for the answer to a riddle that was too deep for him. But it was Jason's mother who really got to me. She had none of her daughters' detachment or her husband's vagueness. Her face said, WE HAVE BEEN BETRAYED. She knew her own mind, and ours too.

After Mass, I started to walk up to Jason's mother to offer my condolences, but I shied off at the last moment. No funeral is without ironies; death itself is an *eirôneia*, a feigning, when set against the fact of the Resurrection; yet as I made my way down the steps, I remembered a line from a book I had read in my own seminary days — something about the hardness of God being more merciful than the softness of men — and it struck me that it was precisely this hard mercy that none of us had the guts to extend to Jason. We were generous with the love that costs nothing: compliments, petty indulgences, the banalities of "affirmation," yet nobody was willing to pay the full price of compassion. Meanwhile, the Church of Jason's boyhood — both the sham-Gothic building we were leaving and that eternal Communion of saints and martyrs — remained solid, still, unperturbed, as a lasting reproach to our softness.[113]

---

[113] Eusebius, "Betrayal: Father Jason's Double Life," *Crisis Magazine*, January 1, 1993, https://www.crisismagazine.com/vault/betrayal-father-jasons-double-life. Fr. Paul V. Mankowski, S.J., wrote this article under the pseudonym Eusebius.

The Truth about the Crisis in the Catholic Church

[The following is the transcript of the speech that I saw Paul deliver in Vero Beach, Florida, in February 2020, which turned out to be the last time we saw each other.]

On April 12, 1959, in a speech given in Indianapolis, then-senator from Massachusetts John Kennedy said, "When written in Chinese, the word 'crisis' is composed of two characters. One represents danger and one represents opportunity." I think it instructive to bring together the notions of danger and opportunity within the same field of view, so to speak, inasmuch as a time of crisis that means new defeats and new victories are equally imminent and equally dependent on human choice. In the context of the crisis in the Catholic Church, I want to examine with you the dangers, the opportunities, and which among the human choices resulting in defeat or triumph you or I might have the chance to make.

The crisis, you don't need to be told, made itself undeniably manifest by the revelations of the sexual abuse of children by priests. The scandal was itself deepened by the scandals of bishops and religious superiors, mendacious denials, cover-ups, revilement of good-faith accusers. But these crimes are only the symptoms of the real crisis, which I would describe as an ecclesiastical deadlock — the counterpoise of contrary forces and objectives within the hierarchy and the governing agencies of the Church that have brought about an impasse or stalemate. No substantive and serious reforms are undertaken because no one trusts the conflicting motives of the reformers. It is a ground-floor mistake to see the crisis as a particularly vexatious large-scale problem, susceptible to administrative correction in secular management terms. In the only important sense, there is no fix. The crisis is unfixable because it is not a problem that a manager can stand outside of. It's not a problem like falling sales or declining SAT scores or difficulty in retaining partners in a law firm. You don't gather in a committee room and toss the problem out on the table and brainstorm about it. It's not a question of alternative means to a given end, but of alternative ends, and the contradictory and mutually antagonistic ends subsist in the very persons — the *only* persons — with the authority to address the problem. Both coaches and players want to score more than their opponents — they want to win games — but when the very question at issue is whether games should be thrown or not, no amount of football expertise can solve it. Rev. Weakland and Cardinal Raymond Burke are not men working in different ways toward the same goal. They want different teams to win. Sometimes our local ordinary will be a Burke, sometimes a Weakland, more often a man who oscillates between one position and the other. Those of us who are not bishops have no say whatever in the concrete decisions made, yet we all, to a greater or lesser extent, have to play along with the fiction that we're all playing on the same team with the same purposes. My gentler, more tolerant friends urge me to make a bad-faith effort at good faith. Better to pretend the candle is lit, they say, than to curse the darkness. Only a bishop, however, can light the particular candle in question. That is another hugely inconvenient doctrine that I, as a Catholic, am compelled to believe. My own bishop, depending on where I happen to be domiciled, may have no convictions at all about the apostolic nature of higher governance and sacramental validity, but it is greatly to his advantage that *I* do.

That said, the crisis provided all of us with important new opportunities when the villainies of Cardinal McCarrick became public knowledge and for that reason discussable. The McCarrick revelations made it possible to talk about his own misdeeds without being reproached for calumny, and they also made it plain that the criminal and his crimes were protected by a network of powerful and covertly iniquitous churchmen at home, abroad, and in Rome. The *New York Times* columnist Ross Douthat wryly admitted his own naiveté in the matter. "It was the early 2000s," he says,

> I was attending some panel on religious life and was accosted by a type who haunts such events: gaunt, intense, with a litany of esoteric grievances. He was a traditionalist Catholic, a figure from the Church's fringes and he had a lot to say about corruption in the Catholic clergy. The scandals in Boston had broken so some of what he said was familiar, but he kept going into a rant about Cardinal McCarrick. "Did you know he makes seminarians sleep with him, invites them to his beach house, gets in bed with them?"

At this, Douthat says,

> I gave him the brushoff that you give the monomaniacal and I slipped out. This is before I realized that if you wanted the truth about corruption in the Catholic Church you had to listen to the extreme-seeming types — traditionalists and radicals — because they were the only ones sufficiently alienated from the institution to dig into its rot. It was also before I learned, from journalist friends, that McCarrick, or "Uncle

Ted," as he urged his paramour victims to address him, had such a long history of pursuing seminarians and priests that a group of Catholics went to Rome to warn against making him Washington's archbishop, to no avail.

So the McCarrick scandal may have taught us nothing new, but it did give us permission to talk about what we had already learned through parallel cases and sharpened the focus of key elements of the crisis. Let me foreground a few. First, we are dealing with collusion, with complicity in sin. The crisis is not an instance of multiple isolated miscreants working mischief on a large scale, but of men in authority concealing, tolerating, and sometimes abetting the crimes of priests and other fellows. I am not arguing for the existence of a conspiracy in a strict sense, a criminal pact secretly but explicitly forged between men who know the other conspirators and who share a common subversive purpose, but there is certainly a network or interlocking plurality of networks operating to protect and promote clerics committing crimes against the Church and against persons subject to their authority.

Second, to use the terminology of Catholic scholar Anthony Esolen, the whole of the "meta-crime" was homosexual. As this is an unfamiliar term, I've provided this visual aid [holds up a white piece of paper with the word "meta-crime" on it], which I produced sparing no effort or expense. It's beyond dispute that the clerical sexual abuse was itself overwhelmingly homosexual. The late Richard Neuhaus put it, "Between men who want to have sex with adolescent boys and men who do not want to have sex with adolescent boys, the former are more likely to have sex with adolescent boys."[114] But Esolen is making a different claim. By the meta-crime he means not the incidences of

---

[114] Richard John Neuhaus, "The Catholic Reform II," *First Things*, June 2004, https://www.firstthings.com/article/2004/06/the-catholic-reform-ii.

sexual predation, but the crime that permitted these other crimes to take place. Esolen explains, "We do not have examples of womanizing priests going out of their way to recruit other such priests, forming a tight little cabal, covering for one another, suborning young men into this wicked way of life, issuing veiled threats against anyone who would go public, and snubbing those who do not approve."[115] Esolen's point is crucial. No sane observer denies the fact that there exist clergy who sin with women, but there is no evidence that they collude in mutual recruitment, mutual advancement, mutual protection. Esolen concludes, "There was no network of abusers of girls. This network was about clergy who wanted to do things with boys and men."

Third, it has become clear that the institutions of priestly formation — that is, seminaries, novitiates, scholasticates — have in many places developed a culture that weakens rather than strengthens the moral fiber of the young men formed in it. This weakness manifests itself not solely or even principally in susceptibility to sexual sin, but in an ignoble moral timidity and an unmanly submissiveness that consents to indignities visited on itself and others, that fails to oppose or denounce injustice when perpetrated by superiors. Here again the unease that many Catholics have been feeling for decades was crystalized by the McCarrick affair, in the mental image of the bishop spooning a series of seminarians on his beach house mattress — an image that points to the astonishing acquiescence of so many men to this treatment. And in the case of any who decline to acquiesce to their advances, there is an equally astonishing unwillingness to make their refusal audible. Fearlessly intelligent initiative is an indispensable condition of moral

---

[115] Quotations from Anthony Esolen are taken from "What the Priest Scandal Is — and Is Not — About," *Crisis Magazine*, September 3, 2018, https://crisismagazine.com/opinion/what-the-priest-scandal-is-and-is-not-about.

leadership. Yet the seminaries operated such that several generations of priests not only failed to acquire such fearlessness but failed to attain the moral imbalance that ordinary men would, including an ordinary resistance to institutional deceit and depravity.

Yet the fact is, some men did protest, and this brings me to my fourth point: the harm done by what I will call the recursive authority loop; that is, a structure of governance whereby a given agency has total power to determine what counts as failure of the same agency and has total control in handling information concerning alleged failures. This brings up the ancient problem of *Quis custodiet ipsos custodes* — who will guard the guardians? Who will audit the auditors? In the days of Marcial Maciel Degollado the constitutions of the Legionaries of Christ obliges its members to pronounce a vow never to make outward verbal criticism, written or otherwise, of any act of governance or of the person of any rector or superior of the congregation, and to inform forthwith the immediate superior of the member who has made such a criticism. Only a saint could be given absolute power of judgment over his own conduct and not abuse it. We know that in the case of Maciel, it did not have a happy ending. Yet the recursive authority loop, while rarely as tight as that of the Legion, operates in other areas of the Church governance as well. The letters of complaint accusing McCarrick of predation were received, stamped, read, and passed up the ecclesiological ladder to the same authorities who made him a bishop in the first place, and who had done so by ignoring similar communications. Even honorable men would find distasteful the task of investigating allegations that, if proved sound, would reflect poorly on their own conduct of office. And here again, the McCarrick affair showed us that this honor was in short supply. The letters of accusation and memoranda had no effect except to make their writers into targets of official vindictiveness.

An old maxim of Roman law says that no man can be a judge in his own cause. Yet, in far too many cases of Church life, *every* man in authority is a judge in his cause. This is true of the administration of religious orders, the careers of diocesan priests, and most particularly of seminary life. The purpose of a seminary is to submit worldly young men to the instruction of prayerful and godly formators, on the assumption that students will be more ill-behaved and unruly and their instructors more sober, esthetic, and virtuous. Yet time and again we are told that it is the seminarians who are shocked by the profane worldliness of their superiors — superiors who, when a complaint of corruption is raised, comprise both jury and judge. The journalist Jason Berry, in his 1991 book on the crisis, has this glimpse into the St. Francis Seminary of the Diocese of San Diego:

> Mary Jones' first inkling of something amiss came in autumn 1980. She left a check for her son, Bob, at the seminary and looked into the piano room. Cushions were on the floor, guys were in togas with wine goblets, not all wearing underwear. "I started crying. A priest came over and said, 'This is not a time when parents are welcome.'" Why did she let Bob continue in this seminary? She continues, "I wanted to preserve our relationship at all costs. It's like those cults. Once you lose communication, you lose it all. When Bob told me he thought he was gay, I went to his spiritual director and I practically tore his apartment up." Crying, she said, "It's not that he's gay; it's whether he became gay because of the seminary. I was the best mother I could be. I educated him in Catholic schools."

Mary's appeals for justice and decency got the same treatment we have come to expect: sympathetic indignation on the part of those with no influence, public affectation of interest on the part of those in authority.

Yet when the sex abuse crisis got to the point where it could no longer be ignored, the men who thrust themselves forward as reformers were, far too often, the perpetrators of corruption, who saw to it that the network would remain intact, and the meta-crime unhindered. Take the notion of seminary screening. At the bishops' meeting in Dallas in June 2002, all agreed that seminaries should do more rigorous testing to exclude potential abusers. But here again, everything depends on the persons you hire to do the screening, which is to say everything depends on your notion of healthy manhood and the role of the priest in Catholic life.

Look at it this way: when you bring your Camry into the dealer's garage and say, "Fix it," you don't need to inquire more deeply into the mechanic's belief system because you and he share the notion of what a well-running Camry is. But if you find your fifteen-year-old wearing his mother's lipstick, you don't drop him off outside the counseling center and wish him luck. You need to know which particular therapist will make it his task to heal him, and you need to know what view of the human person that therapist professes because the putatively healthy specimen the therapist returns to you will vary drastically, radically, on what he believes human life is meant for. For the same reason, it is pointless for your seminary to congratulate itself on more thorough screening. Whom do you screen out and whom do you screen in? The quality of manhood prized by one examiner as tenacity — that is, stalwart adherence to principle, to honor, and to the truths of the Faith — will be condemned by a different examiner as rigidity. "Candidate shows know-it-all attitude towards theology and formation," notes the screening psychologist. "Unsuitable for ministry." So the "rigid" seminarian is rejected at the outset, replaced by one more flexible — more adaptable, shall we say, to the contours of the archbishop's mattress. And here's the rub, the recursive authority loop makes sure this all takes place under the banner of "reform."

It may seem that I have been painting in broad strokes with too little attention to detail. Let me supply some specifics so as to bolster my claims. James Rausch was a sexually active gay man-made bishop at age forty-four and four years later was appointed bishop of Phoenix. In 1995 a Tucson priest and serial sexual predator named Robert Trupia blackmailed the Diocese of Tucson by threatening to reveal his own sexual liaisons with Bishop Rausch, with another Tucson priest, and with an underage male, so as to derail disciplinary measures that would enmesh him in the civil justice system. Dr. Richard Sipe, a psychiatrist and an expert on the clergy abuse scandal, had this to say in a 2003 article about Rausch:

> I interviewed at length a man who is a sexual partner of Bishop James Rausch. This was particularly painful for me, since the bishop and I were young priests together in Minnesota in [the] early '60s. He went on to get his social work degree and succeeded Bernardin as secretary to the bishop's national conference in DC. He became bishop of Phoenix. It is patently clear that Bishop Rausch led an active sexual life that did involve at least one minor; he was acquainted with priests who were sexually active with minors, priests who had at least 30 minor victims each. He referred at least one of his own victims to these priests.

"Did those who knew him," Sipe asks, "know nothing of his life? Perhaps so. But he was in a spectacular power grid of bright men. He was Bernardin's successor at the U.S. Conference, Bishop Thomas Kelly of Louisville was his successor, Monsignor Daniel Hoy and Bishop Robert Lynch, among others, took over his job."

Three points. First, Rausch died young, in office, and in good standing. Second, among those Sipe includes in the roster of his "spectacular power grid" are bishops who, in the wake of the scandals, were commended on the national stage for being in the forefront of efforts for the protection of children: Kelly, Bernardin, Robert Lynch. I forget the third point.

The Sound of Silence

Next, we might look at Lawrence Welsh, a sexually active gay man who was appointed bishop of Spokane at age forty-three. In August of 1986, Bishop Welsh was in Chicago at a Knights of Columbus convention, when he brought a male prostitute to his hotel room, whom he throttled while the prostitute was performing a paid act of fellatio. The prostitute was so shaken that he notified Chicago police, who, in turn, notified the Spokane police, who interviewed Welsh and obtained a confession. By agreement with the metropolitan archbishop, Raymond Hunthausen of Seattle, no charges were filed against Welsh, on the condition that he undergo therapy. There is no evidence that this promise was honored. Hereto, note the effect of the recursive authority loop. Three years later, Welsh was arrested for drunk driving and finally obliged to resign his bishopric. Successor as bishop of Spokane, William Skylstad, when asked in 2002 about Welsh's having choked a Chicago rent-boy, replied, "Obviously he had a very serious drinking problem. Certainly it's very sad behavior associated with that drinking. That would be my observation." Two years later, Skylstad was elected president of the United States Conference of Catholic Bishops. Yet the Lawrence Welsh story did not end with his resignation of Spokane. In 1991, in a move, to my knowledge, unparalleled in Church history, Welsh was brought out of retirement to become auxiliary bishop of St. Paul–Minneapolis, his squalid police record notwithstanding. When Welsh died in 1999, then-archbishop Harry Flynn praised Welsh as "an extraordinary man and faith-filled servant of the Church. He had a special gift for touching others" — I'm not making this up — "with both his humor and his sincere witness to the gospel of Jesus Christ." And, yes, Harry Flynn was also one of the men who shouldered himself into the klieg lights as a great reformer. In fact, Flynn chaired a drafting committee that, at the Dallas assembly in 2002, produced the Charter for the Protection of Young People — a charter that J. D. Flynn of the Catholic News Agency points out deliberately excluded bishops from their disciplinary protocols.

The Truth about the Crisis in the Catholic Church

This brings us back, again, to Uncle Ted McCarrick. The sensational way in which he ended his ministry may incline us to forget that McCarrick, a sexually active gay man, had the public reputation as a pioneer in the campaign to free the Church from the mock of sexual abuse and set it to rights. Journalist Melinda Henneburger regarded McCarrick as "one of the good guys." "Those of us who lived through the horror of the clerical sexual abuse scandals in 2002," Henneberger wrote in July of 2018,

> were so grateful that at least one American cardinal seemed to understand the depth and urgency of the problem. Yes, that man was Ted McCarrick, someone I interviewed a number of times at the height of the scandals in my job as Rome correspondent for the *New York Times*. While too many other Church leaders were still denying, deflecting, minimizing, and blaming the media, he was the first to speak about a "one strike and you're out" policy for new cases of abuse by priests.

Henneberger says that the revelation of McCarrick's true nature was a gut punch to her and she ends on a note of sarcastic disdain: "In 2002 renowned reformer Ted McCarrick said the new standards would tell the laity they must have a role in rooting out abuse. While there are still laity to *have* a role, Uncle Teddy?"

My initial claim was that the true crisis was a kind of ecclesiastical deadlock, a paralysis. I've tried to show that it is precisely the "renowned reformers" who brought the criminal network into being, who keep it alive in spite of urgent calls for a purge, and who have brought about the deadlock in the first place. Recursive authority loop and the dynamics of blackmail make it all certain that the only persons with the authority to tackle corruption and clean out the rot lack the interest or the will to do so. The promised Vatican report on McCarrick to make clear how he scammed the system has been repeatedly and inexplicably delayed. Fr.

The Sound of Silence

Raymond de Souza, pointing to what he calls the rather soviet feel to Roman communications, says that this report will eventually be issued, but after it is released, who will believe what it says? When trustees have shown themselves untrustworthy, how can trust be restored?

If I were addressing bishops instead of laymen, I would say this: the very condition of trusting a man is his total indifference as to whether you trust him or not. That is to say, we trust those who we know will tell us the truth regardless of how we'll react, will keep their promises regardless of how they will appear in the eyes of others. Only a confidence man asks, "How will I get this guy to trust me?" as a distinct endeavor from "What is the right thing to do in this situation?" When a pertinent body is a collectivity like a professional group, we trust the outfit that is hardest on its own members than we ourselves are inclined to be. "They fired Dr. Brown just for that?" "Captain Jones lost his command just for that?" When we marvel that what appear to be trivial lapses to those outside the guild are deemed career-ending offenses to those within, and when we see, not infrequently, that the guild pulls the trigger on its own members even at considerable cost to itself, then we tend to think, "These are serious folks who have a serious mission — a mission they see more clearly than we do." And note: if they surprise us often enough by a severity toward themselves that we don't fully understand, we can accept it as a good-faith decision if occasionally they show a leniency that we don't fully understand. By acting consistently in conforming to objective standards without reference to the impression it makes on us, they've earned our trust.

So, once you've lost someone's trust, how do you win it back? By building a record of what lawyers call "admission against interest." I'm not speaking about the more popular sport of making public apologies for faults committed by one's predecessors in office. By "admissions against interest" I mean voluntarily bringing to light truths about oneself that are damaging, for which indeed one could have no public

The Truth about the Crisis in the Catholic Church

motive besides regard for the truth that goes beyond any possible consequences of its disclosure. Indeed, we have the splendid example of the bishop St. Augustine putting his sins before the world in his *Confessions*. Might bishops follow his example in our own time? Consider how few have admitted, not to their own misdeeds but to having heard rumors of McCarrick's, and you have your answer.

Seventeen years ago, I took part in a discussion about the priest abuse crisis in which I made some somber predictions. At the time I said, "I believe that the crisis will deepen though not dramatically, in the foreseeable future. I believe that the policies suggested to remedy the situation will help only tangentially and that the whole idea of an administrative programmatic approach — a software solution, if I may put it that way — is an example of the disease for which it purports to be the cure." Those same predictions I would repeat today, emphasizing, however, that societal antipathy toward the Church and to Catholic doctrine is increasing every month and is become institutionalized at the same rate. Will the coming hostilities have a happy ending? Yes. It's the periods leading up to that ending that are going to be bloody.

As a Church, we've been here before, and that more than once. Take the case of Rodrigo Borgia, who fathered at least six bastards by married women, made two of them cardinals, bought himself a papacy (he's Pope Alexander the VI), and died one of Europe's richest men in 1603. Yet the moral indignation such decadence roused in a Martin Luther, commendable in itself, made common cause with hatreds that despised the Church not for her vices but for her virtues — virtues true Catholics rose to defend at the risk of their lives.

The French writer Georges Bernanos saw the truth clearly. He says:

> It's a fact of experience that one reforms nothing in a church by ordinary means. If one pretends to reform the Church with these means, the ones by which one reforms a secular society,

he not only fails in his undertaking but infallibly finds himself outside the church. One reforms a church only by suffering for her. One reforms the visible church only by suffering for the invisible church. One reforms the vices of the church only by being prodigal of the example of her most heroic virtues. It's well possible that St. Francis of Assisi was not less revolted than Luther by the debauchery and by the simony of prelates. It's certain that he suffered more cruelly because of them for his nature was very different than that of the monk of Winemark. But he did not challenge the iniquity, he did not try to confront it with self. He hurled himself into poverty and plunged into it as deeply as he could along with his followers, as if to the source of all purity. Instead of trying to snatch from the Church her ill-gotten gains, he overwhelmed her with invisible treasures.

"The Church has need not of reformers," Bernanos concludes, "but of saints."

Heroic sanctity makes itself known in circumstances of heroically endured hardship. And the good news I leave you with is that this hardship is on the way, and the saints will follow. Our Lord has never given us, and will not give us in the future, all the saints we wish. He will give us all the saints we need. Think back to Henry VIII's usurpation of Church prerogatives in 1530s England and the craven capitulations of every single English bishop save one: St. John Fisher of Rochester. Listen to the letter Fisher wrote to reproach the monarch bishops Stephen Gardiner and Cuthbert Tunstall — the team players who sided with King Henry — and ask if it doesn't ring more recent bells.

> Methinks it had rather been our part to stick together in repressing these violent and unlawful intrusions and injuries daily offered to our common mother the Holy Church of Christ than by any manner of persuasion to help to forward

the same. And we ought rather to seek by all means the temporal destruction of the soul-ravenous wolves that daily go about worrying and deflowering the flock that Christ bid to our charge and the flock that Christ himself died for than to suffer them thus to range abroad. But alas, see we do it not. You see in what peril the Christian state now stands. We are besieged at all sides, we can hardly escape the danger of our enemy. And seeing that judgement is begone at the house of God, what hope is there left if we fall and the rest shall stand? The fort is betrayed by them that should have defended it. And therefore, seeing the matter as thus begun and so faintly resisted on our parts, I fear that we be not the men that shall see the end of the story. Wherefore seeing I'm an old man and look not long to live, am I not, by the help of God, to trouble my conscience in pleasing the king whatsoever become of me, but rather to spend out the remnant of my old days praying to God for him?

It took twenty years and the spilling of much innocent blood, but, amazingly enough, the letter worked. It helped change the hearts of the timid time-servers. Let me quote from Church historian James Hitchcock. He says, "By the logic of prudence, as it is now understood, the Church should not have canonized John Fisher, the only bishop who withstood Henry VIII, but instead bishops Steven Gardiner and Albert Tunstall — men who, while not devoid of principle, nonetheless managed to survive the ecclesiastical changes of three reigns. Oh, the fact is well known," Hitchcock says, "that all but one English bishop conformed to King Henry in 1534; much less well known is the fact that in 1559, no English bishop conformed to Elizabeth I, and all were deposed, including Tunstall — a fact which demonstrates the possibility of thoroughly reforming the national hierarchy."

The Sound of Silence

I believe the visible and doctrinal unity of the Church will diminish and will be subject to new loyalties and realignments, roughly comparable to the divergence at present between the German and Polish bishops' conferences. I believe most of these fiefdoms will respond to persecution by compromising or throwing overboard conspicuously dangerous Catholic teachings and practices. I believe organized hostility to the Church will increase to the point where there is no reason at all to be a Catholic, no reason at all to be a nun, no reason at all to be a priest, apart from the unshakable personal conviction that the Church is the supreme dispenser of truth and of spiritual goods. And here I repeat my conclusions from 2003: I believe reform will come, though in a future generation, and that the reformers whom God raises up will spill their blood in imitation of Christ. In short, to pilfer a line from Frank Sheed, "I find absolutely no grounds for optimism, and I have every reason for hope."

Parody: All Things Bright and Fungible

Paul: A friend of mine made this suggestion to me: "You should write something like a James Herriot book for the priesthood: a gentle, loosely structured ramble through the ordinary week of a diocesan Vicar General, say." Here are a couple of sample chapters, or maybe excerpts from sample chapters. Working title: *All Things Bright and Fungible*.

Chapter 6

At times it seemed unfair that I should be paid for my work; for driving out in the early morning with the fields glittering under the first pale sunshine and the wisps of mist still hanging on the high tops of the beeches. The aroma of late-mown timothy greeted me as affectionately as the smile of Corporal Ludkens when I rolled the old Pontiac to a stop and ducked out of the door.

"How's he doing then?" I asked.

"About the same, Monsignor."

We made our way across the parking lot and into the truck-stop lobby past a few drowsy travelers who glanced up in curiosity, and he led me back into the men's restroom, where another trooper, a tall young lad with a look too serious for his years, was posted to forbid entry. Fr. Maehrens lay on his back on the wet floor, alternately panting and whimpering, a bloody handkerchief in his mouth where his upper incisors used to be.

"Wrong customer again, Ricky?" I murmured, while Ludkens and I each hooked an arm and dragged him shoulders-first across the reeking linoleum and out past the stoic sentry. He was wearing a sleeveless shirt, jeans, and running shoes, which I was grateful for, as I didn't want to come back to retrieve a loose sandal or a loafer. Ludkens was softly whistling "Let It Shine" as we passed his cruiser with its flashing roof-lights and came to my faded blue Bonneville. Two heaves got Maehrens onto the back seat. We paused for a moment to catch our breath and rejoice in the sweet stillness of dawn.

"The doc says I shouldn't," sighed Ludkens, cupping his hands to light a Marlboro, "but with truck-stop business I find it helps with the smell." I slapped him on the shoulder to thank him, and he lifted his chin and blew a smoke ring in good-natured acknowledgment. I started the grudging engine of my faithful sedan, moved purposefully onto the ramp and the highway, rolling my window down a few inches to neutralize the odor of Maehrens's hair gel. A warbler gave voice from the birch grove....

Chapter 11

It was going to be a difficult delivery. I knew it as soon as I saw the look in her eyes: pleading, and dark with pain. Her checkbook lay on the walnut lamp table, conspicuously unaccompanied by a pen. I took a deep breath or two to prepare myself for the ordeal ahead.

"What I don't see," she said, "is how the bishop can let Cathedral Catholic High School bring in a pro-abortion graduation speaker when the Church teaches that abortion is immoral."

Gentleness is everything in these situations. "You must realize, Mrs. Riordan, that His Excellency agrees with you 100 percent, 100 percent, and wants you to know that when he offered Holy Mass for your late husband last Thursday, he made a special prayer that God would reward Frank generously for his fearless defense of the unborn..."

Her eyes lowered a bit, and I saw her raise her hand to her throat to touch the holy medal on its gold neck-chain, doubtless a particularly prized gift from her husband. We had now arrived at the delicate part of the procedure.

"The reality is that the bishop deplores Cathedral's choice of graduation speaker. But he found out about it so late that rescinding the congressman's invitation would have caused the kind of publicity and media furor that would have helped rather than hurt the pro-choice cause. And to avoid similar fiascos in the future, His Excellency has decided to create a special Catholic Initiatives Fund — a fund that will permit the diocese to further its mission of spreading the teachings of the Church, especially the hard teachings. But of course, such a bold move requires the cooperation of committed Catholics, and it was, in part, his disgust over the Cathedral High invitation and his resolve to fight back that he sent me to see you personally."

"To me?" she asked, her eyes wide with wonder.

I exhaled. The tough part was behind me. "To you," I said, leaning forward and giving her the soulful, solemn, this-information-does-not-leave-the-room look...

Chapter 13

"Bless me, Father, for I have sinned."

My heart sank. I'd been sitting in "the box" for twenty minutes on a Saturday afternoon, undisturbed, answering e-mails and watching videos on my iPhone, and I figured in five minutes I'd be justified in calling it a day and bolting. The third round of the Masters and a long, tall Chivas Rob Roy beckoned ... and now this.

"It's been two years since the last time I was at confession, maybe a little more ... and I haven't been to Mass much in that time."

"That's not a sin."

"Oh. Okay. And I watched some R-rated movies on Netflix and —"

"That's not a sin."

"I had some impure thoughts and feelings afterward ..."

"That's not a sin."

"And my husband and I —"

"Say three Our Fathers and three —"

"But Father, I mean Monsignor, the real reason I'm here is that on Tuesday I heard a talk, well it was a tape of a talk, by a Father Michael ... Michael Somebody, a friend lent it to me, and his talk was on the birth control pill and why it's wrong, and he explained it in a way so that I understood it really for the first time ever. And so I wanted to come here and make my confession because my husband and I ..."

This was too much. Not only did our parish have Reconciliation Services twice a year to deal with this kind of thing, but I got an iPhone alert saying Lawrie and Mickelson were tied at eight under.

"If you're mature enough to get married you're mature enough to make your own decisions about spacing your children. God wants you to be happy, no matter what Father Michael Somebody says! I absolve you from your —"

"Monsignor, aren't you supposed to give me a penance?"

"Three Glory Bes. And don't forget next Thursday is Las Vegas Night in the cafeteria. In the name of the Father and of the Son ..."

All of a sudden, the dreadful thought came to me that her husband might have drunk the Kool-Aid too and was out there waiting his own turn. I yanked off my stole and switched off the red and white indicator lights and finished the Sign of the Cross on my feet.

Parody: All Things Bright and Fungible

"... and of the Holy Spirit. Amen. Go in peace."

And go in peace I did! As luck would have it, God was on my side, and I made it to the den before the premium coverage started. It was a close call, I admit, but as my seminary rector often repeated, no one ever promised us the life was going to be easy.[116]

---

[116] "All Creatures Great and Small," April 2015.

Baffled in Basingstoke

by Paul Mankowski

[Penned in 1993, after reading a little too deeply into *The Tidings*.]

Dear Miss Manners,

I am a mature and educated woman, but I am at my *wits' end* as to how to solve this delicate situation, and I hope you can guide me. After being in a mutually enriching relationship for several years, my gentleman friend, Brucie, and I have decided to express our sharing in a Ceremony of Commitment for our families and a few hundred of our closest friends. Since Brucie is a Roman Catholic bishop, we can't have it in a church because of their "Dark Ages" mentality, but we rented Brucie's tennis club for a Tuesday evening and their dining room does a scrumptious cheesecake. The difficulty is that I want the child of our love to act as best man. Marcus is only fourteen but plays the alto clarinet and has a sweet smile. But an earlier attachment of Brucie's is making trouble. She wants *her* boy, Eugene, who was conceived while Brucie was still a monsignor. I mean, any tramp can bag a prothonotary apostolic for a night.

The Sound of Silence

Now, the complicating factor is that Eugene is the live-in boyfriend of Brucie's metropolitan, Randall, on the grounds that the scheming bitch Maxine is claiming Eugene has priority over Marcus as being accorded cardinalitial rank. She calls it a "morganatic endowment," if you please, and here she is a bottle-blonde who ends her sentences with "like." Now, most socially sensitive people agree that if Randall were a "top," his dignities would be extended to his Significant Other, but *everybody* knows that Randall has been strictly femme since the Synod on the Laity in '87.

Please don't think I'm one of those persons who always has to have their own way about everything. I only want to do what is right for all concerned. I gave in on the shrimp cocktails at the reception because Randall is allergic to shellfish. Am I wrong to insist on Marcus?

— Baffled in Basingstoke

My Favorite Things

[This song is taken from a longer skit where Shari Lewis is conducting a workshop to help bishops learn boundaries. I wrote to Paul one day when I had a head cold and said, "I feel horrible. Send me something funny and tasteless." He wrote back, "Well, tasteless I can do" and attached the skit. Since names were named in the skit, I am only quoting the song at the end of it.]

[*To the tune of "My Favorite Things"*]

Lads without fathers or lawyers or trousers,
Bellhops who whisper "Your room's ready now, sirs."
Thurifers kissing episcopal rings:
These are a few of my favorite things.

Afternoon trysts to develop my fitness,
Lawsuits dismissed for the lack of a witness,
Liturgists warbling "On Eagle's Wings":
These are a few of my favorite things.

When the Feds sting,
When the perps sing — Lambchop, I-I-I love you:

The Sound of Silence

You don't give a bleat when you're scooped off the street,
But best of all: Sheep — don't — sue!

Acolytes tanning on Provincetown beaches,
Prelates that practice what Barney Frank preaches,
Caddies that treat bishops better than kings:
These are a few of my favorite things.

Workshops to make seminarians tender,
Chat rooms to help me discover my gender,
Halloween parties and Mardi Gras flings:
These are a few of my favorite things.

When the boys tell,
When their moms yell — Lambchop, I-I-I love you:
You're easy to hide in a Buick's inside,
But best of all: Sheep — don't — sue![117]

---

[117] "Restless in Beverly Hills," March 2008.

Final Words

Why Stay Catholic?

A Catholic friend who proofread this book said it had made her heartsick and that, as a convert, she felt as if her Protestant ancestors were looking down on her and saying, "I told you so." That made me worry, because the last thing I want to do is to make Catholics consider leaving the Church because of all the rot. However, I think that shining light on the rot is the only thing that is going to make things get better. The powers that be are not going to do anything to make it better because, as Paul said much more eloquently, the fox is guarding the henhouse. If there is any chance for the Church to be healed, outside of supernatural intervention, it is going to be that the laity demand it. And the laity cannot fight the corruption until they have a good picture of what the corruption is.

I have friends who have left the Church because they could not stand to be in any way connected to the evil that has infested her. The irony is that they were all the most devout friends I had. I'm sure the devil threw a party when they left. If I wouldn't stay for any other reason, I would never give the devil the satisfaction of watching me leave. But if that is not enough to make you stay, let me offer some other reasons.

The Sound of Silence

If you are truly Catholic, you don't need any reason other than the Eucharist. I've often joked that the Catholic Church holds me hostage because, to echo St. Peter, "To whom would I go?" But it is the truth. The Eucharist alone is reason to stay.

Jesus has promised us that the Gates of Hell would not prevail. Right now, it looks as if we're at the two-minute warning in the fourth quarter and the score is Gates of Hell ninety-nine, Church zero. But Jesus does not make false promises. It might take supernatural intervention to save the Church, but the Church will be saved. As the AA quip goes, "Don't quit before the miracle happens." The Church is in need of warriors right now. Don't abandon her when she needs you the most.

I firmly agree with Catholic writer Matthew Nelson:

> Why be Catholic? Because to be Catholic is to be in full union with the one thing that can make you most sane and most happy. A tall claim, to be sure; but it's not an arrogant claim. It's a true claim. I am Catholic because I am convinced the Church is the *only* place I will find the fullness of truth and joy. That's why I'm Catholic: because I believe Catholicism is true.[118]

I support that claim. My days are filled with peace and gratitude, no matter what is going on. I know this is true because of Holy Mother Church — not the façade that has been erected by the modernists but the Church that Jesus founded, with her two-thousand-plus years of consistent teaching; with her saints and martyrs; with her truth that does not change. That Church saved my life and, more importantly,

---

[118] Matthew Nelson, "3 Reasons Why You Should Be Catholic," Word on Fire, September 7, 2016, https://www.wordonfire.org/articles/fellows/3-reasons-why-you-should-be-catholic/.

my soul. That is why I stay and why I will keep fighting for her with everything I have.

Or, as Paul always said about the Jesuits: "*I'm* not going anywhere. *I'm* right."

The End

Acknowledgments

Many people went above and beyond the call of duty to help me write this book, all the while listening to me worry out loud for a long time. First is my family: my husband, Chris; my daughters, Julie and Christine; and my sons, Caleb and Brian. Whenever I take on a new project, it means robbing them of a lot of my time, and they have always been both patient and encouraging. I couldn't do anything without them.

Next on the list is my dear friend Raymond Arroyo, who is an amazing person on so many fronts, but most of all in generosity. This book would not exist without him.

Nor would this book exist without my friend John Francis Clark, who held my hand from start to finish, since I had never written nonfiction before. He provided me with everything from sage advice to editing notes. Most of all, he and his wife, Lisa, provided me with friendship and moral support.

My friend and sorority sister Lynn Cara Schwalje spent a lot of time doing some fine editing — worthy of a William and Mary graduate. She and John helped make the lives of Sophia Institute Press's editors a lot easier.

I owe a tremendous debt of gratitude to everyone at Sophia Institute Press. They are a class act. I am so thankful that they had the courage to publish this book; otherwise, the story of what Fr. Mankowski endured would have died with him.

Friends of Paul who helped me include Kate Adams (who provided hospitality and a lovely tour of South Bend!); Fr. Kevin Flannery, S.J.; Paul's good friend Phil Lawler; my friend George Weigel (who offered early and excellent advice); my wonderful spiritual director, Fr. Sean Raftis; and Paul's high school friend Kurt Nemes. Several other fine Jesuits helped me, and I will do them the favor of not naming them. Paul's family members — especially his sisters — were always very gracious to me when we had occasion to be together.

Fr. Paul Mankowski, S.J. (RIP), changed my life. I owe him so much. I hope this book will repay some of it. I miss you every day, my treasured friend.

Most important of all, the Holy Trinity heard a lot of whining and panic from me, which they returned with every possible grace, as is always the case.

About the Author

In her career as writer, producer, and creative consultant, Karen Hall has worked on numerous series, including *M*A*S*H*, *Hill Street Blues*, *Moonlighting*, *Northern Exposure*, and *The Good Wife*. She has received seven Emmy Award nominations, as well as the Humanitas Prize, the Women in Film Luminas Award, and the Writers Guild of America Award. Her novel, *Dark Debts*, was a Book of the Month Club main selection when first published in 1996, and the twentieth-anniversary edition was published by Simon and Schuster in 2016. She is now developing movies and miniseries through her company, New Voyage Productions. She is married to her high school sweetheart, and they have four adult children and three grandchildren.

CRISIS Publications

Sophia Institute Press awards the privileged title "CRISIS Publications" to a select few of our books that address contemporary issues at the intersection of politics, culture, and the Church with clarity, cogency, and force and that are also destined to become all-time classics.

CRISIS Publications are direct, explaining their principles briefly, simply, and clearly to Catholics in the pews, on whom the future of the Church depends. The time for ambiguity or confusion is long past.

CRISIS Publications are contemporary, born of our own time and circumstances and intended to become significant statements in current debates, statements that serious Catholics cannot ignore, regardless of their prior views.

CRISIS Publications are classical, addressing themes and enunciating principles that are valid for all ages and cultures. Readers will turn to them time and again for guidance in other days and different circumstances.

CRISIS Publications are spirited, entering contemporary debates with gusto to clarify issues and demonstrate how those issues can be resolved in a way that enlivens souls and the Church.

We welcome engagement with our readers on current and future CRISIS Publications. Please pray that this imprint may help to resolve the crises embroiling our Church and society today.

Sophia Institute Press® is a registered trademark of Sophia Institute.
Sophia Institute is a tax-exempt institution as defined by the
Internal Revenue Code, Section 501(c)(3). Tax ID 22-2548708.